Colonialism in Modern America:
The Appalachian Case

Colonialism in Modern America:

The Appalachian Case

by

Helen Matthews Lewis

Linda Johnson

and

Donald Askins

The Appalachian Consortium Press
Boone, North Carolina
1978

The Appalachian Consortium was a non-profit educational organization
composed of institutions and agencies located in Southern Appalachia. From
1973 to 2004, its members published pioneering works in Appalachian studies
documenting the history and cultural heritage of the region. The Appalachian
Consortium Press was the first publisher devoted solely to the region and many of
the works it published remain seminal in the field to this day.

With funding from the Andrew W. Mellon Foundation and the National
Endowment for the Humanities through the Humanities Open Book Program,
Appalachian State University has published new paperback and open access
digital editions of works from the Appalachian Consortium Press.

www.collections.library.appstate.edu/appconsortiumbooks

ISBN (pbk.: alk. Paper): 978-1-4696-4204-8
ISBN (ebook): 978-1-4696-4206-2

Distributed by the University of North Carolina Press
www.uncpress.org

Colonialism in Modern America:
The Appalachian Case

CONTENTS

COLONIALISM IN MODERN AMERICA: THE APPALACHIAN CASE

Helen Matthews Lewis, Linda Johnson and Donald Askins, Editors

TABLE OF CONTENTS

Table of Contents

PREFACE

PREFACE

It is a relatively simple task to document the social ills and the environmental ravage that beset the people and the land of Appalachia. Those data are available in countless documents on housing, health care, education, and land use and abuse. However, it is much more difficult and problematic to uncover the causes of these tragic conditions. The accumulation of descriptive data, while important, fails to provide our most needed information—an explanation of the tragic conditions. Deprived of an understanding of causal factors, we can scarcely respond to any social problem with rational, consistent strategies.

The essays in this volume focus on explanation. That constitutes their strength and weakness. Boldly, the writers, with varying degrees of documentation and journalistic fervor, lay claim to one explanatory model—Colonialism. Viewed through this paradigm, the ills of the region are readily and clearly explained. However, the weakness is also apparent and probably inescapable. No single explanatory model of human action is adequate to deal with the complexity of human social existence. This volume acknowledges the provisional character of all paradigms by including the two final essays by Walls and Plaut that seek to expand the basic Colonial model in an attempt to deal with certain complexities ignored in the Colonial model. This is not a volume which concludes our attempt to understand the Appalachian region in a larger context, but it is an important contribution to our continuing search for more adequate causal paradigms. No serious student of Appalachia can afford to ignore the point of view expressed in these essays.

The Appalachian Consortium Press seeks to encourage a serious, scholarly approach to all issues Appalachian. This is our sole commitment and our justification in presenting this volume on *Colonialism in Modern America: The Appalachian Case.*

Donald N. Anderson
Vice Chairperson
Appalachian Consortium Board of Directors

THE COLONY OF APPALACHIA

The articles in this volume have been selected to illustrate a particular model for the analysis of the social and economic problems of the Appalachian region. Since we have chosen articles which predominantly represent only one point of view, the book can be labelled a biased interpretation. This is true and intentional. It is our purpose to demonstrate the usefulness of one particular perspective for understanding the region. The model has been variously called the Colonialism Model, Internal Colonialism, Exploitation or External Oppression Model. It stands in contradistinction to other ways of viewing and interpreting the problems of the region, most significantly the Deficiency or Culture of Poverty Model and the Underdevelopment Model.

The Culture of Poverty Model attributes regional problems to the deficiencies of the people and their culture. The approach suggests that:

> "Hillbillies" are dumb: They sold their land for fifty cents an acre.
>
> Apathetic, fatalistic mountain people won't try to change their situation.
>
> Poor health, inadequate diet, ignorance cause the problems.
>
> The scum of the cities, the defective or deprived settled the region and developed a defective culture.
>
> A backwards and primitive people cannot cope in the modern world.

Explanations such as these have been used as both descriptive epithets and causal factors to explain the problems of the area and to legitimize the presence of missionaries, poverty warriors, educators, and land and resource buyers.

The planners, economic developers, and government administrators more frequently explain the problems of the area as being due to underdevelopment:

> Isolation and lack of transportation prevent development.

Lack of adequate capital and programs to stimulate
growth result in a lagging regional economy.

There are too many people for the resources.

Lack of incentives for investment and lack of skilled
labor place the area in a poor competitive position.

These explanations lead to programs to improve transportation,
supply inducements for development, facilitate migration, provide technicians and agents who will encourage modernization
and bring in more industries.

The perspective which we select examines the process
through which dominant outside industrial interests establish
control, exploit the region, and maintain their domination and
subjugation of the region.

Appalachia is a good example of colonial domination by
outside interests. Its history also demonstrates the concerted
efforts of the exploiters to label their work "progress" and to
blame any of the obvious problems it causes on the ignorance or
deficiencies of the Appalachian people. We believe that there are
peoples all over the world who have experienced this sort of "development" and consequently live in conditions similar to those
found in the mountains. Thus, they can easily identify with the
process described in this book as the colonization of Appalachia.

Just as exploitation is not new, the attempt to understand
and explain that process as Colonialism is also not new. Richard
Drake in his comments on regional historiography (Jack and Clio
in Appalachia. *Appalachian Notes,* Volume 4, No. 1, 1976,
pp. 4-6) traces the use of the Colonialism interpretation to writers in the Labor Movement in the 1890's and the Populist Movement. In the 1930's in the midst of labor unrest in the region,
such writers as Theodore Dreiser and Malcolm Ross focused on
the outside ownership and exploitation of the area (Malcolm H.
Ross, *Machine Age* in *the Hills,* New York: Macmillan, 1933,
and National Committee for the Defense of Political Prisoners,
Harlan Miners Speak: Report on Terrorism in the Kentucky
Coal Fields, New York: Harcourt Brace, 1932). Drake saw the
colonial interpretation continued through the reform movements which arose in the 30's and crystallized in such leaders

and organizations as Don West, Myles Horton, and the High-lander Folk School.

The value of the Internal Colonialism Model lies in its ability to bring into focus issues of decision-making and control of everyday life that tend to be ignored in the analysis of area problems and consequently in public policy formulation. The other models describe many of the problems and conditions that are the result of domination and exploitation, but they fail to address these things as causal factors. As social scientists, we are seeking *causes* rather than descriptions (or justifications).

Although we attempt to cover the Appalachian area and show that the exploitation takes many forms—from coal mining in West Virginia to tourism in North Carolina, from TVA development in Tennessee to educational development in Kentucky —there is a greater emphasis on the development of coal resources in Central Appalachia. Part of this is because the picture is so much clearer and the process more blatant in the coalfields. Partly it is due to the location of the editors. We feel that the colonial process can be used to explain many areas and situations throughout America where technological, industrial society has controlled the resources and people.

We do not claim that we have presented the last word or that further analysis is not needed. We simply feel that this collection of articles presents a more realistic picture of Appalachia and its problems than can be garnered through the other perspectives. Some may reject this type of analysis as producing despair and depression since the "enemies" or causes of the problems are seen as giant, multinational corporations in league with irresponsible government bureaucracies which are almost unbeatable forces. We regret this unintended result but feel it better to know the real source of the ailment than to waste effort treating the symptoms.

There are frustrations and limitations in the use of the Colonialism Model. We may be guilty of stretching some of the analogies to compare the region with colonies dominated by another country. A very real difference is the ability of the dominated country to eventually throw the invaders out. Even in fantasy, if Appalachia could put up fences, take over resources, and operate them by the people of the area, one questions whether it is better to be dominated by homegrown enterprises than by New York or Philadelphia based corporations? Some of the younger scholars of the area who grew up using and documenting the Colonial Model are beginning to suggest that we need more sophisticated means to better understand the types of economic and political systems which place certain geographic regions or social classes in situations of dependency and powerlessness. The conditions found in the region are seen by these scholars as products of an advanced industrial, capitalist system. The articles by David Walls and Tom Plaut represent this new thrust to develop improved analytical approaches out of the Colonial Model.

The way we define problems determines how we think about solutions. The Colonial Model implies that solutions to Appalachia's problems lie in the radical restructuring of society with a redistribution of resources to the poor and powerless. But we need more research on how this can be done. How can structural change come about to develop a just society? We need a model which explains and examines the relation between economic power, political power, and cultural systems, how they change and how people's perceptions of their situation are formed and changed. Can political power be used to control economic power? We hope this exploration of one model can cause the development of a more precise theory which will lead to more understanding and solutions to the problems associated with living in a colony.

We have divided this anthology into five sections. The first deals with a delineation of the Colonial Model and its application to Appalachian history and experience.

The second section explains how the great wealth of the natural resources within the region came into the hands of "outsiders," men and corporations from places like Pittsburgh, New York, and London. Although coal is the resource most often used to demonstrate the process of resources theft, other profit-bearing enterprises such as timber, cotton, and tourism have left their tragic mark on the people and the land. We have sought articles which would reflect the great breadth of the resources extraction process.

Section III documents the ways in which outside interests

sought to establish their enterprises in the region and the lengths to which they went to politically disarm and culturally discredit those who opposed them. The story told is not so much one of outright deception and swindles (although there were plenty of them) as it is a subtle and deadly process by which a people were convinced of their own worthlessness and thus, in many cases, gave up efforts to defend themselves and their ways of life.

Section IV shows how the region has become increasingly vulnerable to the cultural and economic definitions, interests, and developmental whims of the larger society. It covers a wide range of activity from media, education, and music, to industrial domination of the political process and the Federal domination of the planning process.

The final section is devoted to extending and improving the Colonial Model with an eye to having scholarly analysis lead to proposals for corrective social action.

We are very grateful to the many contributors who so generously gave permission to use their articles, to the Appalachian Consortium Press who agreed to publish the collection, to Borden Mace who patiently encouraged us to complete the project, and to Don Anderson, Ron Eller, Tom Plaut, and staff at Mars Hill College who assisted with the final selection and organization. We wish to thank Ron Heise, who began the arduous task of editing, Eve Tackett, Susie Jones, Reva Shelton, and Wilma Coates, who provided the secretarial skills. The co-editors Don Askins and Linda Johnson completed the selecting, editing and organizing.

Helen Matthews Lewis
The River Farm
Dungannon, Virginia

THE COLONIALISM MODEL

The following article by Helen M. Lewis and Edward Knipe
discusses the nature and use of the Colonial Model and its application to Appalachia. The process of colonialization is outlined
and used as a framework for describing the mountain experience.
Some of the problems of the model and some of its uses in social
movements of the area are discussed.

THE COLONIALISM MODEL:
THE APPALACHIAN CASE

by
Helen M. Lewis
and
Edward E. Knipe

Introduction

The Southern Appalachians is a region of great contrasts. In an area with great wealth in mineral resources, an area which produces one and one-half billion dollars worth of coal in a year, one finds great poverty, sub-standard housing, hunger, and poor health. In an area which has an extensive network of railroads, highly sophisticated machinery, industries linked to the largest, most powerful corporations in the world and a non-farm, industrialized population, one finds low levels of education, a low rate of skilled labor, and a socially and physically isolated people. How does one explain these incongruities? Are the people living in this area some type of cultural throwback? Are these conditions the result of purposive action on the part of a few greedy men wishing to retard future development of the region? Or is

SOURCE: *Paper presented at the American Anthropological Association, 1970.*

AUTHORS: Helen M. Lewis *is a staff member of the Highlander Research & Education Center, New Market, Tennessee. She is a former professor of sociology at Clinch Valley College, and lives on a farm in Dungannon, Virginia.*
Ed Knipe *is an associate professor in the Department of Sociology and Anthropology at Virginia Commonwealth University, Richmond.*

it just a case of a region or area being "behind the times"? Before attempting to analyze the causes of these conditions, we will give a brief history and description of that portion of Appalachia which we are considering.

Inside Central Appalachia

That part of Appalachia with which we are concerned is the portion of the Allegheny-Cumberland mountains in which bituminous coal mining developed. Portions of southwest Virginia, eastern Kentucky, and southern West Virginia form this area and are referred to by the Appalachian Regional Commission as Central Appalachia.

The area was late being settled. Until the Revolution it was an area to pass through or skirt around. The area was inaccessible and offered few advantages to the farmer in comparison with the fertile fields of the Blue Grass. It was covered by extensive forests, the soil was poor, and there was little level land. Those seeking good farming went into the Blue Grass, the Tennessee valleys, or the West.

There was a period of virtual isolation (80-100 years) in the 19th century. The early settlers and their families developed a way of life based upon subsistence agriculture and a social organization based upon kinship. It was a sparsely populated area of small landowners with isolated and dispersed settlements up and down the streams, since the bottom lands provided the only acreage suitable for intensive use. The land was rugged, the soil thin and unproductive, and the slope so steep as to justify the phrase "perpendicular corn fields." The traditional mountain culture which developed in this period has been described by John C. Campbell (1921), Horace Kephart (1913), and more recently by Jack Weller (1965) and Leonard Roberts (1959).

Many changes occurred in the late 1800's and early 1900's with the coming of lumbering, railroads, and coal mining to the area. The first load of coal was shipped from southwest Virginia in 1892 and from Harlan County, Kentucky, in 1911. There were large and rapid population increases in the coal mining counties. The population of Wise County, Virginia, rose from 9,400 in 1890 to 47,000 in 1920. Individuals and families migrated to the coal counties from the nearby farm counties of Kentucky, Virginia, and Tennessee. Some foreign born people were recruited into the coal fields, and Negroes from the South were contracted as laborers.

To house and serve these workers and their families, the mining companies, lumbering interests, and railroads built "encampments" for the newcomers. These "camps" or "colliery towns" were complete with company owned houses, stores, theaters, clinics, hospitals, churches, and schools. In addition to modifying the traditional residency patterns of the local population, a new class of people came to the area with the large coal companies. Chemists, engineers, doctors, and managers were brought into the area as representatives of urban culture. Most of them lived in the commercial and political centers which grew up at rail centers, courthouses, and trading villages. All of these changes resulted in a new system of social stratification hitherto unknown in the traditional mountain society.

Until World War II three different social systems existed side by side in the coal fields of the Southern Appalachians: (1) the original rural mountain settlements, characterized by a pattern of isolated residence and subsistence farming; (2) the coal camps, primarily composed of homogeneous work groups which were socially segregated and economically dependent upon a single extractive industry; and (3) the middle class towns, which were socially and economically tied to eastern urban centers (Lewis 1969). After World War II, rapid and far-reaching changes occurred in the coal fields. Mechanization of the mines reduced the camp population to at least one-half the original. Between 1950 and 1960 there was a 62 percent drop in mining employment in the eastern Kentucky coal fields and a population loss during the 1950's equal to 41 percent of the 1950 population (Brown 1962). The 1960's showed a continuation of the out-migration from the area (Brown 1970). Despite the tremendous out-migration from the area, the rapid technological changes in a one-industry area left a large number of unemployed miners and destitute families.

Along with mechanization the companies began either selling the coal camps' housing to individual miners or destroying the camps. Not only was there a decline in workers and camp population but the ownership of automobiles also made it possible for the workers to commute to work.

Despite the decline in mining employment, coal production has remained high and has boomed in the 1970's. This, however, has not altered some of the basic problems of poverty, unemployment, poor health, and meager education.

In order to analyze the nature of the Appalachian problems, we will review two models which have been used to describe and explain the social conditions of the region. In an attempt to understand some social phenomena, social scientists often construct models of that phenomena. By constructing a model, we are able to evaluate better the framework used by a particular researcher and compare one model with another. Thus, after surveying a number of competing models of some phenomena, we may conclude that one model better explains or predicts that in which we are interested. Or we may be able to combine one model with another so that our understanding is increased.

Models may be constructed in a number of ways. We do not have the space here to review strategies for model construction, but we can say something about types of models. Models may be general or specific, working or non-working. General models apply to a wider range of phenomena than do specific models. For example, the model of the atom shows a general configuration of atomic structure and does not apply to any one atom; on the other hand, a model of a Rolls-Royce automobile applies only to that specific automobile. A working model replicates the action of that which it represents, and it operates on the same principles or "laws," thereby helping us to explain or understand the process of interrelationships among the various parts that make up the model. Like a photograph, the non-working model "freezes" the action which it represents. The dimensions of models can be combined so as to produce a general working or non-working model, or a specific working or non-working model.

If we are to evaluate the merit or effectiveness of a model, we must look for a model that is both general (explains more than just one thing and refers to a class of phenomena) and working (operates in accordance with the principles ruling that which it represents). In the remainder of this chapter we will review two models of Appalachia to determine what value they have in helping us understand the questions we posed earlier. These models have not always been overtly formulated by persons writing about Appalachia. We have taken the liberty of formulating two models; The Culture of Poverty and the Colonialism models, which are representative of dominant perspectives held by those interpreting Appalachia.

Perhaps the most widely assumed model applied to Appalachia is the Culture of Poverty model. Valentine (1968) describes this model as a "Difference" or "Deficiency" model. This model involves describing the sub-culture of the Southern Appalachians and comparing it with the Greater Society. The accounts describe the customs, values, and style of life in a socio-historical tradition. A number of studies have assumed such a model (Weller 1965; Pearsall 1959, 1966; Stephenson 1968; Ford 1965; Ball 1968; Lewis 1968). These studies vary in the degree to which they emphasize the traits as "positive" or "functional" adaptations or as "pathological," disorganized, defeating value systems (Ball 1968). Some emphasize the sub-cultural traits as obsolete as indicated by such terms as "Yesterday's People" (Weller 1965), "Contemporary Ancestors" (Williams 1966), or "Arrested Frontier Culture" (Cressey 1953).

Lesser (1970) finds that most sub-cultural descriptions emphasize only the dramatic and destructive traits of Appalachia (e.g., traditionalism, fatalism) and emphasize the Appalachian people as passive and apathetic carriers of their culture. Henighan (1970), in comparing Weller and Stephenson, finds that Stephenson emphasizes a more "positive" view of Appalachian values. Stephenson (1968) uses the term "contentment" as contrasted to Weller's (1965) term "fatalism."

In an insightful essay, Roach and Gursslin (1967) evaluate the usefulness of the Culture of Poverty model. They suggest that much of the confusion about the culture of poverty is not with the notion of poverty but with the idea of culture. Most researchers begin with the assumption that such a sub-culture exists and then proceed to fill in its description. But culture is more than just description; culture refers to a set of normative patterns that emerge through a group's coping with its environment. Furthermore, the content of this culture must be transmitted from one generation to another. Much of the descriptive material about Appalachia has emphasized a somewhat stilted rudimentary set of normative regulations with little concern for the content of what is transmitted from one generation to another. The assumption is that middle-class or dominant American values are not transmitted in Appalachia.

A more pointed comment on the Culture of Poverty model concerns the purpose served by the model. "If the purpose is explanation, what is to be explained: group life, personality processes, deviant behavior, the origins of poverty, or the perpetuation of poverty?" (Roach and Gursslin 1967, 386). If we are concerned with the causes of poverty, we must view it differently than if we are concerned with the effects of poverty. In the former case, we are concerned with the factors which led to those behaviors described as belonging to those in the culture of poverty. In the latter case, we want to know how these behaviors are transmitted from one generation to another. Description answers neither of these questions.

There is little question about poverty in Appalachia. If we use income as a criterion, we find that the area of Appalachia which we are dealing with has a mean income of less than one-half that of the remainder of the United States. If we use health as a factor, we find that only five of the 60 counties have infant mortality rates lower than the national average; in 34 counties the rate is 20 percent higher than the national rate. The tuberculosis rates in some parts of the area are 10 times the national average. And in 25 percent of the counties there are fewer than 30 physicians per 100,000, as compared with 139 per 100,000 in the United States as a whole. If we use education as a criterion, we find educational attainment is significantly lower than the remainder of the United States. Seventy percent of the adult population have completed fewer than eight years of schooling. If we turn our attention to housing, we find that the rate of construction is only two-thirds that of the national average, and only 33 percent of the housing is sound and is equipped with plumbing. Thus, by almost any standard, the level of living in this area is sub-standard, i.e., at the poverty level.

None of the studies using the Culture of Poverty model tell us why these conditions prevail. And none of these studies inform us why these conditions cause certain values, norms, or behaviors among the people. One could dismiss all of this as nothing but academic folly if it were not for the fact that those persons and agencies concerned with relieving the above conditions often accept the Culture of Poverty model. They focus on the values of the Appalachian and say that these must be changed. This is almost like saying that one needs to stop the bleeding when an artery is severed. However, the application of a band-aid to such a wound disregards the cause of the bleeding in very much the same way that programs designed to change values often disregard the roots of such values.

We do not advocate discarding the Culture of Poverty model when such models (1) make clear what it is they are studying, (2) are concerned with both cause and perpetuation, and (3) do not confuse description with analysis.

An alternative approach to the Culture of Poverty model is the Colonialism model. This model has also been called the Exploitation model (Valentine 1968). Lesser (1970) and other so-called radical critics of the Culture of Poverty model follow this approach. Lesser states: "Essentially, their [Culture of Poverty proponents] argument is that the under-development of the region is a function of Appalachian character rather than the exploitative conditions institutionalized in the region." With the Exploitation model, however, one describes the Appalachians as a subsociety structurally alienated and lacking resources because of processes of the total economic political system. Those who control the resources preserve their advantages by discrimination. The people are not essentially passive; but these "subcultural" traits of fatalism, passivity, etc. are adjustive techniques of the powerless. They are ways by which people protect their way of life from new economic models and the concomitant alien culture. Lewis and Knipe (1970) emphasize certain of these values among Appalachians as reactions to powerlessness; they describe the socio-economic situation as "peasant-like."

There has been a growing interest in using this model to describe the social and economic conditions of the Southern Appalachians and to declare the region a Colonial Empire. Harry M. Caudill, in *Night Comes to the Cumberlands*, calls the Appalachians "the last unchallenged stronghold of Western colonialism." This is not a new claim. C. Vann Woodward (1951) characterizes the whole South as a colony suffering from absentee ownership and economic exploitation. Woodward places the Southern Appalachian colonialism in this context:

> As the 19th Century drew to a close and the new century
> progressed through the first decade, the penetration of
> the South and the Southern Appalachians was begun by
> Northeastern capital and is continuing at an accelerated
> rate. The Morgans, Mellons, the Rockefellers sent their
> agents to take charge of the region's railroads, mines,
> coke furnaces and financial corporations. (Woodward
> 1951)

A systematic account of colonialism has been undertaken
by Blauner (1969). In reference to the American Negro he
makes a distinction between classical colonialism and internal
colonialism. The basic difference between these two is that in
classical colonialism the colonizer moves in from outside, whereas in internal colonialism the colonizer brings in those colonized.
He defines classical colonialism as "domination over a geograph-
ically external political unit, most often inhabited by people of
a different race and culture; when this domination is political
and economic, the colony exists subordinate to and dependent
upon the mother country" (1968, 395). Blauner further distinguishes colonization as a process and colonialism as a system
of relationships that exist between those dominating and those
in a subordinate position. It is the process of oppression rather
than differences in political and economic structure which is
most important.

Blauner suggests four components of the colonization complex. First, colonization begins with a forced, involuntary entry.
Those in the dominant position are not invited guests. Second,
the impact on culture and social organization is greater than we
would expect through cultural contact and acculturation. There
follows, soon after the entry of the colonizer, rather rapid modi-
fications in values, orientation, and the way of life of the colonized. Third, colonization involves a relationship by which members of the colonized group tend to be administered by representatives of the dominant group. And fourth, there exists a
condition of racism, "a principle of social domination by which
a group, seen as inferior or different in terms of alleged biological
characteristics, is exploited, controlled and oppressed socially
and psychically by a superordinate group" (1969, 396).

If these relationships characterize the colonization process, what accounts for the colonized being colonized? Blauner suggests that the main source of domination comes from technological superiority. Those being colonized have resources, natural or human, which are useful to the colonizer. If these resources can be harnessed, the technological superiority of the colonizer is further enhanced, thereby increasing the degree of superiority. Thus the resources of the colonized perpetuate the colonization process.

The Colonialism model shows somewhat more promise when applied to the Appalachian situation than the Culture of Poverty model. Blauner makes it clear what he is studying— domination. He accounts for the cause and perpetuation of the condition, and because he is concerned with processes he goes beyond mere description.

The question now is what information do we have to substantiate the applicability of this model in the Appalachian case. If the model "fits," we should be able to show how colonialism came to the mountains, how it is perpetuated, and, finally, what consequences it has had upon the local culture.

Colonialism and Country Folks

We have already touched upon the beginnings of coal mining in the Southern Appalachians. When the outside colonizers came to the Appalachians in the latter part of the 19th century, they found a society approximating an Asian or African country in its economic foundations. The outside speculators bought land, mineral, and timber rights from illiterate, simple mountain farmers. One important consequence of mining was that it did not open up the mountains. The isolation of the area went beyond just physical isolation; it now included social isolation. The inability of the indigenous population to cope with those representatives of the coal industry and the many fraudulent land deals that were made with the local people stand as bold evidence of antagonistic relationships.[1]

A survival of this early relationship is found in the "broad form" deeds that have been supported by the Kentucky courts. These deeds included "all minerals and metallic substances and all combinations of the same," and they give the unconditional right to remove them by any method "deemed necessary or convenient." This stipulation has allowed companies to strip or surface mine land in the face of strong opposition by the land owners who had sold only the "mineral rights" many years before. The state has used the broad form deeds to support positive legal action against landowners who have attempted to block mining operations. Several cases have made the news in the past few years. Widow Combs placed her body in front of the dozers and ended up in the Knott County jail. Conspiracy charges were brought against Appalachia Volunteers and Southern Conference Education Fund workers who helped Jink Ray and other local landowners successfully stop stripping operations.

Although many writers on Appalachia speak of the outside control of the wealth, the degree and extent to which this is true has been only slightly and sporadically documented. There are no systematic, thorough studies of the land and mineral ownership of the region. This "oversight" itself might be considered "evidence" of the protection which is provided colonizers. Even the Appalachian Regional Commission, after a number of years of data collection and analysis of various aspects of Appalachian poverty and economic potential, has only lately turned its attention to the Central Appalachian area, first with a study of capital resource and a proposed study of land and mineral ownership and taxation (Appalachian Regional Commission 1969). One must go to the "radical" student or "movement" publications or to the Bureau of Mines statistics to find any studies or documentation of such things as coal production.

Kirby (1969), in a study of the tax records of eleven major coal producing counties in eastern Kentucky, found that 31 people and corporations owned four-fifths of east Kentucky's coal. It is estimated that 70 to 80 percent of the southwest Virginia minerals is owned by four or five large corporations. And David Walls (1969, 15) lists seven firms which produce one-third of the coal in Central Appalachia.

More interesting is the fact that many of these "independent" companies are linked in corporate structures. One study (Barkan and Lloyd 1970) for a two-county area in southwest Virginia found a tightly linked chain of railroad men, industrialists, and financiers who own and benefit from the timber and mineral wealth of the area. Diehl (1970) has traced some of the interconnections of ownership in eastern Kentucky and West Virginia. These connections extend in some cases beyond the borders of America to such places as South Africa and to such diversified industries as electronic equipment, chemicals, oil, banks, and auto manufacturers.

The absorption of coal companies by fuel and energy industries reflects the major changes in dominant industries in the United States in general. The early coal companies were controlled by shipping and railroads; later they were dominated by the steel and automobile manufacturers. Beginning in the 1960's and the "Energy Era," fuel and electrical powers began their present domination.

Another indication of outside control of the area is seen by looking at taxation and economic development. David Brooks talks of the role of the coal industry in regional development.[2] He points to the limited ability of mining to provide economic development in a region. Unlike manufacturing or industries in which materials are fabricated or value is added through a production process, mining processes add little value and do little to stimulate other types of economic activities. Since mining is immobile, fixed in space, and limited to its one product, and since the work is arduous and dangerous, it must develop means of attracting or controlling labor. It is advantageous for coal mining to operate in isolation without competing companies. The characteristics of mining lead to a one-industry area with labor tied to the one industry and little development outside the extraction of the minerals. This also leaves no development when the minerals are gone (McKelvey 1968).

Without intervention, mining itself tends to develop certain exploitative or colonial characteristics. Resources generated by coal mining for the local area are meager. In other industries surplus is used for capital investments, which creates new corporations, associations, and other businesses, and develops a middle-stratum of technicians and specialists. This does not happen with coal mining.

Except for wages paid to workers and local taxes paid to the area, coal mining offers little. At one time large numbers were employed in the mines of the area. In 1932 there were 705,000 miners; in 1940 there were 439,000 miners; and today there are only 132,000 miners (Coal Data Book 1968). The mechanization of coal mining and the resulting decline in mining employment in the Southern Appalachians in the 1950's resulted in a wholesale migration from the area and a high degree of unemployment which continues into the 1970's.

In Virginia there are still 8,862 miners in a six-county area. Coal mining is still the main source of employment, accounting for approximately one third of the total labor force. The coal companies paid $56,361,577 in wages in 1968. During the same year, the area produced 36,865,703 tons of coal which, if valued at $4.50 a ton, would total $165,956,000 (Virginia Department of Labor and Industry 1968). The total taxes paid to the area are not known. But one can draw some conclusions from the records of one company. This company in 1967 employed 448 men and mined approximately 2,500,000 tons of coal in four mines. Wages, if all the men worked full time, would have been approximately $3,240,000; royalties to the corporation owning the mineral rights to the land @$.142 per ton would amount to $360,000; and 40 cents a ton to the United Mine Workers' Health and Welfare Fund would amount to $1,000,000. The landholding company and the mining company paid $207,533 in county taxes in 1968. This amount represents taxes on land under development, land not under development, buildings, and equipment. In addition to the four mines, land was leased for stripping, augering, and several truck mine operations. The total outlay for wages, royalties, and taxes was $3,807,533. The value of the coal at $4.50 per ton was $11,128,000. This leaves a difference of $7,320,467. The amount of taxes paid, although small in comparison to gross income, represents 13.5 percent of the tax income for the county in which the company has its operations. Despite their resources, the coal mining counties generate a smaller proportion of the total revenue than the counties in the rest of the Appalachian area.

The corporation having the mineral rights mentioned above is probably the most profitable in America. According to its 1968 Annual Report it netted 64 percent of gross and paid dividends of 40 cents out of each dollar received (Penn Virginia Corporation Annual Report, 1968). Harry Caudill (1968) reports the same corporation as netting 61 percent of gross and paying 45 cents on each dollar received in 1964. He compares it with General Motors which reported a profit of 10.2 cents from each dollar received and paid a dividend of five cents. Caudill claims that this corporation is characteristic of other mineral-owning corporations in the area.

Depletion and depreciation allowances give coal companies a very favorable position. Depletion for coal mined is based on the cost of the mineral properties and estimated recoverable tonnage. In some cases the depletion allowances is greater than the taxes on the minerals and the land. Although the original purchases of most of the mineral lands were made before 1900 at 30 cents to $1.00 an acre, the depletion is figured on the last price paid. When lands change hands, even through a subsidiary, the new cost is the basis for the depletion. This is figured as the percentage of the cost of the land which is mined during the year. Kirby (1969) points out that this is an incentive to sell. An acre bought for 50 cents can be sold in a year of mining for $5,000, thereby increasing the cost depletion allowance considerably.

Another concession to coal companies is the tax on mine equipment and machinery. In Virginia they are taxed at only 10 percent of their value, while the equipment of all others, belonging either to individuals and/or businesses, is taxed at approximately one-third of its value. Here also, resale to subsidiaries can make this even lower for coal companies. A leasing company can sell a $100,000 machine to a mining company which it controls for $10,000; then the mining company will pay tax on 10 percent of that or $1,000. Caudill (1966) reports a similar situation in Kentucky. Through resale to subsidiaries, mining machinery worth $75,000 is valued at $3,000; taxes are less than a miner pays on the automobile which he drives to work to operate the machine. Blizzard (1966) reports taxes low in West Virginia because of the influence of the coal industry. West Virginia has a gross sales tax regardless of profit or loss, but coal companies do not pay on sales made at out-of-state markets, thus excluding most of the coal sales. Machinery and supplies used for coal mining are also exempt from sales tax.

In line with the general tendency of colonists to be exploitive, we find that public spiritedness on the part of coal operations is rare in the area. Coal companies in Virginia are

suing the counties, claiming that assessing "land under development" at a differential rate is in fact a form of severence tax on
mined coal which is unconstitutional. Most of the remarks con-
cerning civic responsibility made by coal company representatives sound like turn-of-the-century rugged capitalism. When
asked about decaying coal camps, burning slag heaps, or disabled
and unemployed miners, coal company executives are heard to
say that they have no responsibility to the area or the people.
Their responsibility is to mine coal as cheaply and efficiently as
possible and to make a profit for the company and the stockholders. They provide employment and housing when needed
and get food stores when necessary to hold employees; they continue these as long as they are necessary to keep workers or are
profitable to the company. Even one of the most public-spirited
executives of a large mining company said that the decision to
begin strip mining was made because it was "the logical thing,
cost wise" (Trillin 1969). This same executive has been quoted
in the *Mountain Eagle* and with great candor in the NET film
Rich Lands, Poor People: "If there is something wrong with
what we are doing in Eastern Kentucky, then there is something
wrong with the country."

The condition of racism associated with the Colonialism
model is well illustrated in Appalachia. Memmi (1967) points
out that it is not only the colonizers but the colonized who go
into businesses that engage in this practice. In the region one
finds that the smaller independent coal operators are even more
conservative in their political and economic ideology than the
outsiders. The *Independent Coal Leader* claims to represent the
small operators; its contents reflect a general negative evaluation
of the local population who are unemployed. It has also taken
rather dramatic stands against any individual or organization
attempting to question the coal industry and its practices. Most
of these small operators are dependent upon the larger companies
for leases or money for equipment or coal sales facilities. A number of local millionnaires have emerged in the area through strip
mining, the selling of equipment, and truck mining. It is interesting to observe how many of these persons make their money and
then retire to Florida. Perhaps Florida serves as the "homeland"
for the native who joins the colonists.

The natives who become colonizers of their own people
must protect themselves by giving an even more disparaging

evaluation of the people than the outsider. While the outsider may become interested in the ways of the natives—collecting quilts, mountain folk tales, and music—and speak with appreciation about mountain culture, the native exploiter is more likely to denigrate his own, to speak of laziness and "sorriness," or to speak negatively of a "certain class" of people, especially those on welfare or those who are unemployed. The native colonizers recount stories of the untrustworthiness and unreliability of their workers. Since these small operators often pay even less than minimum wages, they find themselves in competition with welfare programs.

This is not a new pattern. General John Daniel Imboden was one of the earliest "developers" of the area. In 1880 he bought 47,000 acres of mineral lands in Wise County, Virginia. Later, he bought 21,000 acres for only 35 cents an acre for "certain gentlemen of large means" who were officials of the Baltimore and Ohio Railroad (Henson 1965). A list of property made in May, 1880, reveals that Imboden and his son owned one-sixth interest in over 100,000 acres in Wise County. Imboden purchased land, built the railroad into the coal fields, and later was a lobbyist in North Carolina for the coal interests. After a stint at the state capital in Raleigh he wrote about the elegant people he was meeting. He said he told them about Wise County and "how nice it was. . . and interested them so much that when our road is built they are coming out to see for themselves. They think it must be delightful to see and mingle with such primitive people" (Henson, 7).

One test to determine whether colonization exists is to see whether the colonists utilize the same services they provide for the colonized. The colonizers generally distrust such services in Appalachia, especially local doctors and local hospitals. Local medical personnel are mistrusted because they provide services for miners or country people and therefore inadequate service for they, too, are opportunists or exploiters. A local hospital administrator resents the fact that members of the local board travel 100-300 miles eastward to see "good doctors" or obtain "good medical services" because the "coal camp doctors" are not as good. Other local services and professionals who stay in the area are denigrated. The opinion is that they are no good or they would go elsewhere. Fannon (1963), in "Dying Colonialism," an essay about the native's attitude toward available medical services, points to the native's distrust of local medicine, and sees it as an agent of the colonists. Perhaps the judgment is true. The fantastically poor medical service provided in the early days of coal camps in the Appalachians has been documented (Boone 1947). Today, coal company doctors often refuse to admit the existence of pneumoconiosis or "black lung," and one company doctor was elected to the Virginia House of Delegates and succeeded in getting the disease removed from the Workman's Compensation. Company doctors are said by many miners to be reluctant to report injuries or to diagnose pneumoconiosis in order to protect the company's insurance rates. But they are likely to diagnose it when the person is seeking employment in order to keep the company from "getting stuck" with an already disabled miner.

To continue with examples of conformity between the realities of Appalachian life and the Colonialism model would be pointless. It cannot be disputed that the coal interests came into the region "uninvited," that cultural patterns changed as a result of this intrusion, and that the area is controlled by representatives of the industry. The fact that racism exists to perpetuate this pattern has been illustrated. Since these conditions exist, it would appear that any recommendations for change should take these factors into consideration. Changing the values of Appalachians will not change the system of colonialism nor will knowledge of the situation. Both Radcliffe-Brown and Malinowski suggest that we must know something about those who were to *benefit* from Western colonialism (Harris 1968, 514-567). But they are careful not to question the motives of the British colonizers. Unfortunately, much ethnography has been carried out under colonial conditions; and, in a way, the anthropologist has become as much a colonizer as those having economic and political interests in an area. We tend to study those who resist the least, and colonized peoples are powerless to resist our intrusion into their culture. While the anthropologist often becomes the native's advocate, he may not wish to upset those conditions which enable him to continue his research. "Moderation, compromise and civil service decorum are the ethical bases for the aspiring 'practical anthropologist' " (Malinowski 1945, 161).

Future Prospects

In looking at the two models we find differences in responses to the conditions in Appalachia. Those who follow the deficiency or difference approach (the Culture of Poverty model) work to help and change people. Their object is to change the values of the poor and assimilate them into the middle class or the "greater" culture. Various programs of social work, education, and psychiatry are designed to change attitudes, to motivate, and to assimilate. Those who follow the exploitation or colonialism model emphasize the need to change the structure of society. They advocate the redistribution of goods and resources to give power to the poor. If colonized peoples always rebel, then we must wait and see what happens in Appalachia. Blauner (1967) attributes the revolt of Blacks in America to their colonized position, and Moore (1970) uses the same model to explain the rebellion of Mexican-Americans.

Tom Gish, editor of the *Mountain Eagle* in Whitesburg, Kentucky, talks about colonialism, outside exploitation of the wealth, and the various government programs for amelioration. Although outside corporations still exploit the resources, he feels that the period of blatant colonial control and local domination is past. The coal companies can continue to mine the minerals through control over a few politicians, state courts and lawyers, and they can control labor through collusion with the United Mine Workers. In the meantime, they can ignore and leave behind the many social problems resulting from technological change: illness, injury, powerlessness, and deprivation. These will be handled, along with polluted streams and devastated land, by federal government programs. The early war on poverty programs tried to create political action; such action was frightening to the local power structure and to the corporate interests. These programs have been co-opted or dropped. The focus is now on economic development, assistance, and control. Regional offices of Health, Education and Welfare, of Labor, of the U.S. Corps of Engineers, of the Office of Economic Opportunity, of the Departments of Agriculture and Interior funnel in programs of "assistance" through regional economic planning and development organizations. Gish finds these regional organizations developing more and more like the Office of Indian Affairs, i.e. to control the natives. Perhaps this type of action is a latter stage of colonialism in which those who are left-over, the land and the people, are now wards of the government, living on an Appalachian Reservation.

NOTES

[1]Warren Wright, Burdine, Kentucky, has researched early titles and land transfers in parts of eastern Kentucky. He finds many cases of fraudulent and illegal leases and ownership.

[2]David Brooks, former chief economist, Bureau of Mines, in talks to the Appalachian Seminar, Clinch Valley College, January 1970.

REFERENCES CITED

Appalachian Regional Commission
1968   Research Report No. 8, Preliminary Analysis for Development
       of Central Appalachia. Washington, D.C.

1969   Research Report No. 9, Appendix C, Capital Resources in
       the Central Appalachian Region.   Cheechi and Co., Washing-
       ton, D.C.

Ball, Richard A.
1968   "A Poverty Case: The Analgesic Subculture of the Southern
       Appalachians" *American Sociological Review,* 33:6 (Decem-
       ber), 885-895

Barkam, Barry and R. Baldwin Lloyd
1970   "Picking Poverty's Pocket" Article One, 1, 2 (May), 21-29

Blauner, Robert
1969   "Internal Colonialism and Ghetto Revolt" *Social Problems*
       (Spring), Vol. 16, No. 4, 1969, 393-408

Blizzard, William C.
1966   "West Virginia Wonderland" *Appalachian South* (Summer)

Boone, Joel T.
1947   A Medical Survey of the Bituminous Coal Industry Washing-
       ton, D.C.: United States Department of Interior

Brown, James S.
1962   Eastern Kentucky Resource Development Project, Lexington,
       University of Kentucky

1970   First Look at the 1970 Census *Mountain Life and Work* (July-
       August), 4-8

Campbell, John C.
  1921 *The Southern Highlander and His Homeland* New York: Russell Sage Foundation

Caudill, Harry
  1962 *Night Comes to the Cumberlands* Boston: Little, Brown & Co.

  1966 "Poverty and Affluence in Appalachia: How Absentee Ownership in an Extremely Rich Land Produced a Remarkable Poor People" *Appalachian South* Pipestem, West Virginia (Spring)

  1968 "Appalachia: The Dismal Land" In Jeremy Larner and Irving Howe, ed., *Views From the Left* New York: William Morrow, 264-273

Cressey, Paul F.
  1949 "Social Disorganization and Reorganization in Harlan County, Kentucky" *American Sociological Review,* XIV, 3 (June), 389-394

Diehl, Richard
  1970 "Appalachia Energy Elite: A Wing of Imperialism?" *People's Appalachia* (March)

  1970 "How International Energy Elite Rules" *People's Appalachia* (April-May)

Fanon, Frantz
  1967 *A Dying Colonialism* New York: Grove

Ford, Thomas R.
  1965 "The Effects of Prevailing Values and Beliefs on the Perpetuation of Poverty in Rural Areas" *Problems of Chronically Depressed Rural Areas* North Carolina University: Agriculture Policy Institute

  1965 "Value Orientations of a Culture of Poverty: The Southern Appalachian Case" Working with low-income families, American Home Economics Association, Washington, D.C.

Harris, Marvin
  1968 *The Rise of Anthropological Theory* New York: Thomas Y. Crowell

Henigham, Richard
    1970   Remarks at People's Appalachian Research Collective Confer-
            ence Huntington, West Virginia

Henson, Edward L.
    1965   *General Imboden and the Economic Development of Wise
            County 1880-81* Historical Society of Southwest Virginia
            (February 6-8)

Kephart, Horace
    1913   *Our Southern Highlanders* New York: MacMillan

Kirby, Richard
    1969   "Kentucky Coal: Owners, Taxes, Profits: A Study in Repre-
            sentations Without Taxation" *Appalachian Lookout* 1,6
            (October), 19-27

Knipe, Edward E. and Lewis, Helen M.
    1969   "The Impact of Coal Mining on the Traditional Mountain Sub-
            Culture: A Case of Peasantry Gained and Peasantry Lost" A
            paper read at the annual meeting of the Southern Anthro-
            pological Society, New Orleans, Louisiana

Lesser, Roger
    1970   "Culture: Toward Tomorrow's People" *People's Appalachia*,
            No. 1 (March)

Lewis, Helen M.
    1968   "Subcultures of the Southern Appalachians" *The Virginia
            Geographer* 3,1 (Spring), 2-3

McKelvey, V. E.
    1968   "Appalachia: Problems and Opportunities" Mineral Resources
            of the Appalachian Region, Geological Survey Professional
            Paper 580, Washington, D.C.

Malinowski, B.
    1945   *The Dynamics of Culture Chicago: An Inquiry Into Race Re-
            lations in Africa*, P. Kaberry, ed., New Haven: Yale University
            Press

Memmi, Albert
    1965   *The Colonizer and the Colonized* Boston: Beacon

Moore, Joan W.
>1970 "Colonialism: The Case of the Mexican-Americans" *Social Problems* 71,4 (Spring), 463-472

National Coal Association
>1968 *Bituminous Coal Facts* Washington, D.C.

>1968 *Coal Data Book* Washington, D.C.

Pearsall, Marion
>1959 *Little Smokey Ridge* University of Alabama: University of Alabama Press

>1966 "Communicating With the Educationally Deprived" *Mountain Life and Work* (Spring), 3-11

Penn Virginia Corporation
>1968 Penn Virginia Corporation Annual Report

Roach, Jack L. and Gursslin, Orville R.
>1967 "An Evaluation of the Concept 'Culture of Poverty' " *Social Forces* 45,3 (March), 383-392

Roberts, Leonard W.
>1959 *Up Cutshin and Down Greasy* Lexington: University of Kentucky

Stephenson, John B.
>1968 *Shiloh: A Mountain Community* Lexington: University of Kentucky

Trillin, Calvin
>1969 "U.S. Journal: Kentucky, the Logical Thing, Costwise" *New Yorker* (December 27), 33-36

Valentine, Charles A.
>1968 *Culture and Poverty* Chicago: University of Chicago Press

Virginia Department of Labor and Industry
>1968 Annual Report

Walls, David
     1968-69   Research Bulletins - issues of *Appalachian Lookout* Prestonsburg, Kentucky

Weller, Jack
     1965   *Yesterday's People* Lexington: University of Kentucky

Williams, Jonathan
     1966   "The Southern Appalachians" *Craft Horizons*, X-XVI, 3 (June), 47-66

Woodward, C. Vann
     1951   *Origins of the New South* Baton Rouge, Louisana: State University Press

CENTRAL PREPARATION PLANT
ELK HORN COAL
FLAMING HORSEPOWER COALS
ON THE C&O RAILROAD

Wayland
WASD

THE ACQUISITION OF RESOURCES

Section II: Acquisition of Resources

The first stage of the colonization process is the acquisition of land and natural resources. The following essays describe this process as it has been carried out in different parts of the mountains by different agents in different forms of appropriation: agriculture, tourist development, government forest development, coal development, and the general industrialization of the area.

Ronald Eller in "Industrialization and Social Change in Appalachia: A Look at the Static Image" attacks the interpretation of Appalachia as a passive, static, undeveloped region, left out of modernization and progress. Eller points to the type of industrial development which occurred in the area and the changes which resulted. These changes in agriculture, population, land ownership, and political systems were due to the exploitative, industrial development.

Jack Weller in "Appalachia's Mineral Colony" presents the case for the coal regions of Central Appalachia being a mineral colony. He outlines the destruction and exploitation of resources by out-of-area corporations.

Edgar Bingham in "The Impact of Recreational Development on Pioneer Life Styles in Southern Appalachia" makes the case for the destruction of traditional mountain culture and economic life style by recreational development. He describes the process whereby large developers obtain the land and suggests controls which might retard or prevent some of the exploitation.

Ralph Nader in a letter to Sir Denys Flowerdew Lowson who is Chairman of the Board of Directors of the American Association, a British company owning coal lands in Tennessee, relates the history of the British company's operations. He condemns the policies of the company and suggests ways the company may be socially accountable.

Si Kahn in "The Forest Service and Appalachia" points out that the U.S. Government is the area's largest landowner and the land is developed for timbering and recreation for those outside the region. This has resulted in dislocation and displacement of local population. Lack of land and taxes further limit growth and development of the area. The local population benefits little from national forest and recreation areas. Kahn suggests ways in which the forest service could become a real resource to mountain people.

INDUSTRIALIZATION AND SOCIAL CHANGE
IN APPALACHIA, 1880-1930:
A LOOK AT THE STATIC IMAGE

by
Ronald D. Eller

The belief that time and geography somehow set the Southern mountains off from the rest of the American experience has
been part of our understanding of the Appalachian region for almost a hundred years.[1] As early as the 1870's, writers for the
new monthly magazines which flourished after the Civil War had
begun to develop and exploit a literary image of the region.
Initially drawn to the mountains in search of the interesting and
the picturesque, local color writers such as Mary Noailles Mur-
free, James Lane Allen, John Fox, Jr., and others were quick
to turn the quaint and simple lives of the mountaineers into grist
for the literary mill. Between 1870 and 1890, over two hundred
travel accounts and short stories were published in which the
mountain people emerged as a rude, backward, romantic, and
sometimes violent race who had quietly lived for generations in
isolation from the mainstream of American life.[2]

Implicit in this literary image was a sense of "otherness"
which not only marked the region as "a strange land inhabited
by a peculiar people" but defined that strangeness in terms of

SOURCE: *Paper presented at the Southern Historical Association,
          Atlanta, 1976.*

AUTHOR: Ronald Eller, *a former Rockefeller Scholar at the University
          of North Carolina, Chapel Hill, is a native of West Virginia.
          He is the director of the oral history program and teaches
          history at Mars Hill College, Mars Hill, North Carolina.*

the process of American historical growth. To the urban middle-class readers of *Cosmopolitan, Harper's,* and *Atlantic Monthly,* the apparent persistence of pioneer-like conditions in the mountains seemed to reflect not merely the normal patterns of rural life but "an earlier phase of American development preserved, like a mammoth in ice."[3] Because metaphor was more interesting than reality, the Appalachian present came to be linked with the American past, and eventually the analogy was accepted as fact. By the turn of the century, according to historian Henry Shapiro, the idea that Appalachia was "a discrete ethnic and cultural unit within but not of America" had become a convention of the popular mind.[4] For Americans of the Progressive period who had witnessed the passing of the western frontier, Appalachia became "the frontier we have left within," and the mountaineers were "our contemporary ancestors."[5]

Succeeding generations have periodically rediscovered and reinterpreted the region in the context of their own day, but the static image has remained the standard perception of mountain life. In 1913, for example, Horace Kephart found "our Southern highlanders. . .still thinking essentially the same thoughts, still living in much the same fashion as did their ancestors in the days of Daniel Boone. The progress of mankind from that age to this," he claimed, "is no heritage of theirs."[6] James Watt Raine traveled the "land of saddlebags" in 1924 and again in 1942, and a decade later North Callahan made a similar journey into what he believed was the "happy" but "static society" of the Smoky Mountain country.[7] With the outbreak of the war on poverty in the 1960's, the mountaineers became simply "Yesterday's People"—part of that "other America" of which Michael Harrington wrote.[8] More recently, the rise of the new ethnicity and the counterculture movement have brought attention to the mountain people as just plain "down home folk," and a flourishing minor industry has developed to fabricate such oddities as dulcimers, quilts, log cabins and "Maw's Moonshine Hunie." Of late we have also seen the introduction of courses in Appalachian studies and the proliferation of symposia aimed at diagnosing the "unique" qualities of mountain life. But this revival of interest has done little to alter our traditional views. According to one well known student of the region, Appalachia can still be seen "as a vanishing frontier and its people as frontiersmen, suspended and isolated, while the rest of the country moves across the twentieth century."[9] Marooned on an island of hills, the mountaineer has seemed shut off from the forces which have shaped the modern world. He has lived, we are told, in a land "Where Time Stood Still."[10]

Arnold Toynbee may have offered the most callous assertion of this view when he suggested that the mountain people of the South were little better than barbarians. "They have relapsed into illiteracy and witchcraft," he wrote. "They suffer from poverty, squalor, and ill health. They are the American counterparts of the latter-day white barbarians of the Old World —Rifis, Albanians, Kurds, Pathans, and Hairy Ainus." But whereas these latter seemed to be the belated survivals of an ancient barbarism, "the Appalachians," Toynbee argued, "present the melancholy spectacle of a people who have acquired civilization and then lost it."[11]

Cast in the static role, mountain people have thus rarely appeared as conscious actors on the stage of American history, and almost never on center stage. They are acknowledged to exist somewhere in the background, as subjects to be acted upon, but not as people participating within the historical drama itself. As a result, our efforts to explain and deal with the social problems of the region have focused not on economic and political realities in the area as they evolved over time, but on the supposed inadequacies of a pathological culture which is seen to have poorly equipped mountain people for life in the modern industrial world. Having overlooked elements of movement and change that have tied the mountains to the rest of the American experience, we have blamed the mountaineers for their own distress, rather than the forces which have caused it.[12]

Blaming the victim, of course, is not a uniquely American phenomenon. Rather it is a misreading that takes international form. French intellectuals talk about the Alps, and Spanish intellectuals talk about the Pyrenees in much the same simple if condescending way that urban Americans talk about Appalachia.[13] Indeed, all over the world the terms applied to rural people by urban people have implied either contempt and condescension, or—and this is the opposite of the same attitude— a romantic admiration for the simple, hardy virtues of rural life.[14] Since the Southern mountains were among the most rural areas of eastern America, the Appalachian people have suffered exceedingly from this type of urban provincialism.

Ironically, it was during the same years that the static image was emerging as the dominant literary view that a revolution of dynamic proportions was shaking the very foundations of the mountain social order. In Appalachia, as in the rest of the country, the decades from 1880 to 1930 were years of transition and change. What had been in 1860 only the quiet back-country of the Old South became by the turn of the century a new frontier for expanding industrial capitalism. The coming of railroads, the building of towns and villages, and the general expansion of industrial employment greatly altered the traditional patterns of mountain life and called forth certain adjustments, responses, and defenses on the part of the mountaineers. This transformation varied in scope and speed, but by the end of the 1920's few residents of the region were left untouched by the industrial age.

The effects of this transition were large. For one thing, mountain agriculture went into serious decline. While the size of the average mountain farm was about 187 acres in the 1880's, by 1930 the average Appalachian farm contained only 76 acres, and in some counties the average was as low as 47 acres.[15] This decline was universal throughout the region but was most pronounced in the coal fields and other areas of intense economic growth. Significantly, while the total number of farms increased during these years, the total amount of land in farms actually decreased almost twenty percent as a result of the purchase of farm properties by timber and mining companies and for inclusion in national forests and parks.[16]

Farm productivity and income also changed. While farm production had been the major (and usually the sole) source of income in 1880, by 1930 most mountain farms had become part-time units of production, and the major source of income had shifted to non-agricultural employment—mining, logging, carpentry, and other forms of public work.[17] In Knott County, Kentucky, for example, the income per farm from farming in 1930 averaged only $215, while the income per farm from non-farm enterprises averaged over $342.[18] In 1880 the mountains had been a major producer of swine in the South, but by 1930 swine production in the region had declined to only 39 percent of its former level.[19] Such data suggests that the traditional image of the pre-industrial mountain farm must be altered, and that the small, marginal farm usually associated with the stereotyped picture of Appalachia was in fact a product of industrialization—that is, a more recent development not associated with the purported isolation of the region.

Along with the decline of agriculture came subtle changes in demographic relationships as well. Whereas mountain society in the 1880's had been characterized by a diffuse pattern of open-country agricultural settlements located primarily in the fertile valleys and plateaus, by the turn of the century the population had begun to shift into non-agricultural areas and to concentrate around centers of industrial growth. Between 1900 and 1930, the urban population of the region increased four-fold and the rural non-farm population almost two-fold, while the farm population itself increased by only five percent.[20] A few of the burgeoning urban centers were destined to be temporary communities, such as the big timber towns of Sunburst and Ravensford in the Great Smoky Mountains, but most were permanent structures which had a lasting impact upon mountain life. It is important to point out, moreover, that the majority of these new industrial communities were company towns. In fact, over six hundred company towns were constructed in the Southern mountains during this period, and in the coal fields they outnumbered independent incorporated towns more than five to one.[21]

This rising urban population provided a base for the emergence of a more modern political system in the mountains, one increasingly dominated by corporate interests and business-minded politicians. Where the traditional political order had relied largely on kinship, personal contacts, and a broad-based party structure, after the turn of the century the level of citizen participation declined, and the average farmer or laborer became isolated from the political process. As early as the 1890's, industrialists such as Stephan B. Elkins in West Virginia and H. Clay Evans in Tennessee had begun to gain control of the political organizations in the mountains and to turn the powers of state and local government toward the expansion of commerce and the exploitation of the region's natural resources.[22] As a result, there emerged in Appalachia a contracted political system based upon an economic hierarchy—those who controlled the jobs also controlled the political system, and those who controlled the political system used their power to exploit the region's natural wealth for their own personal gain. This loss of local political control naturally distressed many mountain people and plunged the region into prolonged industrial violence and social strife.[23]

Behind this transition in political culture lay the integration of the region into the national economy and the subordination of local interests to those of outside corporations. Nowhere was this process more evident than in the concentration of large amounts of mountain land in the hands of absentee owners. Beginning in the 1870's, Northern speculators and outside businessmen carved out huge domains in the rich timberlands and mineral regions of Appalachia. By 1910 outlanders controlled not only the best stands of hardwood timber and the thickest seams of coal but a large percentage of the surface land in the region as well. For example, in that portion of western North Carolina which later became the Great Smoky Mountains National Park, over 75 percent of the land came under the control of thirteen corporations, and one timber company alone owned over a third of the total acreage.[24] The situation was even worse in the coal fields. According to the West Virginia State Board of Agriculture in 1900, outside capitalists owned 90 percent of the coal in Mingo County, 90 percent of the coal in Wayne County, and 60 percent of that in Boone and McDowell Counties.[25] Today, absentee corporations control more than half the total land area in the nine southernmost counties of that state.[26]

The immediate effect of this concentration of land holding was to dislodge a large part of the region's population from their ancestral homes. A few former landowners managed to remain on the land as sharecroppers or tenant farmers, and occasionally a family continued to live temporarily on the old homeplace, paying rent to absentee landlords.[27] But a great number of the displaced mountaineers migrated to the mill villages and mining towns where they joined the ever-growing ranks of the new industrial working class. In the Cumberland Plateau, less than a third of those employed in 1930 remained in agriculture. The rest had moved to the mines or into service related jobs.[28] Uprooted from their traditional way of life, some individuals were unable to reestablish permanent community ties, and they became wanderers drifting from mill to mill, from company house to company house, in search of higher pay or better living conditions. Most dreamed initially of returning to the land after a few years of public work, but the rising land values which accompanied industrial development soon pushed land ownership beyond the reach of the average miner or mill hand.

Caught up in the social complex of the new industrial communities, many mountaineers found themselves unable to escape their condition of powerlessness and dependency. By coming to a coal mining town, the miner had exchanged the independence and somewhat precarious self-sufficiency of the family farm for subordination to the coal company and dependence upon a wage income. He lived in a company house; he worked in a company mine; and he purchased his groceries and other commodities from the company store. He sent his children to the company school and patronized the company doctor and the company church. The company deducted rent, school, medical and other fees from his monthly wage, and under the prevailing system of scrip, he occasionally ended the month without cash income. He had no voice in community affairs or working conditions, and he was dependent upon the benevolence of the employer to maintain his rate of pay.

Socially, if not physically, the working class mountaineer was more isolated in his new situation than he had been on the family farm, for industrialization introduced rigid class distinctions into the highland culture.[29] Traditional status distinctions had always existed, but there were few economic differences within the rural population. With the coming of the industrial age, however, the dichotomy between employer and employed became overt. In the company town the miners lived in small dwellings in the hollow near the tipple, but mine superintendents often built palatial structures high on the hillside overlooking the town.[30] Surrounded by elegant trees and well-kept grounds, these homes clearly defined the operator's social rank. In some communities the railroad track literally divided the town in two, separating the more substantial residences of the managing class from the miners' shacks. The social gap between the classes increased, moreover, as managers and professional personnel developed life styles and formal institutions different from those of the working class.

By 1930, therefore, most mountaineers whether they remained on the farm or migrated to the mill villages, timber towns, or coal camps, had become socially integrated within the new industrial system, and economically dependent upon it as well. To say the least, this dependence was not on their own terms—that is to say, it was not a product of mountain culture but of the same political and economic forces that were shaping the rest of the nation and the western world. The rise of industrial capitalism brought to Appalachia a period of rapid growth and social change which those who hold to the static image have chosen to ignore. The brief prosperity brought on by the bonanza that was capitalism broadened the mountaineer's economic horizon. It aroused aspirations, envies, and hopes. But the industrial wonders of the age promised more than they in fact delivered, for the profits taken from the rich natural resources of the region flowed out of the mountains with little return to the mountain people themselves. For a relative handful of owners and managers the new order yielded riches unimaginable a few decades before; for thousands of mountaineers it brought a life of struggle, hardship, and despair. Considered from this perspective, the persistent poverty of Appalachia has not resulted from the lack of modernization. Rather, it has come from the particular kind of modernization that unfolded in the years from 1880 to 1930.

Earlier in this paper I quoted at length from Arnold Toynbee. I would like to end with a quotation from a native mountaineer who found another kind of barbarism at work in the Southern mountains. Writing in *The Hills Beyond,* Thomas Wolfe lamented the tragic changes that had come over his beloved homeland in the years after Reconstruction. "The great mountain slopes and forests of the section," he wrote, "had been ruinously detimbered; the farm-soil on the hillsides had eroded and washed down; high up, upon the hills, one saw the raw scars of old mica pits, the dump heaps of deserted mines. . . It was evident that a huge compulsive greed had been at work: the whole region had been sucked and gutted, milked dry, denuded of its rich primeval treasures; something blind and ruthless had been here, grasped and gone. The blind scars on the hills, the denuded slopes, the empty mica pits were what was left. . . . Something had come into the wilderness, and left the barren land."[31]

NOTES

[1]The author is indebted to the Rockefeller Foundation for research support on this subject.

[2]See Henry David Shapiro, "A Strange Land and Peculiar People: The Discovery of Appalachia, 1870-1920" (unpublished Ph.D. dissertation, Rutgers University, 1966), pp. 250 ff., and Cratis Dearl Williams, "The Southern Mountaineer in Fact and Fiction" (unpublished Ph.D. dissertation, New York University, 1961), pp. 1605 ff.

[3]Henry David Shapiro, "Introduction" to John C. Campbell, *The Southern Highlander and His Homeland* (Lexington, 1969), p. xxvi.

[4]Shapiro, "A Strange Land and Peculiar People," p. v; see Shapiro's forthcoming monograph *Appalachia on Our Mind: The Southern Mountains and Mountaineers in the American Consciousness, 1870-1920* (Chapel Hill, 1977).

[5]Woodrow Wilson, "Our Last Frontier," *Berea Quarterly,* Vol. 4, No. 2 (May, 1899), 5; William Goodell Frost, "Our Contemporary Ancestors in the Southern Mountains," *Atlantic Monthly,* 83 (March, 1899), 311.

[6]Horace Kephart, *Our Southern Highlanders* (New York, 1913), p. 211.

[7]James Watt Raine, *The Land of Saddle-Bags* (New York, 1924); James Watt Raine, *Saddlebag Folk* (Evanston, 1942); North Callahan, *Smoky Mountain Country* (Boston, 1952), p. 74.

[8]Jack E. Weller, *Yesterday's People: Life in Contemporary Appalacchia* (Lexington 1965).

[9]Cratis Dearl Williams, "Heritage of Appalachia," address to the Southern Appalachian Regional Conference (May 13, 1974) reprinted in *The Future of Appalachia* (Boone, 1975), p. 128.

[10]Bruce and Nancy Roberts, *Where Time Stood Still: A Portrait of Appalachia* (Boone, 1975), p. 128.

[11]Arnold Toynbee, *A Study of History* (New York, 1947), II, 312.

[12]See Dwight Billings, "Culture and Poverty in Appalachia: A Theoretical Discussion and Empirical Analysis," *Social Forces*, 53 (December, 1974), 315-23; Stephen L. Fisher, "Folk Culture or Folk Tale: Prevailing Assumptions About the Appalachian Personality" (unpublished paper delivered at the Appalachian Symposium in honor of Cratis D. Williams, Appalachian State University, Boone, N.C., April, 1976); David S. Walls, "Three Models in Search of Appalachian Development: Critique and Synthesis" (unpublished paper, May, 1976, College of Social Professions, University of Kentucky, Lexington).

[13]Roland Barthes, *Mythologies,* translated by Annette Lavers (New York, 1972), pp. 74-76.

[14]Robert Redfield, *Peasant Society and Culture* (New York, 1960), p. 38.

[15]U.S. Department of Interior, Census Office, *The Tenth Census: 1880, Agricultural Statistics*, Vol. III; U.S. Department of Commerce, Bureau of the Census, *Fifteenth Census of the United States, 1930: Agriculture: The Southern States*, Vol. 2, Part 2.

[16]U.S. Department of Agriculture, Miscellaneous Publication No. 205, *Economic and Social Problems and Conditions of the Southern Appalachians* (Washington, D.C., 1935), p. 16; Lewis Cecil Gray, "Economic Conditions and Tendencies in the Southern Appalachians as Indicated by the Cooperative Survey," *Mountain Life and Work*, Vol. 9, No. 2 (July, 1933), 9.

[17]U.S. Department of Agriculture, Publ. No. 205, *Economic and Social Conditions*, pp. 3, 16.

[18]Gray, "Economic Conditions in the Southern Appalachians," p. 10; see also W. D. Nicholls, "A Research Approach to the Problems of Appalachia," *Mountain Life and Work*, Vol. 7, No. 10 (January, 1932), 5-8 and U.S. Department of Agriculture, Publ. No. 205, *Economic and Social Conditions*, pp. 41-57.

[19]U.S. Department of Interior, Census Office, *The Tenth Census:*

1880, Agricultural Statistics, Vol. III; U.S. Department of Commerce, Bureau of the Census, *Fifteenth Census of the United States, 1930: Agriculture: The Southern States,* Vol. 2, Part 2.

[20]Gray, "Economic Conditions in the Southern Appalachians," p. 8; U.S. Department of Agriculture, Publ. No. 205, *Economic and Social Conditions,* pp. 120-121.

[21]U.S. Congress, Senate, *Report of the United States Coal Commission,* Sen. Doc. 195, 68th Cong. 2d. sess., 1925, Table 14, p. 1467; U.S. Department of Commerce, Bureau of the Census, *Thirteenth Census of the United States, 1910: Population,* Vols. II and III.

[22]See John Alexander Williams, "The New Dominion and the Old: Antebellum and Statehood Politics as the Background of West Virginia's 'Bourbon Democracy,' " *West Virginia History,* 33 (July, 1972), 322; Gordon Bartlett McKinney, "Mountain Republicanism, 1876-1900" (unpublished Ph.D. dissertation, Northwestern University, 1971), p. 170.

[23]See Gordon B. McKinney, "Industrialization and Violence in Appalachia in the 1800's" (unpublished paper delivered at the Appalachian Symposium in Honor of Cratis D. Williams, Appalachian State University, Boone, N.C., April, 1976).

[24]Map, "North Carolina Portion of the Great Smoky Mountains National Park, Showing Individual Ownership," Western Carolina University, Archives, Hunter Library.

[25]West Virginia, State Board of Agriculture, *Fifth Biennial Report of the West Virginia State Board of Agriculture for the Years 1899 and 1900* (1900), p. 371.

[26]Tom D. Miller, "Absentees Dominate Land Ownership," in *Who Owns West Virginia?* reprinted from the Herald-Advertiser and the Herald-Dispatch (Huntington, 1974), pp. 1-3.

[27]James Lane Allen, "Mountain Passes of the Cumberlands," *Harper's Magazine,* 81 (September, 1890), 575; Herbert Francis Sherwood, "Our Racist Drama," *North American Review,* 216 (October, 1922), 494; Campbell, *The Southern Highlander,* pp. 87, 314.

[28]U.S. Department of Agriculture, Publ. No. 205, *Economic and Social Conditions,* p. 3.

[29]See Edward E. Knipe and Helen M. Lewis, "The Impact of Coal Mining on the Traditional Mountain Subculture," in J. Kenneth Moreland, ed., *The Not So Solid South: Anthropological Studies in a Regional Subculture* (Athens, Georgia, 1971), p. 28.

[30]Mack H. Gollenwater, "Cultural and Historical Geography of Mining Settlements in the Pocahontas Coal Field of Southern West Virginia, 1880 to 1930" (unpublished Ph.D. dissertation, University of Tennessee, 1972), p. 87; R. H. Lyman, "Coal Mining at Holden, West Virginia," *The Engineering and Mining Journal*, LII (December 15, 1906), 1171.

[31]Thomas Wolfe, *The Hills Beyond* (New York, 1941), pp. 236-237.

APPALACHIA: AMERICA'S MINERAL COLONY

by
Rev. Jack Weller

It must be at least six years ago now that an exchange team of young people came to the mountains from various South American countries. The church group sponsoring their visit called me and asked if they could visit Appalachia, thinking that in all honesty they should have exposure to some less affluent areas of America. There were six in the group—four boys and two girls. In Harlan, Kentucky, in a church basement after some mine and coal camp visiting, we were discussing the economic situation of the coal fields, and how this economic system determined so much else that happens here. Every once in a while they would rap their knuckles on the table. After they did this twice, I asked them what they were doing.

"We're agreeing with you," the South American visitors smiled. "We see that America has its American colonies, too. What your country is doing to Appalachia is the same thing it is doing to us. You come to us and tell us we have resources that you need that we don't, that you will develop them for us, hiring our men and paying them good wages. Then you take these resources, make manufactured goods to sell back to us at high profit, and expect us to be happy while you get richer and we get poorer. And then you wonder why we say, 'Yankee go home!'"

SOURCE: Vantage Point, *No. 2 edition (circa 1974)*

AUTHOR: Jack Weller *is Chairman of the Presbyterian Coalition for Appalachian Ministries. He lives in Hazard, Kentucky, where he is a minister at large for that denomination.*

I suspect that America has several such colonies within her borders. Appalachia is its most prominent one.

A colony, as I understand it, is a group of people with land and resources which are owned and/or controlled by persons other than themselves, and whose resources and productive capacities are used for the advantage of those who control them.

Appalachia is simply our American example of how we use colonization powers in the economic realm all over the world. We strip an area and its people of their wealth under the guise of "developing" them, saying all the time of course that without this development look where they'd be. Yet in essence, we are robbing them of their wealth, impoverishing their people, controlling their economy, politics and people, meanwhile growing rich and powerful in the process.

Minerals, Timber & Recreation

Appalachia is indeed such a colony—a mineral colony, if you will—providing the energy to run the generators, steel mills, power plants, air conditioners, and can openers for an affluent nation while remaining poor itself. Appalachia is also a timber colony, a recreation colony, and an oil and gas colony.

In Central Appalachia, coal is king. There are estimates that over one trillion dollars worth of this black gold has been mined from east Kentucky alone. But in this area, according to the 1960 census (the last one for which these figures are calculated), 6 of the 10 poorest counties in America lie.

Perry County, where I live, the fifth highest coal-producing county in the state, can afford to pay only 14 percent of its public school bill. Letcher County, the third highest coal producer, can afford barely over 8 percent of its costs for the education of her children.

Based on the 1970 census, in Pike County, the highest Kentucky mountain coal producer, the per capita income is little more than 40 percent of the national per capita, and other mountain counties range from that high point to 18 percent of the national per capita.

And, lest we think that coal makes everybody poor, note that Pikeville, Kentucky, a town of fewer than 5,000 people in the heart of the coal fields, has 38 millionaires living within its limits. Other county-seat coal towns have their share of the wealthy also. The Cadillacs and Continentals and Imperials are common vehicles in the mountains—along with the pickups and the refugees from the junk piles that are the vehicles of the common folk.

What has happened in this spiny backbone of Eastern America, that while everyone else has shared the wealth of production, mountain people have been exiles from the American dream? How is it possible that this rugged land and its people have been by-passed, even though they exist within 600 miles of the giant industrial complexes of the North and Mid-West and are so directly connected with their productive capacities?

Reduced to Ruin

Answer: Appalachia is a colony which America has exploited. It is used, stripped of her wealth, raped and reamed and reduced to ruin, while those who gain their wealth from her invest their profits elsewhere and live elsewhere. Let's look at some of the factors involved.

First, Appalachia lost the resources which might have made her rich. Before the turn of the century, giant hardwoods up to six and eight feet in diameter covered the hillsides. Timber agents from the cities were sent to purchase this rich resource to feed the voracious maw of an expanding economy. At this time, when ours was generally a money economy, the Appalachian person still lived in a barter society. He grew what he needed; he made what he needed; he traded for what he needed. So, when timber agents came to buy the trees on his mountains, he was offered 25 to 50 cents a tree for them, trees which on the present market would be worth several thousands of dollars. Perhaps he had a whole mountain side of them—1,000 or more, worth $500 maybe—more money than he had ever seen at one time, and more than he thought he'd ever need. He sold the trees, even helped get them out and floated down the river.

The wealth that might have served his own economy went

instead to make someone else rich. Many fortunes were made in timber in Appalachia, and several large foundations now spread their beneficence back to the region in small amounts for its impoverished people. Granted, our economy runs on the basis of getting the best bargain you can. The Appalachian man wanted a bargain, too, as did those who bought the timber. The advantage lay with the outsider. He alone knew what the trees were worth and what money was all about, while the mountain man often did not.

The same thing happened with the coal. Five to seven mineable seams of coal underlie much of Central Appalachia. The mountain people who owned the land and minerals did not use the coal. They did not know how much was there or how to get it out. They did not know what it was worth. When coal and land agents came to buy the coal, offering fifty cents to five dollars an acre for it, again the mountain man, who was probably poor and hurting for some ready cash, quickly sold it. Besides, he was a farmer using the surface of the land for his living, and when he was assured that he could keep the surface, that all he was selling was something underneath, he made the bargain. Again, that which might have made the people in the mountains rich now belonged to someone else. He sold for no more than five dollars an acre coal which was really worth a thousand dollars or more!

What is more, he also lost the control of those surface rights. For years he paid taxes on that land surface only to find that mineral rights take precedence over surface rights, and strip mining 70 years after the deed was signed proved this fact. He found, too, that oil and gas prospectors could rip up his land, or that pipes could be laid over it. Thus, the mountaineer lost control of all his property.

Out-Of-State Control

I have some figures for Kentucky. The great majority of Kentucky's coal, over one million acres of it, is owned by out-of-state companies. These are land companies, oil, steel, railroads, gas producers, utilities and other corporate giants with stockholders and commitments all over the world—Kennecott Copper, National Steel, Bethlehem Steel, Occidental Petroleum, Continental Oil, Norfolk and Western Railroad. The director of the Area Development District where I live (Hazard, Kentucky) has often told me that no development is possible for our area until the coal industry is willing to relinquish some of its rights and powers in land ownership and control.

The coal companies and the industry, by its very nature, discouraged education of its people at the very time when across America the drive for universal education came into its own. So, when mines shut down and those men tried to find work elsewhere, no one would have them. Educational attainment levels among adults in Appalachia are four years below the national average—another toll exacted from Appalachia's people.

Harry Caudill, author of *Night Comes to the Cumberland*, tells of the annual contributions of the Penn-Virginia Coal Company to a Philadelphia art museum. Philadelphians no doubt pride themselves on having such a fine beneficent citizen-company in their midst. But why doesn't this company do something for the communities and people and area from which their wealth came? It was this company which, according again to Mr. Caudill, returned some 60 percent profit to its stockholders a few years ago. Come visit the community in Kentucky sometime which bears the name and stamp of this company, and see if you would like to live there!

Mine Unsafety

Beyond these brief remarks is the long, brutal tale of mine unsafety: the playing with death by companies anxious for coal, and the playing of politics with the federal laws and regulations and inspectors. Even the United Mine Workers union has its history of betrayal and promises broken. Coal is an industry with a black past, and everything it touches seems to be blackened.

The third factor to consider is the neglect of government in Appalachia. It is almost as if this were a forgotten area of the states involved, or as if these people and this land and this society were of some lower form of life different from the rest and not deserving of the same level of services which the rest of the states get. It was not until the year 1956 that the state of Kentucky assumed responsibility for the education of her children in the mountains. Previous to that time, churches and other outside groups provided the education for them.

When I moved to east Kentucky in 1965, for nearly 700,000 people living in those mountains there was not a single psychiatrist, psychologist, or psychiatric social worker. It didn't mean that our people had no mental illness—only that they toughed it out. Nor was there any work with retarded children, youth or adults, in spite of the fact that our retardation rate is over double the national rate. Hospital beds were less available than elsewhere.

There is one doctor across the nation for every 630 people. In the area of Hazard seven years ago, there was one doctor for every 10,000 people, and the administrator of the Appalachian Hospital called it a "medical disaster area."

In terms of roads, again neglect. In this year, 1973, there is not yet one major modern highway across Southern Appalachia, while across the Rockies, which are real mountains in comparison, there are many.

Little Federal Help

Even the federal government shows a picture of neglect. Fewer dollars per capita flow into Appalachia for education, welfare, construction of public facilities, and recreation than into other areas across the nation.

Tennessee Valley Authority (TVA), the federal agency whose mandate it is to bring to life the valley of the Tennessee River, has for years felt that in doing so it had the right to destroy other valleys in Appalachia in order to get coal for cheap power to its people and industries. The worst offenders in eastern Kentucky in terms of the wholesale destruction of the land and people and streams have been the companies supplying TVA power plants, companies supposedly hewing to the line of their reclamation policies.

Just last May, Senator Fred Harris came to visit eastern Kentucky strip mines, to meet with people, and to hold a hearing. One of the environment control and reclamation men from

TVA was there. He read a fine statement of how TVA had such high standards for land reclamation. Senator Harris exploded. "No man has the right to do to another man what I have seen today. But what is worse, I find that an agency of our own government is doing it," he said.

Perhaps it is not right to say that government at all levels has also exploited the mountains and their people. But, it is right to say that government has allowed this exploitation, encouraged it, and approved it. And no agency of government has lifted its voice to change it.

The record of the Corps of Engineers in the mountains is not bright in their dealings with people needing to be relocated because of dams. People have been offered a low sum for their property by the Corps and then told if they think it is not enough to take the matter to court. Most mountain families, too poor and inexperienced to hire a lawyer and go into courts, take the route of accepting the low offer.

The fourth factor is the worst for us: The church has exploited, too. In Appalachia, as elsewhere in the world, the church has pretty much put its stamp of approval on the "status quo" of exploitation. At one of our Orientation Seminars for new pastors, Harry Caudill said: "You church people put schools all through this area. Rich folk in Pittsburgh and New York reached down in their pockets to make schools for our children, yet daily these children looked out their windows and saw the wealth which was leaving here in those coal cars, but nobody ever asked why. And out of those schools came some of the most reactionary and socially insensitive leaders we have in the mountains today." Harry Caudill is caustic sometimes. Maybe he was judging yesterday by today's sensitivities. But there is much truth to what he says. The church and its leaders have seldom been among those who have stood up to be counted against exploitation. The people in the church have not been the seers and the prophets, in spite of the Gospel in their hearts.

A leader in a southeast Kentucky housing group told a group of Orientation pastors that she no longer attended church. She said: "If I could ever find a people there who cared as much for the people around them as they did for the Kings of Israel I might go back."

I don't want to overdraw this. There are churchmen in the
mountains, lay and clergy, who are at the forefront of the
struggle for justice in the hills, but mostly we are a pretty quiet
and peaceable group who do not ripple the waters much.

Jim Branscome a Berea college graduate, former director of
"SOK," an anti-strip mine group, and now at Highlander Center,
says that he feels one of the worst things about the Appalachian
institutional church and its colleges is that they remove what
anger there is in the souls of those they capture.

"Our colleges and churches," he says, "are in the business
to contribute to the preservation of society without opposing it,
without training their people to place a question mark alongside
everything that society does, thus blaspheming both education
and Christ. They have contributed to one of the most fundamental dilemmas of modern civilization: It is without the preserving aspects of opposition." As the church, we must hear
what this young man is saying to us.

The charge that can be laid most at the door of the church
is cultural imperialism. We have come into Appalachia and have
tried to make its people into patterns made by the rest of the
country. For example, the Presbyterians have a series of churches across the region with a Madison Avenue architect's idea of
what a mountain church should look like—log cathedrals with
stained glass and organs that match the culture about as well as
evening dresses and high-heeled shoes. Rather than affirm the
mountain person for what he was, we looked down at him and
tried to make him something else closer to our own expectations
for ourselves.

On occasion I receive letters from people across the nation,
asking if it isn't about time now to quit these many government
programs with high expenditures in Appalachia. After all, we've
done them long enough. Since the region does not seem to respond, let's spread our American charity somewhere else.

Let's make it clear, however, that these federal dollars spent
in Appalachia are not charity! They are justice—belated justice
at that—giving back to this region a tiny portion of the wealth it
has produced for our country. And, lest we think it to be such
munificence (that word means just a whole lot), remember that

the expenditures of the Appalachian Regional Commission in the 13-state area which contains over 18 million people in the first 7 years of its existence have totalled less than we spent in Viet Nam in one month at the height of the war.

The church must keep our nation's "feet to the fire" about Appalachia. Somehow we must cry aloud for justice, and do justice, and teach justice in our midst. Somehow we must help each other kick off the paternalism that so easily besets the church. Somehow we must do all we can to empower Appalachian people themselves, so they can have a piece of the decisions about their own destiny.

There must be a new burst of energy by the church for the health of the Region.

Jack Weller, author of *Yesterday's People: Life in Contemporary Appalachia,* is minister at large for the Presbyterian Church, Transylvania Presbytery. He lives in Hazard, Kentucky.

THE IMPACT OF RECREATIONAL DEVELOPMENT
ON PIONEER LIFE STYLES IN
SOUTHERN APPALACHIA

by
Edgar Bingham

The American Family Reference Dictionary defines the term *pioneer* as one of those who first enter or settle in a region, thus opening it for development or settlement by others. Therefore, to speak of a pioneer life style with regard to the Appalachian region must of necessity raise the question "which pioneer?" The presupposition which we follow with regard to the term is that followed by most Americans when referring to the pioneers, that being the earlier Europeans who established themselves in the region; and when we refer to remnant pioneer life styles, it is with reference to the way of life which these Europeans established. There is another assumption on the part of the writer which will become increasingly clear in the discourse which follows, and this is the assumption that a true pioneer life style is one that has remained as a characteristic passed on from one generation to the next. This would mean that the life style with which we are concerned is one that is an indigenous part of the mountain people themselves, one which is really preservable only through the cultural continuity of the native human element itself.

At the risk of being narrow in viewpoint, we take the posi-

SOURCE: Proceedings *of the Pioneer America Society, 1973.*

AUTHOR: Edgar Bingham *was born in the shadow of Grandfather Mountain, North Carolina. He has taught for the past 23 years at Emory & Henry College, Emory, Virginia.*

tion that effective preservation of the Appalachian pioneer life style must demand a human continuance, a cultural transfer from parent to child, automatically excluding those who would become mountaineers by purchasing second homes or retirement homes within the Appalachian region. And though we applaud the efforts of those who would preserve Appalachia by making records of the ballads and the folklore, by creating craft centers for the teaching of spinning, weaving, needlecraft, and wood-work, we must distinguish clearly between cultural repositories and living cultures.

Who the original pioneers were in the Southern Appalachian realm is not absolutely known, for ancient peoples had been in the area long before the Cherokees came. But the Cherokees likely pioneered in introducing a different and more advanced existence. They were probably the first farmers, though they were still highly dependent on hunting and gathering. A new pioneer element came in the form of the European hunter and trapper, closely followed by the permanent home-building, sub-sistence-seeking English farmers (along with some Scotch, Irish, French, and Germans), who with their more extensive clearing and cultivation of the land came in conflict with the land-use practices of the natives who were still highly dependent on hunt-ing for their subsistence.

There was much in the Appalachians to appeal to the European pioneers. Some alluvial bottomland was to be found in al-most every valley, and the soils there were deep and fertile. The slopes were covered with some of the world's best hardwood forests which sheltered a variety of game and provided, in addi-tion to the needed timber, supplies of fruits, nuts, berries, and medicinal herbs. Sparkling clear streams fed by an abundance of permanent springs provided excellent fishing. Small pockets of iron ore were widespread, along with constantly available wood for charcoal, and the multiplicity of forges and furnaces is re-flected in names of communities throughout the region. (Gra-ham's Forge and Laurel Bloomery are two nearby southwest Virginia examples.) And the almost complete isolation from the main paths of movement in the Mountain South demanded a high degree of self-reliance, whether in meeting economic needs or in maintaining effective social and political control.

The European life style established in the latter part of the

18th century, like that of the Cherokee whom the Europeans replaced, represented a remarkably good adaptation to the natural environment in which they both lived. Though there were excesses in pioneer land use, such as clearing slopes of timber which was not effectively usable for agriculture or removing trees for fuel which would now be worth small fortunes as cabinet woods (they were weeds to them,for there was no existing market), there was established an essential ecological balance between man and the land which was maintained fairly effectively up until the early part of the present century. And though the population growth was constant, the high birth rates were largely offset by a high death rate and by an outmigration which has increased greatly in this century. Life in the Southern Appalachians remained so unchanged and unchanging up to the present century that Cecil Sharp, an English folklorist visiting the region in 1917, suggested that a fence should be built around the whole province to keep outside influences from altering the culture. Mr. Sharp's concern was timely, for already other pioneers were at work, and this work would alter the landscape in profound ways, undermining in the process the economic framework by which the mountain people lived. These were the corporate-based coal mining and lumbering operations which brought the first easy means of access to the region, the branch railroad lines, designed to remove the rich extractive products found in abundance. And while the overall impact of these operations has left and is leaving this land in a deplorable state, much has already been written about these developments; consequently, we wish to focus our attention on what is a more present danger to mountain life and culture, a danger which has the possibility of becoming even more totally destructive.

The new pioneer in the mountains is the developer of tourist and recreational facilities, and of the more modern invaders, he appears to have the most disturbing influence on the traditional way of life. Like the exploiter of coal and timber, this multifaced monster is also corporate in nature with controlling interests based largely ouside the mountain. And like the earlier invaders, he paints a glowing picture of the economic progress he will bring to the areas affected. The unrevealed story is the fact that the long-range economic benefits (which may still be substantial) go to local business interests associated more or less directly with him. For the majority of the people the

economic impacts are more negative than positive. During the
major building period construction jobs become available; but
after facilities are completed, more or less permanent jobs (often
seasonal) are available as clerks, waiters and waitresses, cooks,
and maintenance personnel.[1] Total employment by recreational
developments is never large and wages are low, lower generally
than in other economic activities, and lower here than in other
parts of the country. Locals not associated with the developments often seek to improve their income by selling farm produce to slightly expanded local markets; and others may start
turning out local craft items such as quilts, bedspreads, and a
variety of toys and trinkets. The primary direct economic impact is and has been to introduce a job orientation no longer
directly associated with the land and to shift the local economy
farther away from the self-sustaining pattern of the past. This
effect in itself is not bad except that it serves to undermine the
spirit of independence so long characteristic of the mountain
people and places them in a position of almost perpetual subordination to the outside dominated financial manipulators,
more firmly cementing the status of inferiority imposed upon
mountain people by the rest of the nation. The imposition of a
more complete money economy with mass produced products
available has led to the abandonment of many crafts and traditions followed in the past.[2] The water-turned grist mills have
all but disappeared, and local farmers no longer try to meet basic
food needs from the farm. The wooden churn, a standard household item a generation ago (for then all farm households supplied
their own butter), is an item of value now only in the antique
shops. Most home orchards have been allowed to deteriorate or
disappear, and even the family garden is often limited to the
more basic items. The introduction of improved communica-
tions and effective advertising has created a town-centered social
focus to replace farm or hamlet oriented activities of the earlier
period. In the past each rural community regularly held barn
dances, quilting bees, corn huskings, molasses makings, and numerous other activiteis which served as strong human-based social
outlets. Now, the lure of the town with its theaters, sports activities, and overabundance of tourist traps draws locals as well as
visitors into the city limits. To suggest that all of this was caused
by the recreational developer would obviously be to stretch a
point, but the leisure-time activities which are development cen-
tered have helped shift the interests of natives away from the
home, farm, and local community. Locals who got together to

pitch horeshoes now spend their weekends around the town.

Far more profound than the creation of alternative economic outlets for mountain people or Appalachian life styles has
been the alteration of the human mix caused by recreation complex developers. Tourism of the earlier period in Appalachia generally demanded little land, most of which was in the towns or
on the town margins. Those of the more recent period demand
vast acreages, incorporating second home developments into new
major recreational complexes with ski slopes, golf courses, fishing
streams, swimming pools, hiking and saddle trails, and even such
unmountaineer-like attractions as racquet clubs. Some examples
of new North Carolina developments were reported in January,
1973, by the *Asheville Citizen*.[3]   Included were the "un-city"
development of Connestee Falls (Realtec Incorporated) encompassing 3,900 acres, with sales to date of over 13 million
dollars; Wolf Laurel, a 6,000-acre resort featuring a central core
of authentic rebuilt native log cabins and including in addition
to homes and homesites, a rustic inn, a golf course, an excellent
restaurant, and ski slopes; and Arrowhead Hideaways on Flattop
Mountain, a 1,000-acre development just begun in 1972.

Research into the control of major tourist and recreational
complex developments tells something about where the profits
go. In the writer's home country of Watauga and Avery counties
in North Carolina, the massive Beech Mountain and Land Harbor
developments are controlled by the Carolina-Caribbean Corporation with home offices in Miami. Peter Barnes and Larry Casalino in a book entitled *Who Owns the Land* have found among
the major developers the names of DuPont, Continental Oil,
General Electric, IT&T, Standard Oil, Gulf Oil, CBS, Eastman
Kodak, and Firestone.[4]   And the number of land purchases
seems to be growing geometrically with each year. One corporation, the General Development Corporation, is reported to control more than 200,000 acres of land (slightly less than an
average-sized Virginia county). And most disturbing to a native
Appalachian is the fact that the area of most rapid takeover is
the relatively unspoiled and most culturally distinctive parts of
the mountain South.   Purchasing operations are economic
blitzkriegs.   Buyers from these large corporations move into
rural mountain areas and suddenly offer prices for land which
unsuspecting natives find difficult to refuse. The prices offered

are in truth inflated in comparison to the value of the land in its traditional subsistence or semi-subsistence farm use (which, for most, form the base of their understanding of land values). Many sell; then they find that land values overall have gone up radically, so they either must give up their former way and become menials for the developer or, as is often the case, they leave the community altogether. Even those who are determined to retain their land find that its value has become so inflated that it is no longer practical to use it for farming, so either they become developers themselves or they sell to the developer.[5] The effect on the human population over recent years has been to replace the natives with "new" mountaineers—mountaineers without a real attachment to the land whose demands or expectations have tended to be in conflict with rather than in harmony with the mountain habitat. Their automobiles, motorcycles, and the service vehicles required to meet their more elaborate demands clog the mountain roads and disturb the rural quiet with the roar of their engines. Their ski slopes have cut huge slashes in the natural cover of the most attractive mountains, and the most appealing trails and associated vistas suddenly become off-limits to the people who have always lived here.

In fairness to the private recreation-residential developers, they see their role as that of making more effective use of land that had little economic value before, not realizing that through their massive developments they are working to destroy most of the characteristics of appeal in the mountain setting. Their cluttering of the landscape with broad highways, ski slopes, parking lots, shopping centers, right-of-ways for the likes of Tweetsie, and buildings ranging from Swiss chalets to pink fairy-tale castles, is making the physical landscape no longer alluring. Those elements of the mountain culture which provided the human appeal are often retained only as museum pieces in settlement schools or as show-place remnants such as in Cades Cove, Tennessee. And once gone, Appalachian culture cannot be recreated even by the most gargantuan human efforts. It might be noted that the federal and state governments have paralleled the private developer and often have cooperated with him in the onslaught against the mountain man and his culture. Cooperation between the Appalachian Regional Commission and the state of West Virginia removed several thousand acres of the most beautiful part of West Virginia from private control and created the multi-million dollar Pipestem recreation complex. The result is a lodge and combination of tourist cabins which the average West Virginian, certainly one native to the Pipestem area, could not possibly afford to use; and moreover, according to Don West, a native of Pipestem, the concession to operate the complex did not remain in the hands of West Virginians but was given to a Chicago firm.

In 1931, Margaret Hitch ("Life in a Blue Ridge Hollow") noted that the development of the Shenandoah National Park had resulted in a displacement (against their will) of the local people, forcing them to move elsewhere! She commented that "within another decade a new era will have begun and the day of the Blue Ridge mountaineer will have passed."[6] We might note that more than a decade has passed since her prophecy was made and the mountaineer is still around, but the forces which are seemingly seeking the eradication of him and his culture push relentlessly forward. The development of the Mt. Rogers National Recreational Area represents another giant stride toward that end. In addition to the hundreds of thousands of acres involved in the original purchase, it was recently announced that the Forest Service intends to purchase an additional 23,000 or so acres. In physical and human terms it means the removal from private hands of parts of three of the most attractive mountain valleys in southwest Virginia, converting them into a complex which would greatly exceed that of the Pipestem development noted above. And as in the case of Pipestem, no preference will be given to local or even Virginia concerns in the granting of concessions to operate within the area. In this case the government goes the private developer one better in that the land desired can be condemned at prices representing only a fraction of its worth for recreational purposes and even less than fair value in terms of present use.[7]

It is inappropriate to suggest that the land-purchasing agents for government-owned recreational developments are intentionally being unethical or dishonest. What does appear to be the case is that they are attempting to purchase land at what might have been a fair price at the time the original land purchases were made for the National Recreation Area several years ago. Prices of all Appalachian land have increased tremendously since that time, and if the land must be claimed, the price should reflect the going rate at the time it is sold. Perhaps more appropriately, the seller should be paid enough to assure his acquiring of living conditions equal to those he is forced to give up. Unless this is assured, the Forest Service or those representing it are not dealing ethically or honestly with the people.

One of the more compelling arguments which could be used by those who would develop Appalachia as a major recreational center for the nation is the concept that land should be used in such a way as to provide the maximum benefit for the greatest number of people for the longest period of time. And certainly the displacement of a few hundred people by the recently proposed Mt. Rogers acquisition or even the displacement of the few thousands (or perhaps ten thousands) by recreation complexes throughout the mountain South is much overshadowed by the growing millions who use the region for rest and relaxation. However, there are other principles involved which have been dear to the hearts of Americans from the beginning of the nation: the principles encompassing the rights of the individual to own land and to the pursuit of happiness. These individual rights are on trial now more than at any time in American history, and in reality it is not the question of the greatest benefit to the greatest number of people. For the recreational complexes that are now being created are luxury complexes which only a privileged few (the 15 to 20 percent who own the bulk of the nation's wealth) can really afford to enjoy. And if the individual rights of the masses continue to be violated for the benefit of these privileged few, then the whole principle of individual freedom is in question.

With regard more specifically to the culture impacts of the recreational developments in Appalachia, the more profound tragedy is that the last and most appealing islands of pioneer Elizabethan culture in the world have become the victims of that most infectious of American diseases, so-called "progress."

There are still others who would suggest that the recreation developers are in reality doing more to preserve pioneer life in Southern Appalachia than the natives themselves by taking land which is subject to overcrowding and poor use by the natives and putting it to more productive use. They point out that pioneer styles are preserved in the rustic external structure of the second homes or vacation cabins, in the replica rail fences and water wheels, and in the much promoted mountain music festivals. But when one goes beneath the surface, the life style of the second-home or summer-home owner is not a life style resembling in any way that of the mountaineer he replaces (notwithstanding the frequent exhortations of roadside advertisers for those passing through to become "mountaineers" by buying lots on English Mountain). His "cabin" with the rustic exterior of the earlier mountain home will be equipped with every appliance, including electric heat. And though he may wear the battered hat and overalls of the much caricatured mountain man, he would be hard pressed to hand tool a baby crib or cut his grass with a scythe. Nor would his wife be likely to know how to card or spin or hand weave a piece of cloth from the homespun. And philosophically the gap becomes broader, for generally the new-comer (outlander) is material oriented and accustomed to manipulating man and the land for profit; on the other hand, the mountain life style, though not shiftless as many would suggest, focuses primarily on meeting the basic human needs of food, clothing, and shelter. The *new* mountaineer must constantly be doing something, from moving the rocks in his rock garden to replacing the natural foliage with that of his choosing (often clashing horribly with the natural landscape), much to the amusement of the native who without benefit of training in meditation can spend hours on end in contemplative observation of the wonders of nature around him. It is probably true that most mountain people are fatalistic, particularly with regard to the natural events which affect their lives, and death is and has been viewed simply as a natural occurrence, even the death that he sees occurring around him.

The Appalachian mountaineer is a product of a cultural heritage which is Elizabethan in origin but which has been modified by the human and physical environment in which he has lived for so long. This is reflected in his speech, his folklore, his ballads, his attitudes toward man and the land, and the harmonious relationship that exists between him and the natural setting he occupies. To assume that he could remain an unchanged element in the mountain setting with communicative inroads penetrating the region on all fronts is not realistic, and no one native to the mountains would want it to be that way. However, it is of major concern and within the realm of possibility that certain desirable Appalachian traits be retained by keeping those born Appalachian as the dominant element within the mountain region.   Also, by developing and encouraging among them (or us—for I am one of them) a pride in their heritage, something of their rich past may be retained or even strengthened.

Though many assume, perhaps correctly, that it is too late to protect Appalachian culture from the devastation wrought by massive recreational developments, there is still some hope that at least important remnants of Appalachian culture may be preserved.   However, the very nature of the native's personality seems to work against it.   It would appear that effective local and regional land planning would be the best avenue, but the highly independent mountain people see this as a socialistic invasion of their individual rights, not recognizing that the basic purpose of planning and zoning would be to protect them against those who have exploited them in the past and will likely continue to do so in the future.

From the perspective of the native looking at his native land, the following are offered as possible approaches to the problems we have noted.

(1)   More extensive wilderness areas should be set aside with the absolute exclusion of developmental enterprises while at the same time assuring those peoples living within such areas the right of continued occupation.

(2)   Regional and local planning agencies, in establishing zoning ordinances, should seek to assure that conditional use permits be required for all major recreational, commercial, and industrial developments.   Public hearings for any such proposed development should be required.   (Exclusion might include family or individually operated shops, service stations, home businesses, etc.)

(3)   Zoning regulations should be established which would require all developments to be cleared by a responsible environmental protection agency.   This is particularly needed in all areas of massive minerals exploitation, massive industrial development, massive housing developments, and in many types of recreation developments (such as in areas where ski slopes are planned).

(4)   Zoning regulations should be established which would

protect good farmland against the economic developer seeking to follow the path of lowest cost.

(5) Lot size limitations should be established in all areas being developed. This action would work against the messy clustering of business establishments in narrow valleys and along roads which can handle only limited traffic.

(6) Rigid controls over size and placement of billboards, glaring roadside lights, and other manifold roadside promotion devices should be established.

(7) There should be a reappraisal of priorities for land use in the entire Appalachian region, with serious consideration given to development of legal devices which would provide protection of the native population against the multiple onslaughts of corporate interests. First in order would be the provision of a publicly supported legal aid system to counter that which corporations are able to employ. Such a provision is desperately needed now by those whose property is being condemned by the Forest Service in the Mt. Rogers National Recreation Area, for they do not have financial resources to fight the actions in the courts.

(8) There should be legal provisions against the replacement of scenic mountain roads with "drive through" super highways directed toward benefitting the outside visitor.

(9) Broadly, a more conscious effort should be made to protect and preserve the rights of the individual against the desires of big business and big government whose primary aim with regard to the Appalachians appears to have been the making of its natural beauty and resources more effectively exploitable by interests which come from outside, and who, by comparison with the natives, can afford to pay well for services provided.

NOTES

[1]At a recent hearing relative to acquisition of additional land for park development by the Forest Service, people in the Helton Creek area adjacent to the Mt. Rogers National Recreational Area asked an official what economic benefits would come to the local people by an expansion of the area. After pondering the question a moment he replied, "Well, the campers coming in are going to want quite a bit of wood for their campfires."

[2]There have been a number of efforts to revive the traditional crafts, but craftsmanship gained earlier by a youngster at the foot of a craftsman father cannot be regained just because a market develops. Crafts schools have been established, but these are seen regionally as museums of the past rather than as vocational institutions where young men and women can develop economically valuable skills. There are a few true craftsmen operating in the tradition of the past, but these make up a very insignificant part of the total Southern Appalachian population.

[3]Nancy Brower, "Recreational, Residential Developments Had a Big Year," *Asheville Citizen,* January 28, 1973.

[4]Peter Barnes and Larry Casalino, *Who Owns the Land?* Center for Rural Studies, Berkeley, California, 1972.

[5]There are numerous examples of tourist-recreational-residential impacts. The writer's sister bought 100 acres of land overlooking Boone, N.C. in the 1950's for $7,000.00 and sold 80 acres of it three years later for $10,000.00. The DuPont Corporation which now controls the 80 acres is selling homesites for $5,000.00 and up. The 20 acres still in the former owner's control is now valued at more than $80,000.00. Alfred McNeill, who lives well outside the Boone-Blowing Rock focus of development, reported in the summer of 1973 that his rough mountain land had gone up in sale value from less than $100 an acre in 1960 to a present value of more than $1,000 an acre. Like many others he would prefer to continue to farm but now is beginning to wonder how long he can continue in the face

of increasing land values and associated increases in taxes.

⁶Margaret Hitch, "Life in a Blue Ridge Hollow," *Journal of Geography*, Vol. XXX, November 1931, 308-322.

⁷The largest number of people to be displaced will be in the Helton Creek area of Smyth County. The writer recently visited the community and talked with a number of the local residents whose land is being sought. Some have already sold at what would appear to be less than fair market value, and far less than what they will have to pay for comparable living situations, and certainly only a fraction of the real value of the land in the light of the recreational development now planned. Charles Blevins owns 8½ acres, much of it good bottom land, and has a good frame house on it along with a number of other outbuildings. The small farm provides essentially all his food needs and a head or two of cattle for sale. The price offered by the Forest Service was $7,300, which would appear to be about one-third replacement value, discounting, of course, the esthetic worth of the mountain setting. There is a fish pond on the place for which Mr. Blevins had recently been offered $12,000. Mr. Blevins also reported that he had sold one acre of hill land within the last year for $1,000.

In talking with others in the valley it would appear that the going rate offered by the Mt. Rogers land appraisers is around $200 an acre. There are few acres anywhere within the developing Appalachians with land values less than $1,000 an acre.

RALPH NADER LETTER

May 16, 1973

Sir Denys Flowerdew Lowson
Chairman, Board of Directors
American Association, Ltd.
56 Gresham Street
London, ENGLAND

Dear Sir Denys:

> O, it is excellent
> To have a giant's strength, but it is
> tyrannous to use it like a giant.
> *(Measure for Measure*
> Act II, Scene 1)

    As a Life Governor of the Royal Shakespeare Theatre, you are no doubt familiar with these lines. The thought has been applied widely—and rightfully—to America's involvement in Vietnam. Yet as that war winds down, another one continues—a quiet, sordid little war in the once-verdant mountains of the states of Kentucky and Tennessee. The victims of this war are the local residents and their lands; the aggressors are "strip miners." And the responsibility falls in large part upon the American Association, Ltd., a British-based landholding and development company of which you are Chairman of the Board.

SOURCE: *This letter was released to the press as a public document on May 16, 1973.*

AUTHOR: Ralph Nader *is the director of a Washington, D.C. based advocacy program for consumer education and protection.*

The American Association, Ltd. controls about 65,000 acres—over one hundred square miles—of coal-rich land in the Appalachian Mountains of Kentucky and Tennessee. This region is famous for a sad paradox: human misery and abject poverty atop and amidst some of the world's most abundant mineral deposits. The explanation is regrettably simple. Appalachia is a colony. The people there do not own the wealth. Large outside corporations like the American Association do. And the prime, almost exclusive, concern of these corporations has been to exploit the region at the lowest possible cost to themselves.

Most of your company's holdings—about 50,000 acres—lie in the isolated "Clear Fork Valley" in Claiborne, Campbell, and Bell counties. Clear Fork is one of the most populated remaining valleys in the coal areas of Central Appalachia, with about 500-700 households in the communities of Fonde, Pruden, Hamblintown, Clairfield, Buffalo, and Straight Creek. Your company owns perhaps 85 percent of the valley there.

In this remote valley, the American Association has displayed corporate profitseeking at its worst. It has permitted wanton and destructive "strip mining"—mining by blasting and scraping away the surface instead of tunneling into a coal deposit. Once-beautiful mountains are now scarred and gouged; foliage is razed; streams are clogged and filled with acid and filth; the inhabitants are endangered by landslides, floods, and polluted water. The difference between what strip mining is doing to the land in Appalachia and what B-52 bombers have done to the land in Southeast Asia is one of degree, not of kind.

And while carting away over 2.2 million tons of coal per year, leaving the region that much poorer, and in ruin, the American Association and the companies to which it leases have virtually ignored the needs of the residents there. They have avoided their fair share of the local tax burden. They have presided over the destruction of job opportunities. They have even blocked the efforts of the local citizens to better their own lot.

Idealism and good intentions—spiced, albeit, with a goodly dose of empire and profits—propelled your firm into Appalachia in the early 1890's. Backed by capital from Britain's Baring Brothers, the American Association founded a town called Middlesboro (after a British counterpart) in the state of Kentucky and set out to make it the booming iron and coal capital of the southern United States. The venture was to strike a bold new phase in British enterprise and in Anglo-American relations. "This is but a transfer of British business to American soil," proclaimed American Association founder Alexander Arthur on November 11, 1890, to visiting dignitaries in the newly-resplendent Middlesboro Hall. He went on:

> I would say that America needs this place and our Anglo-American money, experience and push. Our mines, ovens, furnaces and works you have seen; these comprise our plant. We have also the sinews of body and of money and stand ready, clean-cut, and vigorous, for a generation of progress and success in manufacture, arts, and sciences. *Come and join hands with us in the great enterprise which is worthy of the noblest efforts of us all, native or foreign born though we may be.* [emphasis supplied]

But misfortune, greed, and highly questionable dealings soon shipwrecked the hoped-for "noblest efforts." The financial panic of 1893 dried up the venture's British backing; Middlesboro was sold at auction, and 80,000 acres of mountain and valley land were mortgaged to the Central Trust Co. of New York for $1,500,000.

Then a strange thing happened. The Central Trust filed to recover on the mortgage in 1894, and one J. H. Bartlett was appointed Special Commissioner to conduct the sale. Mr. Bartlett let the property go for but $25,000—about thirty cents per acre. The buyer was, of all people, an agent of the American Association, Ltd., a newly-formed corporation with essentially the same membership as the American Association, Inc. Shortly thereafter, Mr. J. H. Bartlett became General Manager of American Association, Inc. The American Association, Inc. said later that the land had been worth well over one-half million dollars at the time of the sale.

This strange transaction did not go unnoticed. Creditors of the American Association, Ltd. sued the new American Association, Inc. in Claiborne County for "fraud," claiming it had "paid nothing for said property." But the records of this suit went up in flames with the Claiborne County Courthouse. And researchers could find no trace of the suit at the Bell County Courthouse.

The Association had acquired its Appalachian Coal empire through means its founder Mr. Arthur and you might not wish to label a "transfer of British business to American soil." Most records of the era are either missing or else were burned with the county courthouse. But the region is alive with tales of how American Association agents tricked, threatened, or forced uneducated mountain people into giving up their valuable coal land for fifty cents to a dollar an acre. Said one mountaineer recently:

> The American Association said the land was worthless and that they would give my daddy a dollar an acre and we could live on the land and pay rent and they would pay the taxes. We didn't know it but we were standing barely 4' from a seam of coal when the American Association was talking to us.

Local residents say that when the property records burned with the Courthouse, the American Association used the chance to claim property that wasn't theirs.

At first, self-interest bound the American Association, and the coal operators to which it leases, to a sort of uneasy truce with the people of the region. The companies needed men to dig the coal out of the large deep mines. So they had to provide these men and their families with a place to live and at least a minimal level of human services. Usually this level was indeed minimal. The miners and their families lived often in indecent conditions and worked in hazard-trap mines. And they were virtual serfs to the companies that employed them and owned everything around them—their home, their credit at the company store, health care and recreation in the company town, even "justice" at the company-controlled courthouse. In the 1930's your company, along with others, tried to keep these miners from joining a union that could stand up for their rights. Yet, despite all this, the need for able, willing bodies to mine the coal made the American Association and its cohorts show some concern for the region and its people.

But the cord that had kept this uneasy truce together has broken. Mining coal no longer requires people. In fact, people just get in the way. Your company has expressed the desire to rid the area of residents. It will no longer repair homes, and it plans to tear them down in the near future. Yet there is little other housing or even property on which to build housing. Depopulation has replaced paternalism as official corporate policy.

"The people would be better off, and we would be better off, if they would be off our land," said Mr. Alvaredo E. Funk, the American Association's General Manager in Middlesboro, Kentucky.

It began in the 1950's, when a coal market slump forced many coal operators to close down. Medium-sized independent operators, like those that lease much American Association land, were especially affected. Employment in the region dropped sharply. In 1952 there were 1,230 coal mining jobs in Claiborne County; but in 1958 there were but 282. Your company made no effort to provide other sources of employment for the men thrown out of work.

Since the 1950's, the market for coal has revived. More than revived. It is positively bullish. But bullish for the American Association and other coal owners and operators, not for the people of the region where you get the coal. Automation and strip mining have cut drastically the need for miners. At the single large deep mine left on your property, that of Consolidation Coal, 350 men with modern machinery turn out about as much coal as 1,500 men produced at nine mines in 1948. And men are even more dispensable in strip mining. In Claiborne County alone, 200 men can now blast and bulldoze out almost as much coal as 1,500 deep-miners could dig in 1948.

Today with the need for local labor gone, a sort of undeclared warfare has broken loose. The companies to whom you lease are making an unchecked assault upon the land, and in consequence, on its people.

Is it hyperbole to compare your company's presence in Appalachia to a war zone? Consider the evidence.

1. *Environmental Destruction*

Irresponsible strip mining on your lands in Tennessee

harkens dismally of the laying-waste-to-the-land strategies of bygone generals. As you know, a strip miner literally blasts away the sides or top of a mountain. He then bulldozes the debris over the side, and shovels out the coal. The process is fast, cheap, and destructive in the extreme. Landslides block roads and railways, destroy homes and farmlands, and imperil human beings. The blasting alone has cracked the frames and foundations of homes. Streams, choked with silt and debris, flood at the slightest rainfall, leaving harmful deposits on scarce fertile soils. Acid and mineral substances pollute the water and endanger the area's water supply.

"We are afraid to go to sleep when it rains. We just stay up all night," says one Tennessee resident whose property these floods have ruined. In the Clear Fork Valley, some people must boil their water and add chlorine to it to make it safe to drink. And the Campbell County Highway Department has had to spend thousands of dollars clearing a single road after continual landslides.

Is this the experience of people in peace or in war?

Your company, the American Association, currently hosts more strip mining operations than does any other landowner in Tennessee. On your Claiborne County property alone, strippers laid waste to about 3,000 acres before the State passed a law in 1967 requiring that the land be restored. Since then, 1,400 more acres on your land have been stripped, and the reclamation is questionable at best, despite the new law.

2. *Tax Evasion*

While their mineral wealth is literally carted out from under them, the people of this region pay, in measurable and immeasurable ways, for this destruction. State and local governments have to clear the roads after landslides and both roads and bridges after illegally overweight coal trucks have beaten them apart. The people pay for this through taxes and through their own efforts to undo the damage to their homes and property. Yet not only do they get little or nothing, not even jobs, in return, but your company also avoids its duty to pay taxes to meet the costs of local government.

In the United States, local governments depend mainly on property taxes. Especially in Appalachia, where coal is the major form of property wealth, owners like the American Association are expected to pay their share. But it hasn't worked out that way in Claiborne County. Your 44,000 coal-laden acres there represent 17 percent of the county's land area and perhaps 90 percent of the county's coal reserves. Yet in 1970 your property taxes provided only 3 percent of the county's property tax revenue. That year your company claimed to the State Board of Equalization—the board of appeals—that 40,000 acres of its coal-rich land were worth but five dollars per acre. Yet in that one year alone you garnered more in royalty payments from the mining companies to which you lease.

Complaints by local citizens led the Tennessee Board of Equalization to require that coal properties be assessed more accurately. But the figures your General Manager Mr. Funk then supplied the state were dubious at best. Local citizens charged that Mr. Funk's suspicious figures gave your company an almost one million dollar underassessment. The State Board seems to have borne out these claims when it tripled values Mr. Funk reported for properties now leased to Consolidation Coal.

Still, the strip mines on your land are greatly underassessed and undertaxed. Two companies mining your land under lease appear to have escaped taxation altogether, while others seem to have kept all their mining equipment off the tax rolls. As late as 1972 your coal-rich Claiborne County lands that were not being mined were still assessed at only $25 an acre, *less than the least expensive farm land in the county.*

3. Housing

As the major employer in the Clear Fork Valley, and as owner of most of the land, the American Association once provided most of the housing as well. But now that it no longer needs the people, it seeks to get rid of them. It is your company's declared policy to tear down its houses in the valley and not to build new ones. The houses your company still rents, it won't repair. Nor will it compensate tenants who make their own repairs. And the leases it grants are usually for only thirty days, if it grants a lease at all. And the tenant may be evicted without cause or reason.

"I've seen barns in better shape. . . .Why, I've worked farms where people wouldn't keep their animals in barns the shape of these houses," one tenant said recently.

Meanwhile, strip mining destroys those homes and the land on which they rest. Residents count forty-two houses that have been stripped away in the small Rock Creek Hollow alone.

And your company has turned its back on both the immediate distress and the long-run needs of people whose homes are thus destroyed. In 1955 on American Association property, water broke through an old "slag" pile, surged down and destroyed the community of Valley Creek. Two children were killed. Your company offered meager compensation. Just last year your company did not take preventive action when a landslide from a strip mine on your land threatened homes and lives in the community of Buffalo Hollow until local citizens hired an attorney and Granada Television filmed the slide for broadcast in Britain. Even the belated efforts you have taken—which have had little success—are of small comfort to people who have had to evacuate homes on your property before the invading army of bulldozing strip miners. Or to residents such as Lewis Lowe, who now faces perennial flooding along Clear Fork Creek. Or to the people endangered or blocked in by the landslides on such places as Duff Road.

Your manager, Mr. Funk, stated in "The Stripping of Appalachia," a Granada television documentary: "We're ploughing back our share into the development of Appalachia." Ploughing, indeed, there is aplenty. But apparently the only "development" is on a minor part of your holdings in Cumberland Gap across the giant Cumberland Mountain from Clear Fork Valley. Here one finds a new Holiday Inn for tourists, and here a marina and golf course are planned, as your May 19, 1971, Statement to Shareholders puts it "to attract the wealthier citizens of Pineville and Middlesboro." What of the less wealthy residents of your 50,000 or more acres in the isolated Clear Fork Valley?

They could move elsewhere, one might reply. After all, your Statement to Shareholders the following year applauds your contribution to the local housing supply. "We have continued," it says, "our policy of building houses on plots of land owned by us. . . ." But these too are across the Cumberland Mountains. In the isolated valley, housing is scarce because your company owns most of the land and is tearing down its houses. There are very few "elsewheres" for people who wish to remain on the land where they and their parents were raised. And jobs and living conditions in the distant cities are very uncertain.

4. *Preventing Local Self-Help*

To keep the area under tight control, the American Association has blocked the efforts of local citizens to help themselves, to provide for their own jobs and housing. These people have formed a community development organization, the Model Valley Development Council, to better the lot of the valley and its residents. Several years ago, when the Council approached your company to buy land for a small factory, your company would consent to sell or lease only a single small tract. It was covered with slag and refuse from an old mine, and the Association would let it go only if the local people themselves cleaned up the shameful mess. In 1972 the American Association refused to sell or lease land for the people to build homes. Last autumn, American Association General Manager Funk would not consider making just one-half acre available for the community to build a health clinic. Since then (and after wide showing of the Granada T.V. documentary) Mr. Funk has suggested you might lease—but not sell—some land.

But the people are still waiting. Meanwhile your company won't even let them cut trees for wood to repair their homes.

The mere control of so much of this area's land and wealth sets your company athwart any growth or local self help there. The county government is reluctant to provide services like sewers and roads because the population is sparse—sparse largely because of American Association policy. Lack of these services in turn keeps new builders away. And potential industries shun the almost total dependence on your company that setting up in the region would involve.

Your company won't help these people. And it won't let them help themselves.

The American Association's seventy-year occupation of this forgotten portion of Tennessee has resulted, then, in what? Surveys in the valley have shown unemployment at about 30 percent. About 20 percent of the households live on less than $1,000 per year; another 20 percent make less than $2,000. ($9,400 per year was the average family income in this country in 1969.) Homes are being destroyed and land and water are being ruined. Prospects for employment are grim. Prospects generally are grim, with your company looking ahead to 25-30 more years of strip mining and then timber cutting after that.

Does this picture suggest the presence of a responsible citizen or of a greedy aggressor? And what will the picture be in twenty-five more years?—not in the small portion of your land north of Cumberland Mountain where you are building playspots for the rich, but in the depressed Clear Creek Valley where most of your holdings lie?

The bloom indeed has faded from the hopes your countrymen held for the American Association venture in Kentucky and Tennessee. How different the response of two English people viewing the enterprise at the outset and now. Visiting the area of 1891, Sir James Kitson, then-President of the British Iron and Steel Institute, could boast:

> I think we all, as Englishmen, rejoiced to see a town which was being developed with so much sagacity, so much judgment and energy; that was being developed under English auspices and with British capital.

Eighty years later your countrymen were holding their heads a bit lower. After watching the Granada television documentary on your holdings in Clear Fork Valley, a Middlesex, England, woman felt impelled to write a small local Tennessee newspaper:

> I write to tell you how ashamed I am that an English-owned company can so indiscriminately cause so much havoc to a small community. . . .My feelings after watching a recent television programme on the subject were ones of total horror.

> You must realize that I am an English woman of absolutely no importance, but nevertheless, would like

> to use the good offices of your newspaper to apologize
> for the desecration caused by an English company, on
> land in a country that has always had very close ties with
> my own. . . .

It is true that the American Association is just one small part of your nearly L220m ($500,000,000) secrecy-enshrouded corporate empire, of which *Investor's Chronicle* magazine said: "What is quite unknown is how the empire is controlled, how the various companies relate to each other." This empire spans from Australia and Thailand to Canada and the West Indies and includes pursuits so diverse as racetracks, rubber plantations, and equipment for hairdressing salons.

But the policies of the American Association spell the fate of the people and culture of the Clear Fork Valley. And they are now causing embarrassment to people of your own country.

You have shown charitable instincts in many ways. You have served as officer or director of six hospitals. In 1953 you were on the Executive Council of the Lord Mayor's National Flood and Tempest Distress Fund. Until 1948 you were Vice-President of the League of Mercy.

Now you can apply this same sense of responsibility to the corporate realm.

What can you do? Such steps as the following, which you could set in motion at once, could begin to change your company from a hostile aggressor to a more responsible constructive citizen.

1. First, and most important, you should personally visit the region, for at least several days, to see firsthand what your company's policies have done. You should meet with local residents to hear their views and to discuss your company's past actions and plans for the future.

2. Your company should inventory and begin to correct the damage strip mining on its land has done. Especially urgent is the need to correct damage to homes, farms, roads, and water supplies.

3.   You should require all companies to whom the American Association leases to restore carefully and completely the property on which they mine and to repair any damage they do to the people or the region.

4.   You should also require these companies to cooperate fully with tax officials and to provide them with the information necessary to set fair and equitable property tax assessments. Such information should include lease agreements, royalty rates, and survey and estimates of coal reserves.

5.   As a symbol of your desire to compensate the people of the region for the valuable land your agents tricked or threatened their forebears into selling, you should donate some of your 50,000-odd acres for community development.

6.   You should keep in good repair the housing you rent to local people. And you should extend to them fair and adequate lease protection.

7.   You should stop refusing to sell land to local groups seeking to build industry or housing.

8.   You should instruct your General Manager, Mr. Alverado E. Funk, to negotiate with local citizen groups a fair and equitable compensation for all the property taxes which the American Association has avoided in the past.

9.   You should, in the future, consult with these citizen groups about changes in your company's policies in the area.

Such steps will help get your company out of its social red ink in Appalachia. But what of the many other companies you control? Are they too laying waste forgotten corners of the world?

There is a larger lesson to be learned from your destructive Appalachian venture. It is simply to apply to social problems on the corporate level the old adage "To foresee is to forestall." It would be a signal act of corporate foresight and responsibility for you to set up now a special committee to monitor the social impact of all the businesses you control. This committee should comprise both people from within your enterprises and representatives of outside groups who speak for important social concerns. It should have the full authority of your office and should report directly to you.

"Come and join hands with us in the great enterprise which is worthy of the noblest efforts of us all" proclaimed the sanguine founder of the American Association, Alexander Arthur. While the standard since then has fallen miserably, it is not too late to hoist it up again. In fact, the decline, like adversity, could be sweet. It could occasion an ascent to a truly higher standard of corporate action and accountability.

Will you exert your "noblest efforts" to that end? Or will your neglect be the occasion of a mobilized citizenry recovering their future through resurgent legal and political action?

Sincerely,

Ralph Nader

THE FOREST SERVICE AND APPALACHIA

by
Si Kahn

Much has been written about the effects of corporate and absentee ownership on the Appalachian land and people. The massive holdings of coal, oil, timber, land and power companies have been well documented—not to mention the way in which these lands have historically escaped fair taxes. The acquisition of lands by private and semi-public (TVA) power companies has also been well researched.

In fact, however, the largest single landowner in Appalachia is neither a coal/oil corporation, a land or timber company, nor an electric utility, but the United States government. Throughout Appalachia, the Federal government through the U.S. Forest Service owns millions of acres of land. Most of the National Forests lying east of the Mississippi River are concentrated in Appalachia. These include:

State	National Forest	Acreage	Square Miles
Georgia	Chattahoochee	738,076	1,153
Kentucky	Daniel Boone	615,796	962
North Carolina	Nantahala	451,989	706
North Carolina	Pisgah	481,954	753

SOURCE: (c) 1974 by the John Hay Whitney Foundation.

AUTHOR: Si Kahn *is an organizer and musician who has worked for the last 12 years in Appalachia and the deep South.*

State	National Forest	Acreage	Square Miles
Tennessee	Cherokee*	614,107	960
Virginia	George Washington**	1,003,874	1,615
Virginia	Jefferson***	621,473	971
West Virginia	Monongahela	831,329	1,299
	TOTALS............	5,388,598	8,419

This is an area larger than the states of Connecticut, Delaware, and Rhode Island combined!

On the local level, the amount of national forest land in many counties in the Southern mountains is staggering. Within the Appalachian areas of West Virginia, Virginia, Tennessee, Kentucky, North Carolina, and Georgia, there are 37 counties in which the Forest Service owns over 20 percent of the land. In 14 of these counties, *more than 40 percent* of the land is in national forests:

State	County	Acreage	NF Acreage	% NF
Georgia	Rabun	235,520	143,580	61%
Georgia	Fannin	262,160	106,602	42%
Georgia	Union	197,760	95,593	48%
Georgia	Towns	106,240	56,559	54%
Kentucky	McCreary	267,520	154,288	58%
North Carolina	Macon	330,880	149,369	45%
North Carolina	Graham	184,960	111,065	60%
North Carolina	Clay	136,320	59,975	44%
Tennessee	Polk	278,400	150,870	54%
Tennessee	Unicoi	118,400	52,049	44%
Virginia	Bath	345,600	171,996	50%
Virginia	Craig	215,040	115,051	54%
Virginia	Allegheny	285,440	138,070	48%
West Virginia	Pocahontas	603,520	285,474	47%

From the point of view of the U.S. Forest Service, its concentration of land ownership in the Southern Appalachians is

*Includes 327 acres in North Carolina.
**Includes 100,386 acres in West Virginia.
***Includes 961 acres in Kentucky and 18,245 in West Virginia.

highly desirable; it is, in fact, something it has been working toward for a long time. Its basic strategy in the Southern mountains is set out in its official publication, *Guide for Managing the National Forests in the Appalachians*. The guide states in part:

> The concept of the Appalachian Greenbelt is possible because of the unique physiographic characteristics of the area. It is a mountainous green oasis in the Eastern United States from which flows a continuous supply of renewable resources and which provides the large surrounding population with a place to recreate in a natural setting. . . .Summer mountain temperatures are generally 10° lower than the adjacent plains. This factor makes the mountains a highly desirable retreat for city dwellers and other nearby residents.[1]

As this statement makes clear, the national forests are seen by the Forest Service as a resource to be used primarily by the "large surrounding population" of "city dwellers and nearby residents." This includes, of course, the urban population of the Eastern Seaboard. No one can argue that residents of the Eastern cities probably need to "recreate in a natural setting" from time to time. But it is also necessary to remember that *there are some 10 million people living in the so-called "Appalachian Greenbelt!"* What about us?

Well, we're pretty much out of luck, according to the *Guide for Managing the National Forests in the Appalachians:*

> Population losses within the Greenbelt can be attributed to the fact that this area can only sustain a limited number of people year-round. Many of the narrow mountain valleys are unsuitable for industrial complexes. Plans for economic development must recognize the limitations of the area so that over-emphasis on the wrong type of activities does not occur.[2]

The Forest Service is obviously not looking after anyone's interest except its own here. To write off industrial development for Appalachia because of its "narrow mountain valleys" is like saying that Pittsburgh can't support industry because of its many residential neighborhoods. In fact, Appalachia is for many reasons—raw material, electric power, access to population centers, transportation, labor force—well suited for industrial growth. By ignoring the facts, the Forest Service is actively undermining the efforts of the ten million people who live in the mountains for economic, political and social self-development.

But the Forest Service is not reacting to the needs of Appalachian people in its planning for Appalachia. As the *Guide for Managing the National Forests in the Appalachians* makes clear, it is motivated by a very different perspective:

> Pressures on the forest resources and environment within this mountain region come from many users. As long as population growth continues, pressure for products and services from the National Forest lands will grow. Unless definite limits are set for the protection of the environment and use of the resources within the Greenbelt, population pressure will bring about their impairment and eventual destruction. . . .This influence area for the Greenbelt stretches far outside National Forest boundaries. Total planning must consider the overall emphasis area.[3]

The problem with this comment is that the population pressure the Forest Service is talking about comes from *outside* the mountains. After all, population is not growing in Appalachia; the mountains have been losing folks steadily for years. This attitude makes as much sense (especially since the Forest Service is actively encouraging people to use the national forests) as saying that an Indian reservation is threatened by overcrowding because large numbers of tourists want to visit and camp there.

The emphasis of the Forest Service on the needs of people *outside* the Southern mountains has, on occasion, been the root of conflict with local Appalachians. One incident is worth noting as an example of the extremes these conflicts sometimes reach. As reported by the *Atlanta Constitution:*

> Vernon McCall was "the weakest one in the community" of Balsam Grove, a village in the heart of Pisgah National Forest. Vernon, according to Mrs. Leonard Griffin, "is a sick boy. He has epilepsy and he's disabled."

> On February 22, men of the U.S. Forest Service broke

into Vernon's trailer house, dragged out a bed and a few other belongings, and then dug a hole with a bulldozer, rammed his home, his lean-to, his pig pen and his little barn into it and buried the whole thing. Having erased every trace of his home, they planted pine seedlings over it. . . .

The Forest Service claimed the government owned the land, not Vernon, and they had been trying to get him off it since 1968. But the community lawyer said no legal action had been taken to evict Vernon, and local authorities proceeded to charge Forest Ranger Dan W. Hile with willful injury to personal property. . . .

Meantime Vernon, who is 40, has rented a new trailer, and scratches out a living on welfare and what he can make picking and selling ivy. And the seedlings the Forest Service planted over his old trailer have died.[4]

What makes all of this so intolerable is that *the people of Appalachia are the ones who actually pay for these national forests.* Anyone who knows the area is familiar with the irony of high taxes on the one hand and low public services on the other—a situation common to many Southern mountain counties. It has often been noted that in the coal counties this is partly the result of the undertaxation of coal lands. What has not been recognized is that in counties with national forest lands the tax-exempt status of these lands has undermined the tax base and increased the tax burden on local property owners. The following report examines the effects which the national forests in Appalachia have had on the ability of mountain counties to govern and finance themselves.

Federal Lands and County Finances

One of the direct and measurable effects of national forest holdings in Appalachia is the loss of local property tax revenue. At the end of 1972, Forest Service holdings totaled 5,388,598 acres in Georgia, North Carolina, Tennessee, Kentucky, Virginia, and West Virginia. Being Federal property, these lands are exempt from state, county, and city/town taxes. While it is difficult to estimate the exact extent of the tax loss, it is probable that, based on average values for land and effective tax rates in the counties involved, the Appalachian national forests cost local governments nearly $10 million a year in lost tax revenues—revenues that would go to support schools, roads, health programs, welfare, and other public services.

This tax loss has not often been recognized—partly because the Forest Service in its intensive public relations campaigns emphasizes the financial gain to counties from national forest lands. This type of publicity never mentions the fact that these lands are tax exempt; or that they had previously been on county tax digests; or the amount of revenue *lost* to counties when the lands passed from private to Federal ownership. But the fact is that in 1972 the *total* Forest Service payments to Appalachian counties were only $734,641.08—less than 14 cents an acre and well under 10 percent of what the property taxes alone would have been if the land were still in private hands.

The small sums that are paid by the Forest Service to local counties come from its so-called "25% Fund," authorized by the 1911 Weeks Act. This act, in effect, authorized the national forest system by providing for the Federal government to purchase lands necessary to protect the flow of navigable streams, including their watersheds. The 13th Section of the Weeks Act (36 Stat. 961-963) provides:

> Twenty-five per centum of all moneys received during any fiscal year from each national forest into which lands acquired under this Act may be divided shall be paid, at the end of such year, by the Secretary of the Treasury to the State in which such national forest is situated, to be expended as the State legislature may prescribe for the benefit of the public schools and public roads of the counties in which such national forest is situated.[5]

The income from national forests comes mostly from the sale of timber "on the stump," although a certain amount also comes from other fees and from special permits such as those for mining and recreational areas. Unlike the national forests of the Western United States, which produce valuable old-growth sawtimber, the Appalachian national forests have in the past produced trees suitable only for pulpwood. As any mountain landowner will tell you, selling pulpwood on the stump is no way to bring in money. If cut selectively, mountain land will make five to ten cords of pulpwood per acre; if clearcut, it will make ten to twenty cords. The going price for Forest Service pulpwood on the stump in Appalachia is about $2.00 a cord. Selectively cut land can be logged again in about ten years; clearcut land, in about thirty. Thus, on an average yearly basis, the "income" from an acre of national forest land in the Southern mountains is between 66 cents and $2.00.

Aside from the low revenue which this gives to counties, the problem with this system is that it makes "25% Fund" payments—on which counties must depend to help finance roads and schools—completely dependent on an arbitrary factor: how much wood the forest service decides to cut that year. This produces a not-so-subtle pressure on local government to approve the high rates of timber-cutting the forest service would like to set and locally-hated practices such as clearcutting. For example, during the recent struggle over proposed Forest Service clearcutting in the Cohutta Mountains in Fannin County, Georgia —one of the proposed areas in the Eastern Omnibus Wilderness Bill—petitions were circulated which read:

> We cannot afford the loss of revenues that are presently being returned to our county governments by the Forest Service from timber sales. We do not wish to retire our forests from production when we know that the local people will have to pick up the additional tax load; neither do we want the added tax to discourage local population growth, because this is already a problem for our rural areas.[6]

In fact, since timber-cutting revenues in any national forest are lumped together each year before distributing to counties, Fannin County would have received 14.4 percent (its proportionate share of Chattahoochee national forest acreage) of 25 percent (the Weeks Act formula) of whatever income clearcutting the Cohuttas produced—3.6 cents of every dollar of timber cut!

Because the "25% Fund" payments are based on revenue from timber cutting, payments per acre vary widely from state to state and even among national forests within the same state. In Georgia, the Chattahoochee National Forest, which is located within the Appalachian area of the state, made payments to counties of 26.7 cents per acre in 1972. Counties in Georgia's Ocoee National Forest, however, which lies in the state's pulp-wood belt, were paid $1.39 per acre—more than five times what the Appalachian counties received.

Payments vary even more widely from state to state. In 1972, average payments were 41 cents in Georgia (this *includes* the high payment received for the Ocoee National Forest); 21 cents in North Carolina; 17 cents in Kentucky; 15 cents in Tennessee; 5 cents in Virginia; and 11 cents in West Virginia. By comparison, the average payment per acre was $1.03 in California; $2.16 in Louisiana; $1.40 in Mississippi; $2.12 in Oregon; $1.01 in South Carolina; $1.23 in Texas; and $0.95 in Washington. The average payment per acre for all national forests in all states was 58 cents. The average payment per acre for all Appalachian national forests was 13.5 cents, less than one fourth the national average!

Two other ways of looking at this situation help make clear just how discriminatory it is:

> (1)   If counties in Appalachia had received "25% Fund" payments at the national average rate of 58 cents/acre, they would have received $3,125,868 instead of $734,641.

> (2)   If *all* the revenue produced by the National Forests was divided among counties on the basis of their pro-portionate share of National Forest acreage, the Appa-lachian counties would have received $12,503,472 in 1972—seventeen times what they actually got.

Another way of trying to evaluate the fairness or unfairness as well of the constitutionality of the way in which national forest revenue is distributed is to look at it in terms of payment per person to affected counties. After all, "25% Fund" pay-ments were earmarked by the Weeks Act for support of roads and schools, the two items which usually make up the bulk of a rural county's budget. Since the national forest funds *are* Fed-eral payments, it stands to reason that they should be distributed on an equitable basis.

In the 37 Appalachian counties which have 20 percent or

more of their area in national forests, payments per person in 1972 ranged from a low of 9 cents per person (Smyth County, Virginia) to a high of $5.01 per person (Rabun County, Georgia). The average figure was 93 cents per person. Compare this with payments per person made in Western counties with similar populations. These figures ranged from a low of $101.14 per person (Curry County, Oregon) to a high of $437.53 per person (Skamonia County, Washington). It doesn't take much imagination to see what Federal subsidies of this size could mean to education in revenue-starved Appalachian counties.

A further problem caused by the fact that national forest payments depend on timber-cutting revenue is that counties are not able to predict the amount of revenue they will receive in any year. For example, in 1969, during the period of greatest clear-cutting in the Monongahela National Forest, counties received 25.9 cents. In Pocahontas County, West Virginia, this meant that income from national forests in the county dropped from $73,050 in 1969 to $33,931 in 1972, a loss of $39,119. For a county with a population of 8,640, this is a tremendous revenue loss. As rates per acre dropped between 1969 and 1972, other counties experienced similar losses. Throughout the Appalachian region, despite the fact that national forest acreage increased 3 percent in the three years from 1969 to 1972, the amount received from the Forest Service *decreased* $159,070. Of all regions in the country, Appalachia is one of those which can least afford this type of revenue loss.

The loss of this amount of revenue may not seem significant to some people who are used to urban budgets. But it is important to realize that—partly because of the lack of growth due to lack of land—the Appalachian counties in which the national forests are concentrated are among the smallest and poorest counties in the nation. According to 1970 census data, the average population of the fourteen Appalachian counties with over 40 percent national forest land is less than 9,000. Their average rate of poverty in 1970 was 29.2 percent—more than *twice* the average for the United States as a whole. Not one of these counties had a poverty rate less than the national average. In the thirty years prior to 1970, these counties combined lost 13.2 percent of their population, and only one of the fourteen gained population in this period.

These counties are affected not only by revenue loss, lack of public services, high poverty incidence and outmigration rates, but—to add insult to injury—by local property taxes that are significantly higher than those in counties without national forest lands. Looking again at the fourteen counties with over 40 percent of their land held by the Forest Service, the effective tax rate* for these counties is on the average 15 percent higher than the average effective tax rate for the state.** This situation is especially apparent in Tennessee and Georgia. Polk County, Tennessee, for example, with 54 percent of its land held by the Forest Service, has an effective tax rate of $1.38 per $100 compared to a state average rate of $0.90. Of 75 Tennessee counties with single tax rates, Polk County has the fifth highest rate. In Georgia, Fannin County, which is 42 percent national forest land, has the highest tax rate of all counties in the state—higher than the non-municipal rates of Fulton (Atlanta), Muscogee (Columbus), Bibb (Macon), Richmond (Augusta), or Chatham (Savannah) counties.

This situation has not gone unnoticed politically. The Commissioner of Roads and Revenues of Fannin County has made a summary statement of local attitudes toward the problem:

> Fannin County does realize a good many benefits in ways that encourage people to live here, but must also tolerate some serious circumstances. . . .The U.S. Forest Service now owns some 106,000 acres of land within Fannin County and this deprives the county of approximately $150,000 per year in tax revenue. A large portion of this land has progressively been acquired from private land owners who had formerly been paying taxes. This process has resulted in a steady undermining of our tax base.
>
> This example, combined with the tax rate we pay in Fannin County, creates a constant hardship on a lot of

*"Effective tax rate" figures combine millage rates with assessment rates to reach a figure which can be compared with others on a tax rate per $100 of true property value basis.

**In fact, the actual tax rates for these counties exceed comparable rates for rural counties by more than 15 percent, since the state figures include urban and metropolitan counties.

our people who still own a fair amount of taxable property. Every time a piece of property falls into the hands of the Forest Service, the tax revenue formerly received from it is gone for good, and the remaining property owners must share this loss in revenue. . . .They purchase private land as it becomes available with our Federal tax money, and use it, in fact, to undermine the local tax sources where our local revenue must come from to support our local government. . . .

We can no longer ignore the seriousness of these problems. There must be some compatible adjustment when land is acquired and results in a revenue loss.[7]

Responding editorially to the above remarks, one of the local newspapers, *The Blue Ridge Summit-Post,* wrote:

The increase in taxes will no doubt place a great deal of strain on the working man's pocketbook. . . .Our tax rate in the past has been in no way below average standards, yet we, as a county, have profited little from the revenue obtained from it. We see as one of the reasons for our county's tax problem that great land speculator and wild real estate dealer, The Forest Service.

We feel that the state and Federal governments should find a means of returning some of the revenue on this untaxed land to the county, where it belongs. Federal preservation of forest land is a good thing; we believe in some land control; but taxes are taxes, and Fannin County is having to strain the wrong pay check. Our residents work hard for their living, and carrying the load for the Forest Service is not helping the situation. We suggest some type of revenue return to the county on the part of its greatest landholder, The Forest Service.[8]

The Politics of National Forests

The U.S. Forest Service itself has at different times taken different positions on the effect its policies have on local counties. Its usual position is that the "25% Fund" payments are a tremendous benefit to local governments. Their public relations campaign to convince local, state, and national political figures has been so effective that a preliminary draft of *The Last Stand: The Nader Study Group Report on the Forest Service* stated:

> They [local residents] also receive generous public service benefits from National Forest timber cutting. To compensate counties containing National Forest land for their small amount of taxable property, the federal government pays them 25 percent of the receipts from National Forest timber sales within their bounds to support construction of public schools and roads.[9]

To term the token payments which the Forest Service makes to local counties "generous public service benefits" is, to say the least, not particularly accurate (the statement has been deleted from the final report); but the example does show the tremendous extent to which Forest Service public relations has been effective.

At other times, the Forest Service has downplayed the "25% Fund" and emphasized other benefits from National Forests. One Forest Service spokesperson has stated:

> Without any doubt, the many other contributions to the economic development of the Appalachian Region made by the National Forests far outweigh the 25% return to the counties. It is not practical to place a monetary value on many of these contributions. I refer to such things as:
>
>   —Recreation use plus hunting and fishing. . . .In a National Survey of Fishing and Hunting by the U.S. Fish and Wildlife Service in 1965, they placed an economic value on a fishing man-day of $5.60 and a hunting man-day of $6.03. It would be higher today. So, you can see that this item alone would exceed the value of the 25% fund which is used only on schools and roads in the counties having National Forest lands.
>
>   —Watershed protection benefitting local areas as well as down stream flood protection.
>
>   —Employment of people maintaining and administering National Forests plus those employed to harvest timber which we have grown, etc.
>
>   —Construction and maintenance of roads and

bridges which would otherwise have to be maintained by the counties or state.[10]

The inaccuracies in this statement are highly misleading. The
"economic value" of fishing and hunting involves money spent at
local stores which is useful, but not to be confused with county
income from taxes which is spent on education, health, and
welfare.   Clearcutting on national forest lands has destroyed
many watersheds and increased hazards of flooding.   Forest
service employees are paid out of money appropriated from the
Federal budget, which comes from taxes paid by local residents.
No one is "employed" by the Forest Service to harvest timber;
the wood is sold on the stump to woodcutters and timber companies.   Most of the timber on national forest lands was not
"grown" by the Forest Service; it was there when the land was
acquired from private landowners.   Few of the clearcut areas
in the Appalachians have even been reforested.   Nationally, the
Forest Service is 733,000 acres behind on reforesting clearcut
lands.[11]   As for road maintenance, this year alone the Forest
Service closed 60 miles of roads in the Chattahoochee National
Forest out of a total of 1,392. And the damage done to county
and state roads by overloaded trucks carrying timber from
the national forests is a direct cost to local government and a
hazard and inconvenience to local residents.

The fact is that other benefits do not "outweigh the 25%
return to the counties"; they do not begin to compensate for
the loss of tax revenue.   In fact, the *Public Land Law Review
Commission* in its 1970 report to the President and Congress
concluded:

> While benefits are national, the geographical distribution
> of the Federal lands makes their burdens regional and
> local, and, in general, Federal ownership of public lands
> provides no distinguishable benefits to state and local
> governments in lieu of the benefits they would receive if
> the lands were privately owned.[12]

The Forest Service has also argued on occasion that one
third of the United States is owned by the Federal government
and that it would be impossible to make payments for all these
lands.   But there is a difference between many of the western
national forests which have always been public lands and the

national forests in Appalachia, which have been bought up since the passage of the Weeks Act in 1911. Before 1911, *none* of the land now in the Appalachian national forests was owned by the Federal government; all of it was owned privately and was subject to local property taxes. The acquisition over the past 62 years of so much Appalachian land by the Forest Service has meant an increasing destruction of local tax digests, especially in those 37 Appalachian counties where between 20 percent and 61 percent of the land has passed into Federal hands.

It is clear that the national forests are *not* contributing nearly as much as the Forest Service claims to the economic growth of the counties where they are located. The evidence suggests that the opposite is true. The loss of tax revenue has produced a scarcity of public services, including education and health care. The control of so much land by the government has artificially driven prices up for mountain land. Because of the demands for summer homes, recreational development, and land speculation, farming is no longer economically possible in many places. These conditions have helped encourage many young people to leave the area and have prevented many who have left from coming back. Whatever benefits the Appalachian national forests provide to the nation as a whole, for the residents of mountain counties they mean higher taxes and decreased public services. In effect, the people of Appalachia are being taxed to provide recreation and relaxation for people from other wealthier areas. No one can deny that there is a national need for recreation; but that does not make it right that mountain people should have their taxes raised and their public services cut back so that well-to-do tourists can enjoy themselves at no cost.

There are several Federal precedents which strongly suggest that the Forest Service's way of doing business in Appalachia is neither desirable nor necessary. A startling comparison comes when we contrast payments made to counties by the Forest Service with those made by the Tennessee Valley Authority (TVA). In 1972, for example, TVA paid $252,766 to Polk County, Tennessee, in lieu of taxes on the 3,418 acres it owns in the county—$66.05 an acre. The Forest Service paid the county $22,612 for 150,870 acres—15 cents an acre. To put it a little differently, the Forest Service owns 44 times as much land in Polk County as TVA; but TVA paid the county 11 times as much!

TVA's responsibility to counties where it has operations, however, is very different from the Forest Service. The Tennessee Valley Authority Act provides:

> TVA's payments to the respective states shall not be less than the higher of (1) the average of state, county, municipal and district property tax levied by them on purchased power property and on the portion of TVA land allocated for power use for the last two years such property was in private ownership or (2) $10,000. TVA pays directly to counties amounts equivalent to the former county and district taxes derived from power properties purchased as such by TVA and from reservoir lands allocable to power. . . .*These direct payments to counties fully replace tax losses which result from the transfer of such properties to public ownership* [ed. emphasis].[13]

The TVA Act is not the only Federal precedent for the principle of full income replacement to counties. Public Law 81-874, commonly known as the "impacted areas" program, provides under Section 2, "Reduction in Local Revenue by Reason of Acquisition of Real Property by the United States":

> A school district may be eligible if (1) the property was acquired by transfer and not by exchange since 1938; (2) the assessed valuation of such property represents 10% or more of the assessed valuation of all realty in the district at time or times of transfer; and (3) the acquisition has imposed on the school district a substantial and continuing financial burden. Maximum entitlement is the product of the applicant's current expense tax rate applied to the estimated assessed valuation of the Federal property (exclusive of improvements since transfer date).[14]

In fiscal 1969, a total of 106 school districts in the United States received Federal tax replacement payments under this provision. The total paid to these districts was over $3½ million.

It is obvious that it is way past time for the U.S. Government and the Forest Service to begin full compensation to Appalachian counties for tax losses caused by national forest holdings and perhaps to compensate these counties for their

losses in past years as well. This has been recognized by two recent studies. *The Last Stand: The Nader Study Group Report
on the U.S. Forest Service* states as one of its final recommendations:

> To reduce local pressure on the Forest Service and mem-
> bers of Congress to increase National Forest timber
> cutting, Congress should abolish the practice of returning
> 25 percent of timber sales receipts to the counties in
> which the timber is cut. It should replace these payments
> with the more equitable and dependable federal aid to
> impacted areas (now granted to states containing non-
> taxable Defense Department property) to all counties
> embracing National Forest land, regardless of the amount
> of timber cutting.[15]

A much stronger statement has been made by the Public
Land Law Review Commission. In its official report, *One Third
of the Nation's Land,* the Commission states:

> The legislative history of the acts providing for the sharing
> of receipts from forest products and oil and gas, as well as
> other leasable minerals, clearly reflects that the payments
> to the states and local governments were intended as com-
> pensation for the fact that the lands in question would no
> longer be available for private ownership and property
> taxation. . . .Since the *ad valorem* tax system has been
> the foundation for the financing of programs providing
> municipal services, the Commission believes that all
> landowners must share in payment for these services.
> This should not exclude the Federal government as land-
> owner, except where the federally owned land is being
> used for facilities, such as in the case of post offices, to
> furnish services to all the people throughout the country
> . . . .If the national interest dictates that lands should be
> retained in Federal ownership, it is the obligation of the
> United States to make certain that the burden of that
> policy is spread among all the people of the United
> States and is not borne only by those states and govern-
> ments in whose area the land is located. Therefore, the
> Federal Government should make payments to compen-
> sate state and local governments for the tax immunity of
> Federal lands. . . .We find further that any attempt to tie

payments to states and local governments to receipts generated from the sale or use of public lands or their resources causes an undue emphasis to be given in program planning to the receipts that may be generated.[16]

There are a number of other Forest Service practices which often conflict with local needs. One is the charging of fees to use recreational areas in the national forests. These fees range from $1.00 to $3.00 a day, or $10.00 for a "Golden Eagle" passport which allows entry to certain areas for a year. These fees may seem reasonable to tourists, but they are out of reach for most poor families. As a result, local residents are often not able to afford recreational facilities built by the Forest Service in their own counties. One North Georgia mountaineer, commenting on the Forest Service's plan to build campsites in the Cohutta Wildlife Refuge, one of the few wilderness areas left in the Eastern United States, said:

> There's a lot of old mountain people beside me who aren't going to take kindly to the idea of getting a permit to go onto land they call home.[17]

Many Southern mountain residents are also concerned by the rate at which the Forest Service is still acquiring land. A recent example of this process occurred in 1971 in Bland County, Virginia, in the Jefferson National Forest. One Virginia resident and forestry student who has been in close touch with the situation wrote:

> Consolidation Coal Company owned 46,000 acres of land in the county, containing relatively small amounts of semi-anthracite coal. Consol sold the land (finding the coal too poor to be profitably mined), amounting to one fifth of the county, to the U.S. Forest Service, which has incorporated it into the Jefferson National Forest. Combined with the county land already controlled by the Forest Service, it will put nearly a quarter of the county's real estate under government ownership.

> Large opposition to the land sale was expressed by Bland County residents. By the government owning one-quarter of the county, local revenues will be severely hurt. When Consolidation Coal owned the land last year, the com-

pany, a subsidiary of Continental Oil, paid just 14 cents
an acre in taxes, amounting to a total of $6,800.

The Forest Service pays no taxes, but will pay a small
compensation of $3,600—or just eight cents an acre. The
$3,200 loss, opponents say, could destroy the Bland
County budget, which has had severe fiscal problems for
some time.

Most of the biggest supporters of the land sale were non-
residents and outside agencies, including various sports-
men's clubs. The Bland County Board of Supervisors
voted against the land deal twice last year. But a new
Board of Supervisors has now voted in favor of the sale,
yielding to the heavy pressure by outside groups.

So now the land is destined for tourist and recreational
development by the Forest Service. Just how this will
benefit the residencts of Bland County, only time will
tell.[18]

Appalachian working people are also critical of the ways in
which timber sales are conducted. These sales are carried out by
sealed bid. However, the Forest Service requires the posting of a
cash "bid bond" with each bid. On a recent sale in which the
minimum bid permitted was $2,297, the required bid bond was
$300, a hard amount for self-employed woodcutters to come by.
"Performance bonds," sometimes in the total amount of the contract price, are also required. These rules have the effect of
making it extremely difficult for the small independent wood-
cutter to bid successfully on Forest Service timber. The contracts thus go more often than not to the large timber corporations.

Of the Forest Service practices, none is more deeply re-
sented than their use of condemnation proceedings to acquire
homes and farms for national forests. Because of past abuses
of its condemnation powers, the Forest Service's power to condemn land for National Forests was removed by Congress in
1964. This power is retained, however, in the case of national
recreation areas. The pending Eastern Omnibus Wilderness Act
(S.316) would restore condemnation powers to the Forest
Service in the proposed Eastern Wilderness areas. One develop-

ing national recreation area is located in the Jefferson National Forest in Southwest Virginia.   One organizer who has been working with local residents to save their homes and farms from condemnation has written:

> The Mt. Rogers National Recreation Area, as defined by Congress in 1966, covers 154,000 acres in five counties of southwest Virginia. These counties are: Washington, Smyth, Grayson, Carroll and Wythe.   The National Recreation Area (the Forest Service's equivalent to a National Park) is to be developed to accommodate, by present plans, an estimated five million tourists a year by 1990. To do this, the Forest Service has begun acquiring lands for campgrounds, livery stables, lakes, ski slopes and other recreation facilities.   Some of the land has been openly bought from residents who, according to the Forest Service, are "willing sellers." While the Forest Service claims that condemnation proceedings are necessary to acquire land efficiently, many residents resent this practice and point out abuses of it.
>
> The central issue, as many local residents see it, is not simply whether or not there should be a National Recreation Area, but rather the fact that the people are having no say in the plans and developments of their communities and homes.[19]

This lack of local input into Forest Service planning is a complaint heard frequently in Appalachian counties where the national forests are found. Traditionally, the Forest Service has carried out its plans without consulting local government or citizens.   Lately, in response to public pressure from many sources, it has taken to holding "listening posts" at which local residents are asked to present their opinions. These "listening posts," however, have generally been held *after* the Forest Service had already prepared written plans of action for the areas in question.

There is also evidence that the hearings are not taken into serious consideration. At a recent hearing in North Georgia, over 90 percent of the witnesses spoke *against* Forest Service proposals. These proposals would have included clear-cutting vast areas of the Cohutta Wildlife Refuge, despite the fact that this area has been proposed as a Wilderness Area in the Eastern Omnibus Wilderness Bill. Yet, when a transcript of the hearing was requested, the Forest Service replied that it did not plan to transcribe the tape they had made of the hearing. It is difficult to see how a hearing could be a legitimate part of a public planning process when the only record of it is a tape recording in a Forest Service office. This type of practice led one county official to react in a letter to the Forest Service:

> After attending your meeting at Etowah on the Hiwassee Unit, I came away with the feeling that the Forest Service has already drawn up a tentative plan. If this is the case, I think in the interest of saving time and effort, the Forest Service should present their plan and then have hearings before it is adopted. . . .The U.S. Forest Service [has] never attempted to work with local government on future plans for U.S. Forest Service lands within their political subdivision.[20]

Conclusions

It is evident that Appalachian people are bearing an unfair share of the cost of maintaining a national forest system and are getting very few of the benefits. If the national forests in the Southern mountains are to benefit Appalachians as well as other Americans, some changes in Forest Service policy must be made. The following are recommendations which, based on the facts set out in this study, are necessary to achieve this goal.

(1) The Forest Service should make payments in lieu of taxes to all counties in Appalachia (and elsewhere) where national forest lands are located. These payments should be equal to the amount of ad valorem tax these lands would produce if privately owned.

(2) Until such a system is adopted, *all* income from the national forests should be redistributed to the counties in which these lands are located in proportion to the share which each county has of the national total. Such a system would provide each county in Appalachia with national forests approximately sixteen times its current payment. It would also remedy the gross inequalities in distribution of national forest revenues

which now exist among different national forests and states. The present system is a gross violation of the equal protection provisions of the U.S. Constitution and should definitely be challenged in the courts.

(3) To avoid destruction of county economic bases, a limit should be set on the amount of land the Forest Service is permitted to own in any given county.

(4) Admission to Forest Service recreational areas should be free to residents of counties where these areas are located.

(5) The Forest Service should be required to hold public hearings before closing any national forest roads and to show cause before taking action. Procedures should be established through which local citizens, without undue difficulty or expense, can stop such proposed Forest Service actions where they are definitely not in the interest of the *local* community.

(6) Any Forest Service plans for land acquisition, recreational development, road construction, logging, subcontracting, mining, land swaps, special use permits, and other uses of the national forests should be subject to the prior approval of an elected county committee.

(7) The Forest Service should be absolutely prohibited from using condemnation proceedings to acquire any owner-occupied farms or homes in national forests, wilderness areas or national recreation areas. Where such lands have been acquired by condemnation, they should be returned without cost to the previous owners.

(8) Timber tracts should be bid off in small enough lots so that small independent woodcutters can compete. Bid bonds should be abolished and a different system established to guarantee performance that would not discriminate against individual woodcutters. It should be required that 50 percent of all national forest timber be sold to independent woodcutters, cooperatives, or small wood companies which are located in the county where the boundary of timber is located. This will help reduce abuse of the current bid system by the giant timber corporations.

(9)　Where the process of removing national forest timber damages county or state roads, the Forest Service should be required to pay for their maintenance and repair.

(10) Clearcutting, a process which destroys timber, land and water resources, should be totally prohibited on national forest lands.

(11) County and town governments should have the right to acquire national forest lands through eminent domain proceedings to build public facilities such as schools and hospitals.

The situation as it now exists in the Southern mountains violates the letter, and certainly the spirit, of equal protection laws. It is grossly unfair that the financial burden of providing recreation for the Eastern United States should fall so heavily on some of the poorest citizens in the country, yet this is exactly what is happening. It is ridiculous to spend millions for campsites in communities which lack funds for schools, hospitals, health care, transportation, water systems, sewage disposal, and housing; yet this is what is happening.

A number of Appalachian writers have suggested that the Federal government sees Appalachia mainly as a support area for the Eastern Seaboard, providing coal, minerals, electricity, timber and recreation to people outside the mountains. It is possible that in the minds of some economic and political planners, such as the Forest Service officials who wrote the *Guide for Managing the National Forests in the Appalachians,* the Southern mountains exist in the future as one vast Federal holding to be harvested by the coal corporations, the energy conglomerates, the timber and tourist industries. Mountain people are living on top of some of the greatest natural resources in the United States. History teaches that when poor and working people stand in the way of harvesting such resources, they and their interests will usually be moved aside.

On the other hand, the national forest lands in Appalachia could become a real resource to mountain people by providing jobs, land for public facilities, and the revenue for badly needed service programs. Even more, these lands, which have been taken from Appalachian people, could some day be returned to them to live and work on: lands which their grandparents settled and cleared and which their children are being forced to leave.

NOTES

[1]*Guide for Managing the National Forests in the Appalachians,* pages 7, 33.

[2]*Guide,* page 8.

[3]*Guide,* pages 7, 8.

[4]*The Atlanta Constitution,* May 12, 1971.

[5]*The Principal Laws Relating to the Establishment of the National Forests and to Other Forest Service Activities,* page 45.

[6]Undated petition beginning "We, the undersigned are against S.316, H.R. 1758, Wilderness Study Act H.R. 2420 and such Eastern Wilderness bills. . . .," author's possession.

[7]*Blue Ridge Summit-Post,* Blue Ridge, Georgia, October 11, 1972.

[8]*Ibid.*

[9]*The Last Stand: The Nader Study Group Report on the Forest Service,* pages V-13.

[10]Letter from W. W. Huber, Chief, Division of Information and Education, Southeast Region, U.S. Forest Service, dated January 18, 1971.

[11]*The Last Stand,* pages III-9.

[12]*One Third of the Nation's Land: A Report to the President and to The Congress by the Public Land Law Review Commission,* page 238.

[13]"TVA Power: Payments in Lieu of Taxes," TVA Information Office, Knoxville, Tennessee, November, 1972.

[14]"Administration of Public Laws 81-874 and 81-815: Nineteenth Annual Report of the Commissioner of Education," Office of Education, U.S. Department of Health, Education and Welfare, Washington, D.C., June 30, 1969.

[15]*The Last Stand,* pages VI-37.

[16]*One Third of the Nation's Land,* pages 4, 236, 238.

[17]U.S. Forest Service "Listening Post" on Cohutta Mountains Unit, Chatsworth, Georgia, August 1, 1972.

[18]Letter from Dave Tice dated January 22, 1973.

[19]Letter from Dave Tice dated February, 1973.

[20]*The McCaysville Citizen,* McCaysville, Georgia, September 23, 1971.

THE ESTABLISHMENT OF CONTROL

Section III: The Establishment of Control

The following five essays detail the process by which outside interests develop political, economic, social and cultural control over the Appalachian region. The articles point to the control over schools, courts, media, and the role of missionaries and local modernizing elites who assist in the take over and help set up systems of control.

In the first essay, Helen Lewis, Sue Kobak, and Linda Johnson outline the colonization process and illustrate it from the history of Southwest Virginia. The two most resistant aspects of mountain life were religion and the family, both of which became defensive and reverted inward in order to protect their members from the colonization process.

John Gaventa in "Property, Coal and Theft" discusses the way in which outside owners establish control through the media and control over the infrastructure. He uses examples from Middlesboro, Kentucky, and the development of dependency and powerlessness.

Warren Wright in "The Big Steal" describes the methods which were used by coal buyers and land speculators to secure the titles to coal lands of Eastern Kentucky. He presents evidence of legal chicanery and the development of dubious titles to the land and the use of the judiciary and political system to secure their ownership.

Anita Parlow in "The Land Development Rag" describes the economic, political, and social intrusions made by land developers in Watauga and Avery counties in North Carolina and outlines some of the attempts at resistance made by farmers to halt the development.

Mike Clark in "Education and Exploitation" points to the role of local colleges in training local people to control the area for the colonizers. Schools teach new values, adjust students to the new life style and produce workers for the system.

FAMILY, RELIGION AND COLONIALISM
IN CENTRAL APPALACHIA
or
BURY MY RIFLE AT BIG STONE GAP

by
Helen Matthews Lewis
Sue Easterling Kobak
Linda Johnson

The Southern Appalachians has been called "the last un-challenged stronghold of Western colonialism." (Caudill) In re-cent years this concept or refinements of it—"neo-colonialism," "imperialism," or "third world pillage"—have been applied to the region (Lewis and Knipe 1970; Dix 1970; Simon 1971; Diehl 1970; Lesser 1970; Burlage 1970).

This paper is an attempt to look more closely at the coloni-zation process in Central Appalachia and to look particularly at

SOURCE: Paper presented at the American Anthropological Association, Toronto, Canada, 1972.

AUTHORS: Helen Matthews Lewis is a staff member of the Highlander Re-search and Education Center, New Market, Tennessee. She is a former professor of sociology at Clinch Valley College, and lives on a farm in Dungannon, Virginia.
Sue Easterling Kobak, an early Appalachian activist leader and farmer, helped organize the Appalachia Free University. She is a former Appalachian Volunteer in southwest Virginia, and currently teaches in the Dungannon, Virginia, schools.
Linda Johnson, a native of West Virginia, is the co-coordinator of the Grace House Learning-Training Center, St. Paul, Vir-ginia.

the two most resistant aspects of traditional mountain culture, the family structure and religion, to see in what ways they resisted or adapted to the process or how they were used as instruments of colonial domination.

Central Appalachia—which is made up of eastern Kentucky, southern West Virginia, southwestern Virginia and northeast Tennessee—was the most isolated part of the Southern mountains. Except for a few outposts, the area was not settled until after the Revolutionary War. Mrs. John C. Campbell describes the area and its early settlement and characterizes the people living in the mountains as descendants of colonial English, Scotch-Irish, and German stock, "the advance guard of the great migration to the west who were seeking land, liberty, game."

> Many settled and remained in the area from the pure chance of a "broken axle" but more stayed from choice. The population spread back up among creek and branch, wherever a little bottom land was to be found, fresh game or new springs of clear water. Traditions brought from lands across the sea blended with customs and prejudices bred by the frontier existence and were maintained during a relatively long period of isolation following the original settlement. (Campbell 1925, 9-13)

Whether mountain culture should be properly described as a culture transmitted unchanged from the founders or an adaptive culture which developed in response to the isolated mountain conditions, descriptions do convince us that there was in the area at that time a society and culture different from the mainstream American way of life and certainly different from that of the outsiders who came into the mountains with industrialization. Since the outsider noted peculiarities, emphasized differences, and described the oddities, it is very hard to find reliable and clear descriptions of early family structure or religion in the mountains.

Raines (1924,X) in his book *The Land of Saddlebags* states that "while the rest of the nation has grown far from our revolutionary ancestors, the Mountain People have been marooned on an island of mountains, and have remained very much the same as they were at that time."

A sociologist visiting the hills of Kentucky in 1898 (Vincent 1898) describes a society based upon hunting and subsistence agriculture and a social organization based upon kinship. There were isolated mountain families living up coves and hollows with strong ties of kinship built upon three or more generations of intermarriage. Brown (1952) describes the traditional mountain family structure as a "family group," conjugal families living in family kin groups which formed small neighborhoods. The kin relations were extensive and complex, and neighborhoods acted as mutual aid societies. The groups were isolated, stable, self-sustaining, localized groups.

Although the family was described as strongly patriarchal with a highly differentiated division of labor between men and women, there were many family cooperative activities in work, recreation, and visiting. Men and women had to substitute for each other; and both needed to be strong, resourceful, and self-sufficient. Women's work was an integral part of the total operation, and although her work was hard, it was also hard for everyone in the family. There was an equalitarian simplicity in the terms used by husband and wife: "the woman" and "the man"; or "my woman" and "my man."

It was a life which stressed both independence and cooperation. The family and also the individuals had to be self-sufficient and independent and must not *depend* on others for help; one must be prepared to manage somehow by himself, but when he could, he helped. To be a good neighbor on a friendly, *equal* basis, "accommodating," was very important. Visitors to the mountain home frequently remarked on the lavish hospitality, generosity, uncompetitiveness, openness, directness, and simplicity of the mountain people. They were described as free from self-consciousness, dignified, quiet, reticent, and courteous.

The early church was characterized by writers as separatist, immersionist, hardshell, strongly Calvinistic, anti-missionary; the people were literal interpreters of the Bible, rejecting infant baptism and placing emphasis on experience. Vincent found theological discussions popular in the family,and he felt these satisfied the appetite for metaphysics and offered opportunity for intellectual exercise and discipline (1898, 18).

The church or meeting house served as a gathering place;

the monthly or less frequent meetings were an opportunity for sociability and a time to hear a preacher and have funerals preached. It served more as an occasional gathering place than an ongoing organization, although in the "settlements" the church served through monthly business meetings the function of a civil court, sanctioning the behavior of the members and disciplining those who fought with neighbors, abused their brothers, used rough language, or retailed ardent spirits (Henson 1972). There was little church machinery; and the mountain values of simplicity, equalitarianism, and democracy were reflected in the ceremonies of footwashing and laying on of hands. The insistence on untrained ministers who were given special authority only through the spirit also reflected an antielitest bias in mountain society. Services were informal, congregations could sing down the preacher, people could wander in and out of services, but every preacher was given a chance to preach. Rhythm and eloquence and emotional ecstasy were admired and encouraged in the preacher. This emotional extravagance has been thought by some to be contradictory to the portrait of the stolid, impassive, dignified mountain man; but perhaps this unselfconscious ability to display emotion was in keeping with an unsophisticated, straightforward approach to life. Mrs. Condon (1962, 88) reports that the Presbyterian church grew slowly in Harlan County because people thought the members were distant, cool, and unfriendly.

Though the area experienced gradual alterations between its settlement and the turn of the century, the biggest changes for the area came about 1890 as a result of the railroad, lumbering and coal mining, and the missionaries. Mrs. Campbell writes that at the turn of the century "suddenly the retarded frontier was rediscovered by two classes: those who saw the natural resources and sought them regardless of the interests of the natural owners; and those who with missionary zeal rushed in to educate and reform" (1925, 9). Mrs. Campbell, herself one of the missionaries, points to the "natural" alliance of exploiters and missionaries who came together to the hills.

John Fox, Jr., a writer of romantic novels and a member of a coal-developing family which came into the mountains at the turn of the century, supports this natural alliance:

> The railroad comes first as an element of civiliza-

tion, but unless the church and the school in the ratio of several schools to each church quickly follow, the railroad does the mountaineer little else than great harm. Even with the aid of these three, the standards of conduct of the outer world are reared slowly. A painful process of evolution has been the history of every little mountain-town that survived the remarkable mushroom growth which, within the year of 1889-90, ran from Pennsylvania to Alabama along both bases of the Cumberland. (1901, 209-10)

The process of colonization as it occurred in the Central Appalachians generally followed these stages:

1. Gaining entry: invasion and securing of the area or resources

2. Establishment of control: removal of opposition and resistance to prevent expulsion of invaders

3. Education and conversion of the natives: change the values and social system of the colonized

4. Maintenance of control: political and social domination

THE FIRST STAGE: Gaining Entry

The invasion was well planned and well executed almost before the natives knew what had happened. A well-trained force of lawyers, surveyors, geologists, and land buyers came into the mountains and millions of acres of mineral and virgin timber lands passed into the hands of development companies at from 30 cents to one dollar an acre. Even Franklin Delano Roosevelt, just out of Harvard, abstracted titles and surveys in Harlan County for his uncle, Warren Delano (Condon 1962). Vanderbilts, Fishes, and other big financiers from the Northeast visited the mountains to help secure mineral rights and building rights and make arrangements for the railroads. Thomas Nelson Page of Richmond, Virginia, in a speech to the Daughters of the American Revolution in 1910 urging them to give money for missionaries in the mountains, describes the coming of the exploiters:

> When the outer world has reached them, it has
> mainly been to trade upon their ignorance and rob them
> of what should have been their wealth. There are lands
> which were bought of them for a few dollas an acre,
> which are bonded now as many thousands, and the justi-
> fication for such legalized robbery at the hands of preda-
> tory wealth is that which is as old as Cyrus—that is was of
> more use to the taker than to the lawful holder. It is
> small wonder that they are suspicious as to the advances
> of civilization where the advance couriers are the land
> agent and the coal prospector—little wonder that, when
> evictors come under color of ancient patents to drive
> them from the lands which their fathers have held for
> generations, they should break out in feuds and vio-
> lences. (66-67)

In the early days there were few to criticize the methods.
In 1924 Raines describes the situation as follows:

> The mountain people are suffering from the ruthless
> exploitation of large financial interests. These foreign
> juggernauts may have secured their coal and timber lands
> for a song, but taking money from those that have no
> special use for it is not a fatal damage. The deadly sin is
> the thrusting of a ferocious and devouring social system
> upon an unprepared and defenseless people. (236)

Others interpreted the invasion as something akin to manifest destiny: "It is a region of vast resources that has been
blocked out of the wild by a great people and held in trust, as it
were, for the modern capitalist to develop and utilize. Its people
are beginning to see the dawn of a new day" (MLW, 1-1-1925,
2-3).

In the process of entry, both the missionaries and the industrialists were amazed by what they found. They sought to understand and to categorize the mountain people and culture. Letters
were sent home, reports were sent to church boards, and newspaper articles were written about the development. Picturesque
stories appeared in magazines.   Some were horrified at the
illiteracy, the lack of schools and medical facilities, and the

limited diet; they were appalled by the lack of roads, the isolation, the lack of conveniences, and the hard life of the women;
they were intrigued by the songs, beautiful weaving, quaint
language, marriage and funeral customs, and unorganized church
meetings; they were admiring of their courage, honesty, directness, and lack of sophistication. But always the mountain people
were compared with "back home": the educated and professional middle-class, the urban homes and situations from which
they came.

The biography of one of the early missionaries, Rev. Murdoch of Buckhorn, relates his first trip home after seeing the
mountains (May 1946):

> His heart and mind bursting with things to tell his
> Brooklyn friends. They were jotted down on a folded
> piece of paper. A kind of vivid moving picture of the
> crowded months since he left them. There was the
> mother who watched over her son to keep him from using
> profanity while shoeing his horse; children chewing tobac-
> co, other children going barefooted in the snow; the rich
> veins of coal laid bare along the creeks, destitute families
> in rickety cabins, burial without ministers, whole dis-
> tricts without schools, the silent forest at the head of
> Squabble Creek, the flowers and birds along the trails,
> the character sketches of some of the people he had met
> in his travels.

Such terms as arrested development, retarded frontier,
remnant, a distinct relic, a peculiar people, survivals, ancestors,
backward, and limited outlook were commonly used. Mrs.
Campbell writes that a conventional world was charmed with
its picturesqueness and startled by its illiteracy and disregard for
law. "It could not understand how people could at once be a
feudist and man of integrity and responsibility in his neighborhood. How they could be illiterate, yet have a real and deep
culture. Personal experiences led to undiscriminating generali-
zations on the 'finest of Anglo-Saxon blood' and the 'off-shoots
of degenerate refugees and criminals.' No people have ever
played more completely the mixed role of villain and neglected
hero in the public eye" (1925).

John Fox, Jr. played a large part in stereotyping the mountain culture for the outside world and justifying the imposition of power and control over a native people. He, like most of the newcomers, was both admiring and denigrating. He describes the Southern mountaineer as truthful, honest, courageous, hospitable, peaceable, and a man of law—yet known for his moonshining, his land-thieving, and his feuds. But he goes on to blame the Civil War, the revenue service, and the "system of land laws that sometimes makes it necessary for the mountaineer of Kentucky and Virginia to practically steal his own home" for making the mountaineer a "criminal" (1901, 209). The invasion brought in the outsider and opened up the mountain culture to view, and the mountaineer became aware of himself as different. He began to compare himself with the newcomer and learned to judge himself as inferior.

Jean Ritchie (1955) describes the development of the schools and its effect on her family:

> The settlement schools and the railroad began to bring the ways of the world to us in a kind of steady trickle. . . .The settlement schools [brought] in level-country people who settled among us and whose ways of doing things, whose very speech and actions, helped us to see that there was a different kind of life than the hard one we knew. (pp. 225ff.)

An editorial in *Mountain Life and Work* (April 1925) criticizes "unauthorized characterization by professional writers and unscientific reformers which built up among the mountaineers what the psychologists call an inferiority complex. It has found expression in the humble submission to outside invasion and in the eager acceptance of small favors and paltry benevolences."

ESTABLISHMENT OF CONTROL

John Fox describes, either naively or arrogantly, the process whereby the newcomer gained control and subdued the native population. In an article entitled "Civilizing the Cumberland" (1901, 209ff.), he describes how in Big Stone Gap, Virginia, the "sternest ideals of good order and law were set up and maintained with Winchester, pistol, policeman's billy, and whistle through a unique experiment in civilization." A volunteer police guard, a private army, manned by the young newcomers, was organized. Fox describes it as a police force of gentlemen: "aristocrats and pultocrats," American and British, lawyers, bankers, real-estate brokers, newspaper men, civil and mining engineers, geologists, speculators and several men of leisure. All were college graduates (Harvard, Yale, Princeton, University of Virginia) "who had come into the mountains of Virginia to make their fortunes from iron, coal and law." They were first organized to put down a strike of mountain workers at a newly established brick plant in the Gap. Fox then relates that they became precision troops who guarded jails against mobs, cracked toughs over the head with billies, lugged them to the calaboose, and appeared as witnesses against them in court the next morning. They turned a mountain crossroads town where mountain boys frolicked and fought into a quiet, respectable outpost of high society.

Since the developers wrote most of the history, there are few accounts of native opposition in the record. John Fox does mention that there was considerable hostility and dislike for the newcomers, and he mentions that fighting clans tried to make the "furriners" leave the county. He says that the strike of mountain workers became a confrontation between the newcomers and the mountaineers, and the opposition of the local people was readily discouraged by the newly formed guard. He relates how the newcomers were harassed, the guard mocked by the mountain "toughs," and the townspeople frightened and inconvenienced by the "wild jayhawkers from old Kanetuck" who were accustomed to coming to the Gap to sow wild oats and fight with the boys from Wise and Lee counties. He also reports that with the organization of the guard and the establishment of town ordinances which outlawed drinking, shooting, and yelling, all this was changed and mountain people were practically prevented from entering town (except as "meek sheep"). "It arrayed the town people against the country folk. . . but with each element of disorder there was a climax of incidents that established the recognized authority of the guard."

The hanging of a local bad man, Talton Hall, became a ceremonial display of power, thereby showing the legal conquest of the mountains through a confrontation with and defeat of the family-clan system. "Never had a criminal met death at the hands of the law in that region." The badman was a Kentucky feudsman and his clan was there to rescue him from the gallows. The guard won, and Fox points out that it showed "that a new power had come in the little band of 'furriners,' high-spirited, adventurous and well born, who had taken matters into their own hands, and subdued local lawlessness" (p. 25). The guard extended its "benign influence" throughout the area, and other boom towns formed similar organizations. After that, the natives, "the easy-going, tolerant good people, caught the fever for law and order." This early show of force and organization of political control made it possible in later years for the owner-operators to rely on the local authorities to protect their interests and maintain the needed law and order. After that, natives did most of the policing, and not until the unionization of the mines did the outsiders again have to take up guns to protect their interests.

The establishment of control may not have been quite as rapid or efficient in other parts of the mountains, but the pattern was much the same. The technological superiority of the newcomers made conquest inevitable. The shrewd manipulation of the machinery of law made the newcomer the supporter of law and order while the native became an outlaw. Since the newcomer wrote the history, the colonizer is "adventuresome" while the native is "tough."

Raines was to write later: "The Mountain Man that attempts to redress the injustice of the law by using the rifle is no more guilty in his lawlessness than is the millionaire corporation that uses shrewd lawyers instead of rifles" (1924, 144).

EDUCATION AND CONVERSION OF THE NATIVES

The role of the missionaries and educators was an important one: to make legitimate the exploitation, to eliminate some of the worst abuses, and to educate and change values so that the people would accept the new ways. John Fox recounts another incident of resistance to the newcomers and the use of religion to win over the natives. He reports that when the first printing press was taken to a certain mountain town in 1882, a deputation of citizens met it three miles from town and swore that it should go no farther. An old preacher mounted the wagon and drove it into town.

There are other reports of resistance to the missionaries, and some ministers were run out of communities and their churches burned. The preachers and church boards soon found that women were more welcome, especially if they had any skills such as teaching or nursing, for the mountain people were eager to acquire teachers and health workers who could most effectively reach the people. A former missionary reported that women were sent in to "pave the way" for the ministers. She rode horseback all over eastern Kentucky without fear of any harm, whereas the preachers would be run out. She started schools and clinics, but she knew that she was really there to pave the way for the preacher to save souls.

In a report in 1915 of the Conference of Southern Mountain Workers (an inquiry into their needs, and the qualifications desired in church, educational, and social service workers in the mountain country), one churchman writes:

> I place first [in needs] academic schools rather than Sunday schools for the reason that the former have the stronger appeal and are less liable to sectarian objections and denominational opposition. In this kind of school it is possible to successfully mold the character of the young and to prepare them for more efficient life-work. Through the young, it reaches out into the home and social environment of the parents. Next in importance, I place the Sunday school. It is a more plastic and adaptable agency for reaching the young and adult mountaineer than church services. Its approach is more immediate and acceptable. Well organized and tactfully conducted, the Sunday school's religious and social enterprises can come in closer touch with the homelife and social habits of children and parents. (p. 11)

Jean Ritchie relates the story of the arrival of a strange woman into Hazard in 1895, driving a wagon and traveling ahead of the railroad:

> Folks couldn't rightly make out why she had come all that weary way up into Perry County; she had no people here that anyone could see. . .she was friendly, "nice-spoken," "a little bit nosey," "visited nearly every family," "stayed the night," "would pitch in and help,"

and sometimes she'd come right out and rail at them over
doing something a wrong way or a hard way and show
them a *better way*. Miss Pettit had such a way about her
that she got by with it.

After several years of summer visiting, Miss Pettit returned
with tents and other women and started teaching school. They
held classes on how to cook, sew, mend, darn, and take care of
sick folks. They read the Bible and talked about the evils of
drink. The *Women,* as they were called, developed both Hindman and Pine Mountain Settlement schools.

Jean Ritchie relates a story about her grandfather which
was told by the Women and published in books describing the
development of the settlement school. It is a story which has its
counterpart in other parts of the mountains and takes on the
nature of a legitimizing myth. It relates how a mountain man
came to support the Women and their school and to claim them
as saviours for his people. He walked long distances across the
mountain; and he said: "I growed up ignorant and mean; my
offspring was wuss; my grands is wusser, squandering their
time drinking and shooting; and what my greats will be if something hain't done to stop the meanness of their maneuvers, God
only knows. Women, I am persuaded you air the ones I have
looked for all my lifetime. Come over on Troublesome, Women,
and do for us what you air a-doin' here" (p. 227).

Another missionary, Alice Lloyd, from Boston, came to a
Presbyterian Mission, Hope Cottage, on Troublesome Creek.
Another old mountain man, Abisha Johnson, went to Hope
Cottage and begged Alice Lloyd to teach his children to live "not
liken to the hog but unliken the hog" and gave her 150 acres
for a school on Caney Creek.

Many other women made similar treks. Deaconess Binns
of the Episcopal Church came to Nora, Virginia, on the first
train that ran on the line to teach in the schools and start Sunday
schools. In 1905 an Englishwoman, Miss Toddy Collins, who became known as the Angel of Happy Hollow, walked across Big
Black Mountain from Kentucky to Roda, Virginia, a mining
camp, to begin a church and a school, preach funerals, make
coffins, and mother the sick. The Women were usually wel-
comed by the coal operators who provided houses and buildings

for churches and schools.

An Iowa minister came to Beverly, Kentucky, which he described as "the wildest part of the Cumberlands." Following the gleam "to this neglected place where lawlessness and ignorance reigned," he built schools and churches and became known as the Shepherd of Red Bird Mission (MLW, January 1929, 17).

The missionaries were sincere and dedicated to educating mountain people, nursing the sick, caring for orphaned children, and assisting families in many ways. They also had a profound effect upon family life. Jean Ritchie reports that families moved closer to the settlements to be able to send their children to the schools. The Women made a great impression on the people with their stylish clothes, the pretty furniture, and the nice way they talked. Jean Ritchie and her sisters were impressed: "What if I could grow up to be like that. . . .It was like the whole world was opening up like a blossom" (pp. 230-231).

One story is typical of how a community sought their help: "At the request of the community, who were asked in a public meeting to vote on it, a church famous for its high standards was induced to begin work there. It sent a well-trained, consecrated woman as full-time religious worker. A congregation was organized and a school with several teachers. Every year a fresh crop of young people go out from the community to the mission schools to train themselves for worthwhile service" (MLW, April 1929, 13).

The missionary and settlement schools were successful in educating a whole generation of teachers and middle-class leaders for the mountains. In a brochure about Konnarock Training School in Virginia, Mr. Kenneth Killinger says: "These schools lead and train youth in Christian womanhood and manhood, developing Christian leaders who will ultimately raise the spiritual, social, educational, cultural, and economic standards of the mountain people." The training at some of the schools was so successful that an educated native, an extension worker for the University of Kentucky, could look back at his people and state that through Junior Club work he was finding that what was really wrong was "laziness or we may call it, lack of industry" (MLW, July 1925).

The missionaries worked on two levels, which insured their influence in the development of the education, health, and social service systems. First, they came as direct representatives of the church and started a denominational church school, or they started Christian schools of no particular denomination in order to avoid direct conflict with local preachers.

Second, the missionaries would work in the already existing school system for no pay, as did Deaconess Binns of Nora, Virginia. Deaconess Binns worked for the school board for 35 years for a dollar a year. Thus, her efforts to start a Sunday school and various recreational programs for children met with community approval. It was through this method that an Episcopal church was started and maintained until her death in 1968. All the schools and missions offered various other services besides the rudiments of education. People in the communities quickly learned that they could go to these missions to receive health care and free used clothing and to leave orphaned children, etc. These and other services had been taken care of in the past by the family and community. Now, missionaries with much better facilities were able to "show-up" the meager efforts of the past. In their eagerness to be accepted by the community, many missionaries were overgiving, which placed people in dependency relationships, since missionary help was the only alternative to the hard life of the past.

There was another side to the training. The mountaineer became overwhelmed and ashamed of his culture. Fox was to relate that as religious and educational agencies work on the mountaineer "he is cowed by the superior numbers, superior intelligence of the incomer and he seems to lose his sturdy self-respect" (p. 50).

Raines reports that more than 200 schools, orphanages, academies, and colleges brought in by church boards had been established by 1924 (pp. 176-77). He points out that most were boarding schools which provided greater opportunity to mold the habits and thoughts. The schools included household and garden chores, religious training, and constant supervision. He describes the curriculum in what he calls the "brought-on, non-indigenous schools."

Most of the cultural people coming into the moun-

> tains to teach unconsciously use the same methods and
> the same materials to which they were themselves accus-
> tomed. . .which are poorly adapted to the super-rural
> conditions in the mountain area. They either urge the
> mountain pupil away from the mountains or overwhelm
> him with hopeless discouragement. In either case, they
> unfit him to remain at home. (p. 181)

It was these schools which developed a dual society where children had one relationship and identity at home and one at school.   The schools, books, and teachers represented another world, another history, and another literature.   Some of the teachers attempted to preserve certain aspects of mountain cul-ture such as crafts and music.   Jean Ritchie reports that "if it hadn't been for the settlement schools, many of the old moun-tain songs would have died out when the ways of the world came in on us.   But the Women loved our music and plays so that they became a regular part of the life around the two schools" (Pine Mountain and Hindman, 231).

Other teachers, however, found no singing and a complete lack of suitable good songs in the mountains (MLW, July 1925, 3).   One teacher found children singing "I've Been Working on the Railroad," an "obviously unchildish song," and only two out of 23 students knew "Annie Laurie."   This teacher brought in a progressive music series and promoted such operettas as "The Windmill of Holland" and "The Quest of the Pink Parasol." Such denials of mountain culture made native children ashamed of their heritage.

Churches and missionaries gave some support to certain harmless aspects of native culture. This fact served to soften the impact and ameliorate some of the abuses of the system, the denigration of mountain culture, and the development of feel-ings of inferiority by mountain people.   The churches and schools, however, taught the values of organization, planning, hard work, and thrift.   They made the industrial process legiti-mate by blaming the ills of the system on the mountaineer him-self.   He must learn to be more "cagey" (not so gullible and taken in by the land sharks); he must learn to be more thrifty and hard-working, more respectful and cooperative with the mine operators.   Although some of the missionaries saw clearly the ex-ploitation, they still had great faith in progress and the benefits of industrialization.

The superintendent of mountain work of the Presbyterian Church wrote in MLW, January 1929, of the tremendous multiplication of industries, some of them of gigantic scale and from alien sections and nations. He saw a need for the states to provide safeguards against the exploitation of their population, for "only as church and state move hand in hand will industrialization become an unqualified blessing."

Some were more critical. Perry Davidson, writing in 1926 in MLW, says:

> Coal, the chief material wealth of the section, is now owned by outside capital. It is doubtful if any of the profits accruing from the exploitation of this natural wealth will be reinvested in the welfare of the mountain people. No great agricultural prosperity is to be hoped for. The timber is gone. This narrows prospects, but let's not despair.

> And this is his solution. Maybe there is oil below the coal, and if it is struck the native will not let the "furriner" outwit him next time. (January 1926, 10)

In an industrial round table of the Conference of Southern Mountain Workers in 1926, the group agreed that the industrializing of the mountain resources had been deadening to the constructive instincts and had inhibited the forming of habits of thrift and a feeling for conservation. This group hoped to obtain the cooperation of the heads of companies in working out remedial programs. The consensus was that the employers have hearts and that they vaguely realize the evils of their industrial system but do not know what to do about it. The feeling was that if they were approached in the right way they would welcome counteractive influence.

Another Episcopal missionary, who earlier worked among the Indians of Canada before coming to his mountain post, worried about the fact that mining was not constructive and that recklessness took the place of thrift; the miner did not learn to save. "While the accumulation of money is neither the most desirable thing or the only desirable thing, it is a good indication

of a man's habits, and a man who tries to save a little can be depended upon to fight temptation against slackness of life and
conduct" (MLW, January 1926, 22).

Some few missionaries thought the church should be more
vigorous in warning the mountain people of the danger of large
corporations and also in preserving parts of the native culture.
One missionary who came as early as 1876 wrote with appreciation about the mountain people:

> They need the inspiration of the outside world
> without its greed and corruption. . . .they are closer to an
> original type of American manhood than any other sec-
> tion of our country. They should not be changed in their
> fundamental characteristics. . .they need to be warned of
> the danger of disposing of their large mountain holdings
> for a song. Corporations and trusts are a constant menace
> . . . .they threaten the mountaineers by transforming them
> into a servile class. (An Inquiry, 20)

The missionaries saw the family and church as problems to
be resolved (Tadlock, 3). The superintendent of mountain work
of the Presbyterian church found the native church non-progres-
sive and without any activities other than monthly preaching by
uneducated ministers with an emphasis on doctrine unrelated to
life. "But industrialism has brought its nucleus of Christian
people, pastors, evangelists, church and independent schools
which are centers of religious progress. . .with modern church
programs, efficient pastoral leadership (MLW, January 1929,
20-23).

Even those ministers who admired the primitive, simple,
real worship found the lack of organization of the churches a
drawback; services were not regular enough and preachers were
ineffective and inefficient. Here again, the outsider judged the
family and churches as needing to be better organized—or disrupted—if the native was to be fully integrated and assimilated
into modern society.

The missionaries formed themselves into an organization
called the Conference of Southern Mountain Workers which began publication of a magazine *Mountain Life and Work.* In the
first issue (April 1925, Vol. 1-1) a statement of philosophy, A

Program for the Mountains, was included. It summarizes well their attitudes and programs:

> First the program for the development of mountain resources by mountain people: . . . .Northern and Eastern artisans and capitalists are our friends and we invite them among us but we must not permit them to crowd us out and take away our heritage and birthright. There is no insinuation that this heritage and birthright are being dishonestly taken from us. They are simply slipping from our hands because of our inability to hold them. We can hold them only through education, skill and efficiency. These three acquirements must become our possession if we would develop the mountain resources.

> The program for "The perpetuation of Mountain Home Life Along the Lines of Our Own Best Traditions" emphasized the development of God-fearing homes where education is encouraged and love reigns; homes wisely planned. . . .the creation of beauty. . . .building upright character. . . .conveniences to relieve the drudgery of wife and mother. . .the precepts and examples of law abiding citizens are held in reverence and everything derogatory to peace and order and neighborly good will is discouraged.

> In the program for "A Religion that Functions Actively in the Life of the People" churches should work at a common task and jealousies and competitions should be forgotten. The churches should promote unselfish devotion to the welfare of neighbors and the cause of Christ. There was a need for a religion felt in politics and business and to motivate the civic life of people. . . .patriotic enforcement of law by ballot box and community backing of public officials. . . .election of God-fearing, country-loving officers who will do their duty. Training the youth that bravery and heroism are not expressed by intimidation, revenge and killing. (pp. 20-21)

Throughout the program, the emphasis is on the need for education, skills, efficiency, planning, law and order, material conveniences, fear of God and a sense of duty, all very helpful values for the new society.

THE CHURCH AND FAMILY RESISTS

Both the family and church became defensive and reverted inward in order to protect members from the sudden influence which came with the development of industrialization. Some of the characteristics and "problems" ascribed to children and families today by psychiatrists, educators, and social workers can possibly be traced to this process whereby the family tries to preserve traditional mountain culture and resist or adapt to the colonization process.

In outline one can point to the following reactions and ways through which the family system has resisted colonization:

1.   The family and kinship group became a refuge for its members.

2.   The family became more resistant to certain changes and developed sabotage techniques.

3.   Used as a refuge, the family resulted in overprotection of children.

4.   The family and family groups in neighborhoods became defenseive, exclusive, and closed.

5.   The family and family groups became the center for "underground" mountain culture.

6.   The family and family groups encouraged biculturalism.

Each of these reactions will be discussed briefly. Some of these conclusions can be documented from other reports and studies of family and children in the mountains, but many of these remarks are highly impressionistic observations based on our experience growing up, being educated, teaching, living, and working in the area.

1.   The family becomes a refuge. In studying the families in the Southern Appalachians and Appalachians in the cities, researchers have continued to find the society familistic, kinship ties strong and viable, loyalties to kin taking precedence over

"civic" responsibilities, kin groups acting to ease migration problem and to provide a home base for the returning migrant (Brown 1971; Ford 1965; Pearsall 1959; Coles 1971).

In the coalfields, where there are few alternatives for employment, the family offers the only alternative means of support. If one "can't take it" any longer, he will be accepted back home and cared for until he has the strength to go back into the mines, locate a new job, or migrate to (or reenter) the city. Rather than being destroyed by industrialization, the family and family ties remain or perhaps in some cases become stronger as the family requires more commitment on the part of members. The Appalachian is expected to be loyal and help members of his family whether he likes them or not.

This family loyalty can also be used against the family. Industries soon learned to use family loyalties to minimize criticism of industrial operations. One will not endanger a relative's job or criticize a situation in which a kinsman is involved. Mine operators, for instance, have learned to hire through families to find loyal workers; they also hire from a number of families to cut down on criticism of strip mining within a community.

2.   The family becomes resistant to change. Family members restrain their members from taking social action. There is little revolt or conflict since one is afraid to disrupt the only remaining refuge. A number of persons have commented on the permissive mountain mother, and some have suggested that she is afraid to discipline her children for fear of a disruptive conflict. Many school social workers and nurses have commented on mothers who say they can't make a six-year-old go to school, eat proper food, or go to the dentist. This has a contradictory aspect in that the child is taught to rebel against certain institutions such as health and school. The child seems to be trained by the mother to be "willful," and the mother seems to take pride in a child who cannot be controlled. This serves to cut down conflict within the family and also keeps the child at home as he rejects the institutions.

3.   The mother frequently becomes overprotective. She holds the child close and makes him feel guilty about leaving home or developing new ideas. Memmi remarks that this is a problem in other colonial situations. "The soft warmth of clan

reunions is satisfying and one is afraid to leave it." Looff (1971) in his book *Appalachia's Children* agrees with Memmi (p. 99) that the "young remain glued to family which offers warmth and tenderness and clutches and emasculates him."

4. The family and neighborhoods become more exclusive and closed. Early visitors—including industrialists, missionaries and tourists—found great hospitality, open goodwill, as well as the beginnings of cautious suspicion. The mountain people learned to distrust. Semple (p. 610) reports that people were beginning to resent the coming of "furriners" among them on the grounds that outsiders came to spy upon them and criticize and "tell-tale" as they put it. A cautiousness toward outsiders has been encouraged in the family. "Listen and don't talk" is widely used as a protection. One can also put down an outsider's idea with, "You are not one of us. You don't understand." This is a form of defensive racism, and the burden of understanding is placed not upon the Appalachian but upon the good shepherd in wolf's clothing who desires to "help" mountain people. This can lead to the family's becoming oversensitive to criticism, more negative, more unchanging and traditional in approach to problems.

5. The family becomes the bulwark against the loss of native culture. Memmi points out that what is saved may be meagre or it may go underground since the colonial falsifies history, extinguishes memories, and devalues native culture. Since he stresses differences, he is always compared with something "better"; therefore, the native becomes ashamed of his heritage and draws less and less from his past, which results in a "present orientation" according to Pearsall, Weller and Ford. The Appalachian takes on the myth perpetuated by the industrialist that there was nothing here until coal came in to develop it.

The main aspects of the culture which were fought for and were the hardest to change were mainly patterns of relationships which can be described as basically *non-competitiveness*. Family members and neighbors depend on each other, but it is a dependence which also encourages independence or "let the other fellow alone." People help each other in time of need; they share the load; but this help is not imposed nor organized and leaves room for independence and individuality.

The family also develops ways of holding down conflicts, "talking things over," and face-saving games. Disputes must be settled amicably; therefore, certain things are never mentioned and certain behaviors are ignored.

Equality is maintained through treating all children the same and providing them with equal inheritances wherever possible (Brown 1952). The only consistent exception is "baby," and if land is passed on to only one child, it will more often be the youngest, who in exchange stays home to care for parents.

To keep a sense of equality and non-competitiveness, a "local success" or ambitious hillbilly almost has to leave his family and neighborhood and live with the colonizers. In his small neighborhood he will be sabotaged and people won't help him. He will be put down as not neighborly and "out for himself." Perhaps this explains why the local success seems to become more exploitative than the outsider. He goes against his rearing, he is punished, and he retaliates and must find his support from the outsiders.

Equality is still important. Mountain people resist experts, titles, and people who put on airs or get above their raising.

6. The family encourages biculturalism. The schools create a duality—a world different from the family environment. Branscome speaks of the "annihilation of the hillbilly" by the institutions. Many mountain youth remember the shaming process when they had to deny their "mother tongue," reject their music and their religion. Memmi (p. 108) says the colonized turns away from his music, the plastic arts, and, in effect, his entire traditional culture—the consequence of which is ambiguity. Smathers talks of two routes the educated mountaineer can take: cultural schizophrenia or cultural transvestitism (biculturalism). Mountain children are taught early to act properly in public and be hillbilly at home. Mountain people learn to deal with medical, welfare, educational, governmental institutions and speak their language and use their techniques. They learn to use institutions, outsiders, etc. selectively. But the strain is great. The mountain person is taught how to use the hillbilly stereotype for his own protection and to confound, aggravate, harass, and thwart the colonizer. (They leave the program planner wondering why that didn't work.) One example is the stereotype of

laziness, dependency, and irresponsibility which the Appalachian has learned to manipulate effectively in order to sabotage the colonizer's attempts to organize the mountaineer into pseudo-participatory democracy rituals which further splinter Appalachian solidarity.

The mountain church also went through similar reactions. Briefly, the church also became defensive: the native minister reacted against his characterization as ignorant and uneducated by making lack of training and education positive values. Local preachers attacked the incoming trained clergy for their "high larning" and accused them of being lacking in "spirit."

The church resisted the social consciousness which was being promoted by outside religious institutions; therefore, the church became more fundamental and rigid in doctrine. It saw the establishment churches as supporting a system, political and economic, which was destroying a way of life. Its best defense was to become less worldly.

Few outsiders felt comfortable in the primitive Baptist services; therefore, keeping their services expressive became a good protection. The church maintained equalitarian rituals and strict rules of behavior which set them apart. Mountain people still do not belong to Presbyterian, Episcopal, or town Methodist churches unless they have become middle class professionsals or successful businessmen.

Other churches (which became more popular with younger Appalachians) developed in the area, including Free Will Baptist and Pentecostal churches. In these churches, foot-washing is still maintained as part of the ritual; the services are informal; there is still shouting and expression of religious fervor; and preachers still "preach." They now have Sunday schools, sing more popular gospel songs, and even train and pay their preachers; but the city churches are still shunned as coal operators' churches, too fancy and elegant for plain country folk.

But while helping to preserve certain aspects of indigenous culture, the native church refused to become involved in politics or to be critical of the economic exploitation of the area; this fact has worked against change in the *status quo*. Memmi (pp. 99, 101) finds that in a colonized situation both religion and the family serve as refugees and save the colonized from the despair of total defeat. He feels that the native society gets in a bind; in order to preserve or save the collective consciousness, it must shut itself off, live isolated. In so doing, it hardens, petrifies, and "degrades its own life in order to save it."

This appears to be only partly true in Appalachia. The church and family still reflect and teach basic mountain values of equality, non-competitiveness, and family-neighborhood solidarity. These positive and viable aspects of the expressive church and the solidary family may be powerful allies in and the basis for a revitalization movement in Appalachia.

Mike Smathers suggests that "resistance strategies" should be considered as positive strategies for the future saving of Appalachia. Those committed to the liberation of Appalachian people might well study the ways in which the mountain family and church have continued to resist the institutions in order to give help to controlling the new "developers": federal government, tourism, and T.V. The new missionaries, the new professional planners, educators, and community organizers might well look at their roles in the new development to see how they also may be aiding and legitimizing the further destruction of Appalachia.

REFERENCES CITED

Blauner, Robert
1969 "Internal Colonialism and Ghetto Revolt," *Social Problems* (spring) Vol. 16, No. 4, 393-408.

Branscome, James
1971 *Annihilating the Hillbilly*, Huntington: Appalachian Movement Press.

Brown, James
1952 "The Farm Family in a Kentucky Mountain Neighborhood," Kentucky Agricultural Experiment Station Bulletin 587, Lexington, Kentucky (August).

Brown, James S.
1971 *Mountain Families in Transition*, Penn State.

Burlage, Rob
1971 "Developers and Colonizers" in David Walls and John Stephenson, *Appalachia in the Sixties*, Lexington: University of Kentucky.

Campbell, Mrs. John C.
1925 "Flame of a New Future for the Highlands," *Mountain Life and Work* (April, pp. 9-13).

Caudill, Harry
1962 *Night Comes to the Cumberland*, Boston: Little and Brown.

Coles, Robert
1971 *Migrants, Sharecroppers, Mountaineers, Children of Crisis*, Vol. 2, Boston: Little and Brown.

Condon, Mabel Green
1962 *A History of Harlan County*, Nashville: Parthenon.

Conference of Southern Mountain Workers
　　1915　The Southern Highlands:　An Inquiry into their needs and
　　　　　qualifications, desired in church, educational and social service
　　　　　workers in the mountain country.

Diehl, Richard
　　1970　"How International Energy Elite Rules," *People's Appalachia*
　　　　　(April, May).

Dix, Keith
　　1970　"Third World Pillage," *People's Appalachia* (April, May).

Egerton, John
　　1966　"Alice Lloyd:　The College That Can't Be," *Louisville Courier
　　　　　Journal*, October 23, 1966, pp. 7-12, 26, 27.

Ford, Thomas R.
　　1965　Value Orientations of a Culture of Poverty:　The Southern
　　　　　Appalachian Case.　Working with low income families, Ameri-
　　　　　can home economics association, Washington, D.C., pp. 57-69.

Fox, John, Jr.
　　1901　*Blue-grass and Rhododendron*, New York:　Scribners.

Henson, Edward L., Jr.
　　1972　*Gladeville and the Mountain Stereotype 1856-1860*,　Virginia
　　　　　Cavalcade (spring, 21:4, 30-35).

Lesser, Roger
　　1970　"Culture:　Toward Tomorrow's People," *People's Appalachia*,
　　　　　No. 1, March.

Lewis, Helen M. and Edward E. Knipe
　　1970　*The Colonialism Model:　The Appalachian Case*, paper read at
　　　　　American Anthropological Association Annual Meeting, San
　　　　　Diego, California, November 22, 1970.

Looff, David H.
　　1971　*Appalachia's Children*, Lexington:　University of Kentucky.

Mahy, Gordon G., Jr.
　　1946　*Murdoch of Buckhorn*, Nashville, Tenn.:　Parthenon Press.

Memmi, Albert
    1965   *The Colonizer and the Colonized*, Boston: Beacon.

Mountain Life and Work
    1925-30   Files of back issues, Conference of Southern Mountain Workers.

Page, Thomas Nelson
    1910   *The Mountaineer of the South, American Monthly*, June 1910.

Pearsall, Marion
    1959   *Little Smokey Ridge*, University of Alabama.

Raines, James Watt
    1924   *The Land of Saddle-bags*, New York: Council of Women for Home Missions and Missionary Education Movement of the United States and Canada.

Ritchie, Jean
    1955   *Singing Family of the Cumberlands*, New York: Oak Publications.

Semple, Ellen Churchill
    1901   *The Anglo-Saxons of the Kentucky Mountains: A Study in Anthropology*, Harper, VI, 588-622.

Simon, Rich
    1972   "An Historical Sketch of Migration in Appalachia," *People's Appalachia*, Vol. 2, No. 3, July.

Smathers, Mike
    1972   Talk at rural sociology meeting on Appalachian Research, Baton Rouge, Louisiana, August 25.

Tadlock, E. V.
    1929   *Coal Camps and Character*, January, 1929.

Vincent, George E.
    1898   "A Retarded Frontier," *American Journal of Sociology*, IV, 1-20.

Weller, Jack
    1965   *Yesterday's People*, Lexington: University of Kentucky.

PROPERTY, COAL, AND THEFT

by
John Gaventa

> If I had to answer the question, *"What is slavery?"* and if
> I were to answer in one word, *"murder,"* I would im-
> mediately be understood. I would not need to use a
> lengthy argument to demonstrate that the power to de-
> prive a man of his thoughts, his will and personality is
> a power of life and death, and that to enslave man is to
> murder him.
>
> Why, then, to the question, *"What is property?"* may I
> not likewise reply *"theft,"* without knowing that I am
> certain to be misunderstood, even though the second
> proposition is simply a transformation of the first?
>
> . . . .Pierre-Joseph Proudhon, 1840[1]

In Appalachia, property is theft.

We can understand the meaning of this relationship of
poverty amidst wealth by looking closely at the example of the
Clear Fork Valley, stretching between Pine Mountain and Cum-

SOURCE: *A revised version of the article, "In Appalachia: Property Is
           Theft," printed in* Southern Exposure, *Vol. I, No. 2 (summer-
           fall, 1973).*

AUTHOR: John Gaventa *is a staff member of the Highlander Research
           and Education Center, New Market, Tennessee.*

berland Mountain and lying on the border of Kentucky and
Tennessee. Here one finds the results of corporate exploitation
at its worst. Once a booming mining area, automation and strip
mining have left 30 percent of the population unemployed.
Mountains are gouged by the relentless blade of the bulldozer
and blasts of dynamite. Streams are filled with silt and flooding; timber and wildlife are destroyed.

Not just land, but a way of life is eroding. Thousands have
had to leave to find homes and jobs in the cities of the North and
to make way for the strippers. For those who remain, houses are
poor, and incomes for over 70 percent of the population are less
than $4,000 annually.

Within that same valley in Bell County, Kentucky, and
Claiborne County, Tennessee, approximately 85 percent of the
land—50,000 acres—is owned by a single company, the American
Association, Ltd., of London, England. From its land, over 2.2
million tons of coal a year are carted away, mostly to Georgia
Power and Duke Power. And from the royalties on that coal,
thousands of dollars a year are exported to the company's London headquarters. Yet, there in the midst of England's "Wall
Street" the wealth may scarcely be noticed. The chairman of the
company's board of directors, Sir Denys Flowerdew Lowson, a
former Lord Mayor of London, controls an estimated 88 such
companies around the globe; and he personally is listed as chairman of 40. The American Association is one of the smallest of
his concerns. To the people of Clear Fork Valley, however, the
company represents tax evasion, destruction of land and jobs,
and the denial of the future; to Sir Lowson, however, the company's listed value represents a piddling one half of one per cent
of his estimated personal wealth.

It is no misnomer that one of the American Association's
parent companies should be named London Foreign and Colonial
Securities. But its English nature should not detract from its
similarities with the other absentee property owners of Appalachia. By looking at the historical development of this micro-
colony in Clear Fork Valley and the meaning of its colonial control in the modern day energy demanding world, we can learn
something of a situation common to much of central Appalachia.
And by understanding the micro-colonial relationship, we can
learn something not only about Clear Fork but also about the

relationship of other regions to the energy conglomerates.

The Making of a Micro-Colony

It is an irony of history that many of the first settlers to come to the mountainous areas in and around Cumberland Gap were the rebels. In the Appalachians they found a place to escape the rapid industrialization of England and of Europe and to establish a new way of life, free from the exploitative social relations which they had known before. As Jack Weller describes in *Yesterday's People,* some of the settlers came from the Levellers movement in Britain, where they had challenged the power of their English landlords, and they came "in rebellion against a form of government that imposed its rule from the top."[8]

Yet their freedom in the frontier mountains was changed in the late 1800's when coal and iron ore were discovered and demanded to feed the new wave of westward industrialization. In the Cumberland Gap area it was a young Scottish-Canadian capitalist, Alexander Arthur, who foresaw the Gap as an iron, coal, and steel center to feed the rapidly growing South. Backed by capital from Britain's Baring Brothers, a company was formed, the American Association, Ltd., which in turn transformed the Yellow Creek Valley of Kentucky into the booming coal town of Middlesborough, named after its British counterpart.

Rarely has there been such a colonial boom. Between 1888-1892 over 20 million dollars of British capital poured into the area. Railroads, furnaces, industry, hotels, streets, and lavish halls were built. Thousands of people—many from England, others from the east, some from the south—poured into the area. The town was quickly dubbed by its promoters and others as "The Magic City of the South," and in 1892 its magic was valued on the British stock exchange at over 40 million dollars. Founding Father Alexander Arthur, who came to be known as the "Duke of the Cumberlands," proclaimed to a group of investors on November 11, 1890, "This is but a transfer of British business to American soil."[9]

And, indeed, soil they had acquired—an estimated 80,000 acres in the Yellow Creek, Clear Fork, and other valleys, all rich with coal and timber. The most famous historical account of the development of the area, *Wilderness Road* by Robert Kincary, simply states that the company acquired the land within a few months. In fact, modern day courthouse deeds show perfected titles. But there is more to the story. Residents describe, still with anger, how the agents tricked, threatened, or forced the uneducated mountaineers to give up their land. Some mountaineers, not knowing or even caring about the value to the industrial world of the wealth beneath them, "voluntarily" sold the land for 50 cents or one dollar an acre. An entire mountain, from which Consolidation Coal now supplies the American Association almost $200,000 yearly and Georgia Power over 1,000,000 tons of coal yearly, was reportedly traded to an agent of the company for a hog rifle.

Other mountaineers were victims of legal tricks. One method, oral history reveals, was to have someone jailed and then offer to post bond in return for his land. Where there was resistance, force was used. Residents tell stories of how the company men would burn their fathers out if they wouldn't sell. And though many of the courthouse records of this era have been burned or have disappeared, it is not uncommon for a local Appalachian to look out from the front porch of his company-owned house and remark, "See that mountain? They stole it from my daddy."

"Property is theft," but to endure, theft has to be legitimized. In Middlesboro, as in the modern era, the tools of legitimacy were the concentration of power in the hands of a few and an ideology of boom and progress to attract the support of the many.

Certainly, the American Association had the power in the boom town. It retained controlling interest in everything—banks, industry, railroads, even the Four Seasons Hotel in which were hosted the recreational shenanigans of the rich. One is reminded quickly of modern plans for development of Appalachian playgrounds. Anyone who had or who wanted any part of the economic benefit of the new society was dependent on the will of those few who controlled it.

With the dependency on the economic controllers, though, also came a supporting ideology of progress, civilization, and response to social need. Arthur proclaims it this way:

> I would say that America needs this place and our Anglo-
> American money, experience and push. . . .We have also
> the sinews of body and of money and stand ready, clean-
> cut, and vigorous, for a generation of progress and success
> in manufacture, arts, and sciences. Come and join hands
> with us in the great enterprise which is worthy of us all,
> native or foreign born though we may be.[10]

The *New York Times* and other publications applauded the development. For *Harper's* magazine it represented "a summing up
of the past and a prophecy of the future. . . .the last of the
mountaineers passing away before the breath of civilization."[11]

Like other traditional colonialists, the virtues of this "civilization" were unquestionably better than the past, somehow
less-than-human, ways of the "natives." The imagery from
the same *Harper's* article demonstrates this equation by the
colonizers of progress with economic boom, of human dignity
with the material gain:

> As I stood one day in this valley, which has already begun
> to put on the air of civilization with its hotel and railway
> station and mills and pretty homesteads, I saw a sight
> which seemed to complete the epitome of the past and
> present tendencies there at work. . . .
>
> . . . .creeping slowly past the station—so slowly that one
> knows not what to compare it to unless it be the minute
> hand on the dial of the clock—creeping slowly along the
> Wilderness Road toward the ascent of the Cumberland
> Gap came a mountain wagon, faded and old, with its
> dirty, ragged canvas hanging motionless, and drawn by a
> yoke of mountain oxen which seemed to be moving in
> their sleep. . . .
>
> On the seat in front. . . .sat a faded, pinched and meager
> mountain boy. . . .His stained white face was kindled into
> an expression of passionate hunger and mental excite-
> ment. For in one dirty claw-like hand he grasped a small
> paper bag, into the mouth of which he thrust the other
> hand, as a miser might thrust his into a bag of gold. He

had just bought with a few cents he had perhaps saved no
one knows how long some sweetmeat of civilization which
he was about for the first time to taste. . . .

So it is easy to see how for the American Association the
combination of monopoly and ideology fused to portray it not
as a colonizer or controller but as a conscientious and necessary
contributor to the social good. A *Scribner's Magazine* article in
1890 reflects this social view. The American Association "leases
its mining and other properties but does not and will not sell
them. This fact is evidence of the interests which it has and will
always have in the prosperity of Middlesboro." The company
controls the coal commerce from "the raw state of the earth's
bed until the final and finished result is in the hands of the consumer. . . .To this parental character of the American Association" the article concludes, "and to the comprehensive protection with which it pursues the course of industry is largely due
the prosperity of Middlesboro."[12]

For those to whom the economic dependency brought re-
wards, the ideology of progress brought responses of loyalty
appropriate to the "parental character." In 1891 local newspapers report that a three-hour mass meeting was held to express
appreciation to the officers of the American Association. Held at
the Opera Hall, it was the "largest and most enthusiastic meeting" ever witnessed and one at which quite a number of "the fair
sex graced the scene."[13]

For those mountaineers who did not accept the new ideology, such progress meant the intrusion into and colonization of
their culture. But their protests and situations were ignored,
justified as a "social cost," or pitied by those who saw them as
"left out of the mainstream." The literature of the city's development says little of its effect on the mountain people. But
one 1905 account describes the colonization of the free life of
the mountaineer in rationalities frighteningly similar to what one
might hear today:

The Association have between 200 and 300 tenants of
mountain people and are on the best of terms with them.
The Association has not always treated them fairly and
justly, but has gone out of its way to assist and to encourage; they have responded by being true friends,

assisting the Association in protecting its property. It is
much regretted that these people have not yet got the
advantage of schools and churches to which they are
entitled.[14]

The Yellow Creek and Clear Fork valleys had been colonized.
Through the power of property the propertyless had been made
the powerless. Not only is property "theft" but it is also the
ability to legitimize itself: to make colonization acceptable.

But the glory of the Magic City of the South didn't last
long. Money from London dried up. The American financial
panic of 1893 hit the hills of central Appalachia. A 1911 issue
of the Middlesboro newspaper describes in retrospect: "It may
be doubted if ever in the history of boom towns there had been
so great a collapse." The properties in the town of Middlesboro
were auctioned off and the 80,000 acres of land were mortgaged
to the New York bank and a Mr. J. H. Bartlett was appointed
auctioneer. At that point, the American Association changed
its name from Limited to Incorporated yet retained essentially
the same shareholders. In the auction, an agent for the "new"
company bought back for $25,000 what had been mortgaged
for $1,500,000 only a few months before. Shortly thereafter,
J. H. Bartlett became general manager of the American Association, Inc.

The strange transaction did not go unnoticed. Creditors of
the American Association, Ltd. sued, claiming "fraud," rigging
of federal courts, and perjury. The outcome of the suits is
undetermined; the records went up in flames in one courthouse
and seemed to have disappeared from the dockets in another
county courthouse.

Though the company had lost its property, it hadn't lost the
power to steal it again. Middlesboro as a company town was
gone, but the company had regained 80,000 acres of surrounding coal-rich mountain land, and on that property it could
continue to control its colony.

A Modern Day Colony

It was last summer and Lewis Lowe looked out at his small

one-half acre of land located along the Clear Fork Creek, now covered with strip mine silt deposited on it from the latest flood. For the last few years, he hadn't been able to farm much on his land. "Strip mine mud. . . .nothing will grow on it," he said angrily. And today he was thinking of leaving, of moving out of the mountains where he had lived the close to seven decades of his life to an unknown town somewhere. "You'd think we were animals or something, the way they've treated us . . . .the strippers and the Association."

His life represented much of what had happened in the eighty or so years since the Middlesboro bust. The coal mines and company towns had come to the Clear Fork Valley. For 46 of these years, along with hundreds of others like him, Lewis had worked "from sun up to sun down, worked in almost every mine around, I did." Then, though, it was other companies, those that leased from the Association, that were the "villains." They owned the stores, ran the mines, built the houses, extracted most of the profits, and supplied the Association handsome royalties. These companies needed the labor of the men like Lewis; and though exploitative in the many slave-like ways of the coal camp era, they provided jobs and camouflaged the controlling palm of the behind-the-scenes, landowning American Association. But in the 1950's came the coal slump. For a variety of reasons, the deep mines closed down as they did in much of central Appalachia.

In its relentless, ugly way came reminders of who it was that still possessed the property upon which the companies had operated. In 1952 there were 1,230 coal-mining jobs in the county; by 1958 there were only 282. The American Association no longer had the need for men on its land, and, therefore, it no longer provided the employment that had subdued the recognition of the colonizer. Most of the men had to leave the valley to try to find work in the cities of the North; the American Association made no attempt to provide or even to allow alternatives.

Lewis had wanted to stay and did until the company told him one day in the dead of winter that he, his wife, and six kids would have to leave in three days. The strip miners were coming in, and they used bulldozers. People got in the way. Twice Lewis was evicted, forced to leave the land that he had tilled with his hands and labor. The home, the garden, the spring that through his work had come to be his now were to be shoved aside by the bulldozer. He didn't get any compensation; after all, they said, it was the company's land. Finally, in 1960 he had found and saved the money for the small place where he now was and had tried again to create a peaceful home that he could call his own. But now, the stripping had caught up with him again, and he was thinking of giving up, of leaving for good.

Here in the life of a single miner comes a human example of what is meant by "property is theft," for Lewis Lowe was propertyless, and those who had the property had controlled, manipulated, and finally defeated his will, expression, and pride as a human being. Here also in Clear Fork Valley in a larger sense is an example of the insidious power of absentee corporate ownership that is the murder of Appalachia.

We have already witnessed the fundamental form of theft. In the valley today over 2 million tons of coal a year leave to provide over 10 per cent of Georgia Power's fuel, all from the land of this single London based company. Much of the coal is deep mined from a single Consolidation Coal mine, owned in turn by Continental Oil. The rest comes from strip mining by only a few profitable firms, mines which were originally owned by a set of mountain elites but which have now been acquired by the energy conglomerates. Royalties on all the mining, from 20 cents to $1 a ton, are carted away to offices off Bank Street in the financial district of London.

We have recognized this form of inequity, and most of America today has accepted the ideology that legitimizes it. But there are other forms of theft in the colonial relationship which grow from that inequity of property that inevitably means the inequity of power. Consider several examples.

Property Tax Evasion. Traditionally (and theoretically) the normal social mechanism for sharing or redistributing wealth is taxation. For local governments, property taxation is the major source of revenue, and, supposedly, property is taxed at an equal rate so that those with large amounts of valuable property pay more than the owners of small amounts of less valuable property.

But it hasn't worked that way in the Clear Fork Valley.

There the American Association owns 17 percent of the land surface of Claiborne County and perhaps 90 percent of the county's coal reserves. Yet in 1970 its 44,000 acres provided only 3 percent of the local revenue. Even after citizens' challenges demanded that the law be enforced, the situation remained similar. Vast areas of untouched coal reserves were being appraised at $25 an acre, less than the least expensive farmland in the county.

And Claiborne County is no exception. In 1971, the nine land companies that controlled 35 percent of the land surface and approximately 85 percent of the coal reserves in Tennessee's five major coal-producing counties accounted for less than 4 percent of the local revenues. In West Virginia, Kentucky, and Virginia—despite laws to the contrary in every state—property taxation has failed to reap the benefits of the immense property wealth for local government.[15]

These are the counties that need local revenues the most yet get the least. Consequently, the amount of money they have available for education, health, welfare, housing, and for the means and services of human development is far less than the national average. The local small non-mineral holders pay an unfair share of taxes; they pay for loss of services; and they pay in innumerable other ways for the destruction caused to their roads, streams, and lives as the wealth is carted away.

Property means not just poverty for the propertyless; it means the power of the colonizer to avoid traditional forms of sharing that property. Theft of revenue means more than a loss of money; it means in Appalachia the denial of the basic services and means for building independent local communities.

Strip Mine Theft. The American Association hosts more strip mine operations than does any other landowner in Tennessee. Almost 5,000 acres of its land have been laid waste by the devastation of bulldozers and dynamite. In central Appalachia itself an estimated 600,000 acres of strip-mined land have been left unreclaimed.[16] And as in the Clear Fork Valley, it is on the property of the absentee owners, who escape the consequences, where most of the stripping is done.

To many outside of the mountains, stripping is viewed as an

environmental issue, and indeed it is. The strip miner literally blasts away the sides or top of a mountain; debris is bulldozed over the side, and the exposed coal is shoveled out. While the process is fast and highly profitable, it leaves the mountain a gaping sore; ecological cycles are upset; timber may take several hundred years to recover; streams are filled with silt and acid. Reclamation, though ostensibly possible, is expensive and rarely carried out in the mountains. It is, as some have put it, "like putting lipstick on a corpse."

To many Appalachians, though, stripping is more than an environmental issue. It is an economic one. Folks look back to the days of the deep mines when there was work, and to that deep mining many would like to return. "We've been deprived of our livelihood," says J. W. Bradley, a former deep miner and now a leading figure in the anti-strip-mine effort. "The strippers came in under falsehoods and stole our jobs from us," he says. And, in fact, the Report of the President's Council on Environmental Quality in March, 1973, observes that if stripping in the mountains were stopped today, there would be jobs for three times as many men in Appalachia in deep-mining and probably at higher wages.

But for mountain folks the destruction of stripping is the destruction of something even more basic. For people who have always lived close to the land, who have built their lives and their communities around the freedom and confines of the mountains and the streams, stripping is the symbol of destruction of a way of life, a culture. "Every time we see a bulldozer go into the mountain, it's like someone has stabbed a knife in our heart," explained one mountain woman to a group of city folks. Stripping, economically presided over by the absentee property owner, is theft of both a *means* and a *way* of life.

Theft of Alternatives. As if the theft of wealth, of taxes and services, of a means and way of life were not enough, another most insidious theft is the denial of alternatives to the Appalachian. The carving up of the mountains by a few owners means that others have no choice in building their futures; they are subject to the will of the large landowners.

In Clear Fork Valley it isn't enough to say that Lewis Lowe can go elsewhere; there aren't any elsewheres, at least in the mountains. There in the valley, Alvarado E. Funk, the General Manager of the American Associaton, has announced a policy of depopulation: "The people would be better off, and we would be better off, if they would be off of our lands," he said. And, because of a lack of jobs or homes, or because of the destruction wrought upon them by the land-use practices of the corporate owners, people are forced to leave.

In the valley people are trying to hang on and to provide alternatives. A non-profit community development council has sought for five years to provide the alternative by building new industry and homes. Yet for five years they have been denied any land upon which to build. Just last year the American Association would not even consider freeing one-half acre of its 50,000 acres in the Clear Fork Valley for a clinic. Nor are many other industries interested in coming in. Also, large blocks of land kept unused deny smaller landowners services such as roads and sewers and the chance of their own development.

The outmigration of thousands of people from the mountains over the last twenty years hasn't been a matter of choice for most. They've moved to make way for the bulldozer, and now there's talk of having more of them move again to make way for recreation, to allow folks to escape the now overcrowded mountains.

Theft takes many forms. Here in the Clear Fork Valley it is not only what is done but what is *not* done, *not* allowed, that prevents possibilities of new industry, developments, futures by and for the Appalachian people.

What then is the modern day colony? It is theft by the property owner of the resources, of taxes and a base for community services, of a means and way of life, of the possibilities of choice for the colonized propertyless. As was true in the 1890's it is either ignored or rationalized to the rest of the nation by an ideology, the need for energy, or the need for the South to grow, to "catch up." But hidden beneath the ideology is the dependency of the propertyless on the property of others and threat of destruction of a land and a people. In Appalachia, the corporate property holder, like the slave owner, holds the power to deprive "will and personality," a power of "life and death." In Appalachia, property is theft.

Energy and the Nation: The Making of a Macro-Colony?

The colonization of people by the energy conglomerate extends to others in America, outside the Appalachians. One ought to be able to learn about the nature of social thievery and the process of colonization from history. In the development of the energy industrials and in the "boom" in the South today are signs of a macro-colony, parallel to the development and boom of Middlesboro, the micro-colony of the 1890's.

The first similarity is that the energy conglomerates or their representatives, particularly the oil industrials, are buying up all the land and minerals they can get in Appalachia and the West. Jim Ridgeway's new book *The Last Play* gives a good account of the recent major transactions: Consolidation Coal by Continental Oil, Island Creek Coal by Occidental Petroleum, Peabody Coal by Kennecott Copper, etc. There have been countless others on a smaller scale. And in some instances the form of barter is similar to that of the 1890's: One company offered an Indian tribe in Montana a health clinic in return for several million dollars worth of minerals.

Not only are these few corporations gaining vertical control, but they are developing horizontal alliances—with the landowner, with the fuel company, with the energy producer. Like the American Association in the 1890's, control is being gained by a few from the product to the final good of electricity. Other industries in the South and the nation are becoming dependent upon the energy conglomerates for their own economic strengths and futures.

A second similarity of the energy boom is that this dependency on the economic concentration in the hands of a few is supported, even concealed, by a prevailing ideology: the demand for energy for progress and growth and defense, the fuel crisis, etc. The United States has only 6 percent of the world's population yet already uses some 46 percent of the world's energy. Yet we have no suggestions for cutting back on the use of energy, only the need for more and more fuel. Not only can the fear of an "energy crisis" be invoked, but with the capacity to advertise, to create demand and to control supply in the same hands, the ideology can be self-sustaining—and profitably so to the sustainers.

Thirdly, like those riding the bandwagon of the Middlesboro boom, the combination of dependency and ideology have brought support of emotional loyalty from the general American consumer. The boom has been a quick one; the sequence of events in the last year alone has been dazzling. All the major weeklies—*Time, Newsweek, Business Week*—have declared a fuel crisis. *Time* magazine sponsored a conference to consider solutions to the crisis to which several dozen representatives of the energy conglomerates, Nixon's key energy advisors, and *two* environmentalists were invited. Shortly thereafter, Nixon's famed "energy speech" declared the need for *more* tax loopholes, for *relaxation* of environmental controls, for more social thievery to "solve" the "crisis." Generally not wanting to interrupt growth or in the belief that their lights would grow dim, the American public accepted the steps, or others like them, as necessary.

And, like in the Middlesboro boom, little attention is given by the press or the public to the destruction of a land and people back in the mountains. In cases where the plight is noticed, the colonization and depopulation are justified as "necessary social costs." Attempts at correction aim only at "allowing" the Appalachian to join the already overcrowded and mountain-directed mainstream.

The analogy of the energy boom to the boom of the Magic City in the 1890's is not meant to say naively that energy sources and use are not major social problems. They are. But it is meant to show that the present ownership of energy resources and the supporting ideology of "energy crisis" can be used to disguise social thievery from the urban public as well as from the mountaineer. Consider the following three examples.

Labor. Georgia Power's union and race policies brought to our attention by the "Georgia Power Project" or Shell's response to demands of its refinery workers for better working conditions show that in the name of "energy crisis," workers can be exploited. As in the coalfields, the demands of labor are discounted as minor compared to the national needs for energy supply.

The Consumer. The growing monopoly within the energy industry means that prices can be increased for the consumer without bringing any benefit back to the coal fields. Usually, for instance, it is the function of the Federal Power Commission to control price increases of electricity. But hidden within their code is a provision known as the "fuel-release" clause. Essentially, this clause means that wherever the price of fuel (coal) increases, the consequent price of power (electricity) can be passed on to the consumer, no questions asked. The effect is obvious: if a large stripping operation on American Association land raises the price of coal to Georgia Power, then Georgia Power can raise the price of electricity to the public. The extra cost is born by the consumer, but the profits don't go back to the people of Clear Fork Valley or to reclaim their mountains. They go to increase the wealth of the already wealthy few who own, produce, and supply the coal and power.

The "Energy Crisis." Energy companies justify strip-mining destruction by claiming the need for cheap fuel to supply the consumer. Yet, only approximately 10 percent of Appalachia's coal can be stripped; the rest must be deep mined if it is to be recovered. Moreover, stripping "for the cream" damages the mountain in ways that will make far more expensive and dangerous the deep mining required for "the rest of the milk." While the Appalachians are being destroyed, the consumer is being duped. The lack of a rational fuel policy today means that he will have to pay extra costs tomorrow. Someday, as was the case in Middlesboro, the quick, cheap profits will be over. But while the companies will retain their control, the consumers who accept the credibility of their colonizers will have to pay for and suffer the losses.

Yes, just as we could see in Middlesboro the founding of a micro-colony out of which have grown ever more insidious forms of thievery, we can see in the modern boom for coal, energy, and "progress," the building of a macro-colony whose similarities to its predecessor ought to sound a warning: property is theft and not just in Appalachia. In the current context, it becomes chief collaborator with other energy industrials in theft from labor, from the consumer, from the future, and from others throughout the nation as well.

A Bit on De-colonization

There is a difference today in the Clear Fork Valley as

there is in the rest of the mountains to the time of the 1890's, however. People are resisting and a movement is building.

The movement takes many forms. In the Clear Fork Valley, citizens have begun to challenge for the first time the American Association and its London holders. Some gains have been won, including the acquisition of some of the company's property with which the local community development council can build a fresh future growing from within rather than controlled from without.

In the five major coal-producing counties of Tennessee, Save Our Cumberland Mountains, a grass-roots organization of some 200 people, has in the past two years begun to challenge forcefully the tax evasion, strip mine destruction, and economic and political controls exercised by the large land companies in their areas. Led by J. W. Bradley, SOCM, like many other groups throughout the mountains, is an attempt by the people of Appalachia to regain control of their land and their lives. Whether expressed through working for union reform, fighting strip mining, developing community-controlled industry, or demanding welfare rights, people are angry. Organizations are building.

There are those who have compared the mood in the mountains today to the pre-dawn of the civil rights movement—waiting for a spark, a leader, or the right combination of social events that make such movements happen. Those who learned from the failures of the 1960's, though, know that such movements must come from within, must be led and fought by Appalachians, and cannot be fought from the outside.

Just as the 1960's provided for non-blacks in the South a brutal awakening of consciousness to the meaning of the statement "slavery is murder," perhaps from the 70's the South can come to recognize that in Appalachia "property is theft." Just as the murderers of the slaves aren't necessarily in Mississippi, the colonizers of Appalachia aren't necessarily in Appalachia. Perhaps with this recognition we can see that whether we are mountaineers, workers, or consumers, urban folks or rural folks, we face in the energy conglomerate the same thieves. And if there can come that understanding, there can also come the hope that a movement for decolonization of Appalachia will spark a struggle for radical change of structure and of ideology in the rest of the South and the nation.

NOTES

[1]Proudhon, Pierre-Joseph, *First Memoir* - Quoted in Selected Writings of Pierre-Joseph Proudhon, Stewart Edwards, ed., Elizabeth Frazer, Trans. London: Macmillan and Co., 1969, p. 124.

[2]Schmidt-Bleek, F., "Towards a More Beneficial Use of Coal," Appalachian Resources Project, University of Tennessee, 1972.

[3]Gaventa, Ormond, Thompsen, "Coal, Taxation and Tennessee Royalists," unpublished study for the Vanderbilt Student Health Coalition, 1971.

[4]Kirby, Richard, "Kentucky Coal: Owners, Taxes, Profits," a study in Representation Without Taxation," for the Appalachian Volunteers, March 11, 1969.

[5]McAteer, Davitt, "Profile of West Virginia as a Colony," unpublished study, 1971.

[6]*Dun's Review and Modern Industry*, April, 1965, p. 40.

[7]*Capital Resources in Central Appalachia*, prepared for the Appalachian Regional Commission by Checchi and Co., Washington, 1969.

[8]Weller, Jack, *Yesterday's People*, University of Kentucky Press with the collaboration of the Council of the Southern Mountains, Inc., Lexington, 1966, p. 11.

[9]Speech by Arthur, November 11, 1890, published as a pamphlet by the American Association. The other historical material comes from cited works or from my own research in local newspapers, courthouses, library records, and interviews.

[10]*Ibid.*

[11] Allen, James, "Mountain Passes of the Cumberland," *Harper's Magazine*, copyright by Harper and Brothers, 1890, p. 8.

[12] "Southern Lands: Middlesborough, Ky.," *Scribner's Magazine*, November, 1890.

[13] Recounted in *The Middlesboro Daily News*, August 19, 1965, pp. C-22.

[14] Tipton, J. C., *The Cumberland Coal Field and Its Creators*, Pinnacle Printery, 1905.

[15] For further information, see "Property Taxation of Coal in Central Appalachia," A report for the Senate Subcommittee on Intergovernmental Relations from Save Our Cumberland Mountains, Inc., prepared by John Gaventa.

[16] Schmidt-Bleek, Appalachian Resources Project.

References are provided only for direct quotes from other printed works.

THE BIG STEAL

by
Warren Wright

The historian Frederick Jackson Turner has suggested the year 1890 as the end of the American "frontier." I suggest, not to contradict the Turner thesis but as a slight supplement to it, that 1890 marks the opening of a certain portion of the Appalachian frontier: that portion of eastern Kentucky to which John Fox, Jr. refers in the title of his novel *The Heart of the Hills.* These are the mountainous coal-mining counties where the topography at the head of the watershed in Letcher County lies little less than perpendicular and only gradually improves in the direction of south central Kentucky, westward toward the Bluegrass area, and northward toward Ashland and the Ohio River's tributary system.

It is not hard to understand the isolation, the late development of this region (if such a word as "development" can be tolerated for the moment). The western surge—American expansion—simply split like a river current on the problem of southeast Kentucky terrain and surrounded it like a huge boulder in the channel, flowing in the more natural paths to the north and south. Of course, there were other contributing factors in the isolation. Other than the rugged terrain, there were no immediate prospects and little allure for those inclined to the plow,

SOURCE: *Paper written in 1970.*

AUTHOR: Warren Wright, *former executive director of the Council of Southern Mountains, has engaged in years of private study and preaching in mountain non-denominational churches. He is currently investigating social and judicial history.*

to stock-raising, and later to the precious mineral rushes. The riches of the timbered hills were by-passed, the coal strata and other minerals were at first unknown, and few, then as now, appreciated the aesthetic qualities of the Cumberland atmosphere.

We can therefore say, with a degree of assurance, that southeast Kentucky was settled, very thinly and for an abnormally long period, by a rather distinct social type. We may not here take time for much observation or comment or proof, but it is the significant and apparent fact that the Daniel Boone "type" was of necessity the earliest settler. (Isolation carried forward the character process; organized industrial rapacity preyed on what it found and completed the process of southeastern Kentucky society.) It is noticeable that not even Boone tarried in the mountains when he came leading groups in from North Carolina, but he pressed on toward central Kentucky. The few who came and stayed generally followed Boone's trail from North Carolina, coming in through southwestern Virginia; lesser numbers came from Pennsylvania and western Virginia. A few came in directly from Europe; one of my great-grandfathers came directly from Ireland, and a great grandmother came from Holland. I would but make the point in regard to all these: The mountains typed them all to a degree which it may well be doubted is known in its singularity anywhere else in the States. When I credit this result to the mountains, I mean to signify the national isolation, the personal loneliness, and—if a metaphysical idea may be permitted in a sociological thesis—the natural atmosphere of the Cumberlands.

In 1964, after a period of about four years of research in local history, in the state judicial system, and in the region's sociological aspects, I mapped a section of Pike and Letcher counties, a section perhaps five miles in length and comparably much narrower. This mapping was aimed at coal-title research and at a history of the development of the coal empire. It was quite interesting for me to find the first land patent ever granted in the mountain hollow where I was born and had grown up, interesting to attempt to fit these records of 1832 to the easier work of the following decades. I mapped many of the patents of the 1840's, and each decade's history grew more discernible as I found and located the natural objects (for authenticity), both on paper and on the ground.

I discovered that shortly after the Civil War a little flurry of interest in the awareness of the mineral wealth was manifested, unbelievably, by a trio of local people. These men established leases or options of record on hundreds of acres near Jenkins. These leases, of necessity, could but expire and cease to be of legal import; railroads and capital were still far in the future. Twenty-five years of subsequent isolation brought the history to 1890 when, for the Elkhorn Valley of Pike and Letcher Counties and the Shelby Valley of Pike County, the speculators came in a rush.[1]

R. M. Broas from New York organized the first mass-buying venture. Whether he was buying for himself or as a direct agent for those to whom his "titles" were transferred eleven years later, I have not discovered. He was fairly well furnished with money by the standards of the day. From records of Pike Circuit Court and from material in the Appellate records (Northern Coal and Coke Co. v. C. S. Nield, et al.) it appears that he had "about 20 corps of engineers (surveyors). . . .besides abstractors and attorneys examining titles." His daily payroll was asserted to be four hundred dollars, which perhaps reveals why he chose to deal in leases rather than fee purchases or outright mineral severance deeds. One dollar per acre was paid to consummate the transactions by consideration, and provisions for paying two more dollars per acre "when and as mined" were written into the documents. Not only did this dollar per acre permit Broas to reach twice or thrice as far in acreage grasped, the question of taxation, either on the surface or on the dormant mineral reserve, was left to the lessor. Although any unbiased arbiter could easily perceive that such a lease, granted for a period of 999 years, was an open contravention of Kentucky statutes on "perpetuities," the leases were upheld then in the subverted court system and were more definitely upheld as late as the 1950's when Pike Circuit Judge Jean Auxier ruled that in all effect the leases were "deeds." This occurred in the face of the mountain court record books wherein the documents had been listed as "leases" for sixty years.

At once the Court of Appeals upheld Auxier, and since the substance of the perpetuity statutes had already been voided, there was a sophistry truth in the reasoning. The law against "perpetuities" had ruled that no instrument, in general, was valid that did not provide consideration that could be utilized by the grantor in a reasonable time, presumably his lifetime. Here was a lease consideration wherein the lessor's grandchildren to the point of economic infinity could not obtain consideration, *and then only as the coal was mined* (i.e. perhaps ten dollars one year for the mining of five acres and ten dollars in the next century for five more). Nor was the injustice to such grantors the only reason for denial of such transactions; public policy was very much at stake. A wealthy corporation could thus, at a minimal expenditure, tie up and obviate hundreds of thousands of acres or other resources in opposition to the state's or the nation's need.

In reference, however, to the removal of public resources and public necessities from the normal availability to the public, the perfect illustration is supplied in the thousands of unsightly shacks and broken men with broken families visible to those who merely pass through southeast Kentucky while the denuded hills, though despoiled, still hold plentiful means of subsistence and self-respect for men who are trained for no other work. But the Broas leases still stand, 16,500 acres of them in Pike and Letcher counties.

By my computations, Broas' agents obtained leases for prospecting and mining, generally on the standard form partially described heretofore, 5,167 acres in the head of Shelby Valley between May and August, 1890. These leases comprised part of the area mapped, where the titles were fully or partially abstracted in my research project. Condensing all the material upon which this report is based to the smallest amount of space, I believe it worthwhile to indicate the outstanding facts of just two days of the Broas activity: May 12 and May 15. The following instruments were executed in Shelby Valley (all but one) and show on May 12:

Jacob Sanders and Mahulda (leased) 471 acres—coal only—her signature by mark;
William Vanover and Sarah—313 acres—coal—signed by marks of both lessors;
Wm. Vanover, Jr. and Dicy—182 acres—coal—her mark;
James and Mary Elkins—147 acres—coal—her mark.
    On the 15th:
Isaac and Elizabeth Belcher—177 acres—coal—both lessors' marks;
James and Sarah Estep—272 acres—coal—her mark;

Reuben and Bethena Johnson—207 acres—coal—both signatures
by marks;
Richard and Elizabeth Branham—191 acres—coal—her mark;
G. H. and Dove Belcher—70 acres—coal—her mark.

It will be noted that not one of these wives was able to affix
a handwritten signature to the Broas leases; it must not be assumed that the five husbands who apparently did were able to
either read or write. It is a pathetic fact that men then were
proud of being able to sign their names, and any facsimile was of
course a legal signature. From further research related to valid
titles, I was able to establish as fact that but three of the men
were able to read and write from among the eighteen lessors
above, but three were legally competent. And that is, I would
suggest, a fairly representative figure for the mountain society of
that date.

The instruments above were duly acknowledged by a local
notary, but the witness required for all instruments signed by
illiterate grantors was the agent of Broas, certainly not a dis-
interested party. Incidental to the lease executions, the agent
drew and the notary took acknowledgment of two *quitclaim*
deeds between certain of the parties designated, and with one
most interesting citizen whose activities are yet furnishing spice
to the odors of Pike Circuit Court. A quitclaim deed from
William and Sarah Vanover to James Estep was witnessed by
Morse, the Broas agent, and signed by the marks of both grantors. This deed gave Estep "color" upon which to base the lease
he was executing; Morse was accepting a dubious lease and helping to bolster it up by a quitclaim brazenly drawn on the same
day.

The other quitclaim was drawn to the enterprising mountaineer I mentioned above; this instrument quitclaimed a property of description too vague to be located to the benefit of
one Denny Vanover, who as his numerous remaining nephews
assured me, would "make you a deed to anything; just point out
what you wanted." I understood, and my future research indicated that I properly understood, that had Denny lived in New
York City he would have sold the Brooklyn Bridge perhaps fifty
times. Morse did not take Denny's lease that day; I doubt that
the survey, which was to enclose 352 acres *acquired through him,*
was yet completed. It was a more delicious fact, still apparent

after eighty years, that Denny owned but 100 acres in the center of Three Mile Creek, and *that* under a "cloud" when he happily leased Broas the entire left fork of Three Mile Creek, 352 acres. I had the honor and pleasure of placing these facts in Pike Circuit Court for the benefit of the present owner of the so-called surface, who, should he be able to find an attorney of integrity in the noble old Common-wealth, *may* be recognized as the owner in fee, able to purchase a quarter million dollars worth of chewing tobacco. (I would not wager highly on his chances; the case has lain dormant for four years, stalemated by his inability to find counsel and the court's uneasiness about dismissing the material I inserted in his counter claim.) (Bethlehem Minerals Company vs. John Johnson, Civil Action 7288, Pike Circuit Court.)

The color (i.e., color of title, which I mention above in regard to the Broas leases) is an important element in the policies and operations of the coal companies. "Color" means no more than suggestions of title; it may be the flimsiest of title ground upon which to take a stand—such as a quitclaim, as above, from a person who obviously has no right or even a claim to transfer. If the receiver of such an instrument can make any showing of accepting it in good faith and as having some element of value for him, he can use it as "color of title." And there is no criminality ordinarily in giving a quitclaim deed, certainly when rendered to a person of average intelligence and competency; the grantor merely passes whatever right he has in any subject matter to a grantee, without professing any right or giving any warranty. Such a deed could give title to a fortune or might not be worth the ink in its writing. Under Kentucky law, I can quitclaim my interest in this college for a thousand dollars, if to a competent grantee, and no criminal charge will lie to the instrument. And what is the interest of the mining companies in such deeds and others insufficient as to valid title? This: The illegal mining of a tract of coal under color of title means that *at worst* the operating company will be forced to pay but standard royalty, usually around twenty-five cents per ton, which would have been but good business for it in the beginning; it *may* never be called to account, which is better yet. But without color of title, a company would be responsible for all coal extracted and liable at the then present market price at the *pitmouth*. One of the many interesting angles of the Bethlehem-John Johnson Case is that the company must now mine the coal on the merits of its case; its title has been challenged and color cannot avail if the landowner successfully maintains his title in court.

Let us consider for a moment the relation of the Big Steal (in eastern Kentucky) to lawful execution of deeds and leases. In Corpus Juris Secundum the commentary reads:

> More inadequacy of consideration is not a ground for the cancellation of a conveyance of minerals or mineral rights, but where a gross inadequacy of consideration is shown, and also weakness of mind, illiteracy, and inexperience of the grantor, and where misrepresentations have been made by the grantee, courts of equity may grant relief by way of cancellation. A mineral conveyance may be cancelled where the minds of the parties failed to meet on the amount of the purchase price. (Sec. 163, P. 350, Vol. 58)

The pertinent citation reads:

> In case of fraud, overreaching or other circumstances justifying equitable relief, court will readily cancel transactions by which speculators procure from indigent and illiterate grantors for nominal considerations, conveyance of . . . mineral rights in farm land which has been made subject of oil and gas leases to reputable oil companies. (Durbin v. Bennett, D.D. Ill., 31 F. Supp. 24)

Though I am somewhat doubtful of the existence of any "reputable oil company," it is clear that this federal principle would tear the Big Steal all to Hades, even at this late date. I have demonstrated the degree of illiteracy in the Broas lessors. How indigent were they? It is very likely that some of them lived on dirt floors. What about the considerations? Much has been made of the position that the rediculously low prices were *then* reasonable, that a dollar then was worth ten, even twenty, today. The essential element in the case is inadvertently given by Appellate Judge E. C. O'Rear, serving the mineral interests on the Frankfort appellate bench as he had served them *in the very buying of that subject matter on which he sat.* Not seeing the application of all he wrote in a lengthy opinion sustaining a Pike County Judas (*who had ordered that the validity of the Broas leases should not be SPOKEN AGAINST*), O'Rear said:

> These conditions have attracted and will doubtless for
> some time continue to attract investors and speculators.
> *Another natural consequence is that prices for such
> properties will be advanced under present improved con-
> ditions, very considerably over what was even a high price
> for the same properties a few years ago* [Emphasis mine] .
> (NCC v Nield, Pike Circuit Court)

Contrary to his own words in an earlier portion wherein
he opined that Broas had purchased with mere hope in the "future," the eminent jurist is recognizing that the speculators already know the value of a southeastern Kentucky dollar, that it
is but waiting on the completion of the rail line to climb like a
rocket, and this is what justice must compute the *consideration*
on. This factor alone takes us back to the Corpus Juris commentary: "A mineral conveyance may be cancelled where the
minds of the parties failed to meet on the amount of the purchase price." (Of course, none of this law nor those facts matter,
but they furnish us with a sociological study.)

One other factor remained in the list of possibilities toward
cancellation; it was the question of misrepresentation.   An
earlier but near relative of that same Auxier who ruled against
Pike County in the Broas situation of the 50's prepared sworn
evidence in an early move *against* the Broas transactions to the
effect that part of the consideration of the leases had been
Broas' assurances that the railroad would arrive in five years and
then mining, hence payment, would forthwith begin. Misrepresentation of another type, a humorous and pathetic type, was the
lessee's solemn covenant that all gold found in the leaseholds
would remain under title of the grantors. In spite of all these
factors which alone or cumulatively warrant cancellation, we
would do the mountain people an injustice to assume that they
supinely submitted to the Broas steal once it became a matter
of public knowledge. Efforts were made to break the leases in
court, attempts were made to return the dollar-per-acre payments, and some lessors openly resold to willing grantees over
the Broas documents of record. (The leases were truly void for a
half-dozen legal considerations which are offered in the above,
but the corporations had conspired with state government as an
initial move; in the entire history of the Big Steal only one
significant ruling has been awarded the landowners: i.e., lateral
and subjacent support which I hope to discuss briefly. In that

time, only Governor Breathitt of the 1960's has established a
record among his predecessers of openly standing with and for
the people and *that* only in the latter half of his term.)

Let us consider the prospects of a newly-arrived speculator
or buying agent, one who is in the first wave into the mountains
and is "in on the ground floor." If he is from the North or East,
as I imagine all were, he has never seen such a country, such potential, for even the steep hillsides may be propitious. (Coal
would be dumped directly into rail cars.) Only on the West
Coast could the value of the timber stands be surpassed, though
the lumber men had arrived earlier, seeking only the very best of
the best types. The black walnut and yellow poplar had been
cut heavily, and the best of the white oak is gone, but the eye
could not from any distance perceive the difference. There are
no roads worthy of the name; wagons can be used, or sleds, but
the creeks are forded, not bridged. Through the decades of
isolation only the creek bottoms are cleared and some of the
"cove" fields. The timber grows down to the creeks, hanging
over the paths and wagon trails.

The tentative earlier prospecting had quickly established
an important truth; no great care need be exercised in buying.
The coal was there, everywhere; the only difference would
be in grade, and none of it was worthless. So one could buy
freely as to site. Buy from site to adjoining site future mining
fields by accretion. But buy anywhere as opportunity offered
to make the capital reach as many fools as possible.

Here was a people who had known but six-month or seven-
month schools as the annual custom. But this means less than we
might expect. The severe winters could cut that time to four
or five months, and distance was very much a factor in atten-
dance. Many families did not even choose to send their children,
though others were more than willing. Short-term "writing
schools" sometimes supplemented the regular term; these might
last as little as ten days. Eighth grade students could teach, and I
suspect that in earlier days anyone who could read and write was
eligible.

The mental capacity of the people thus ranged from an
understandable illiteracy to a vicious stupidity in some cases.

(There were the exceptions; I have learned of men who could plot land surveys and there were men who left the mountains and returned as doctors and lawyers. These exceptions were probably rare indeed earlier than 1890.) But the buyers found a general atmosphere of geniality; they were expert in breaking down the innate suspicion. They addressed the victims by their first names; they placed themselves inside the obligations of hospitality, for many, even among the violent types, considered themselves responsible for the safety and feelings of a guest— even if he was sleeping on a cornshuck mattress and being fed cornbread and salt bacon. For these mountain people to see a hundred dollars in cash at one time was a life experience; and in addition to the lack of education, they were and are yet exceptionally naive. As much as they may distrust outsiders in general, they have the strangest veneration for education (even if hidden under hostility). At that time, it is to be doubted that a single one knew the implications for the future in the mass selling; many thought the coal existed in only one seam; some thought it existed only in certain places.

I have written all this in regard to the buyer and his advantages to illustrate his one great disadvantage, that which has been a burden on the back of the industry up to this date, and that which would have changed the regional social system had not the industry prepared for its potential troubles by aligning with state government and maintaining either an alliance or a rapport unto this very day. The industry's problem was this: *There were no legal means of obtaining titles to the great coal strata.* There was comparatively little population; this was good in a way for the region was "open." But relative to population, there were but few settlers per lineal mile on the creek systems; there were even fewer claimants of property, for incredible as it may sound, this region has always had a "renter" class, even when land warrants and patents could be obtained for a pittance; sympathetic county surveyors would come to the farm, survey one line and geometrically calculate the other three, back to the starting point, to lighten the cost of the patentee. But there were those who had never obtained land. I have concluded that it was seldom indeed that this class stayed on one location long enough to perfect a title by residence. These who were later called "renters" did not then necessarily have to rent; they were often squatters, moving from one creek to another as the whim or necessity moved them.

Furthermore, many of those who considered themselves to be landowners were definitely not. The mountaineers honored each others' deeds (in general), but these were often based on original squatting or arbitrary claims, and the continuity that would have perfected preemption or adverse possession had often been broken to spoil the possible or pending title. Even when absolutely valid patent titles had been obtained, men would sometimes abandon them and others might obfuscate the record by patenting over the same lines, unwittingly or knowingly breaking the patent laws.

But titles, as far as corporations are concerned, *must be obtained through individuals, through title holders.* So the industry knew its problem in advance, knew that only in a region so deprived and isolated could it hope to grasp and maintain such a tremendous chunk of the national wealth. The entire governmental system was subverted to maintaining this national swindle, and on the local level the two parties took on the aspects of two bloated swine fighting in the swill trough, careful never to turn it over—for who knows but what we might win next election. From the Court of Appeals down to the average police court, the judiciary became a class of parasites whose only necessity for a show of legal knowledge lay in the cases wherein two non-political people had suits of private nature, and both were evenly matched as to influence and access to money.

Returning directly to the Broas leases and other sources of title, I sought to make the point that titles may only be obtained where they exist, and for the massive purposes of the industry there were no massive title sources. It was realized from the first that continual title improvement must be a goal and remain an integral part of operations for years. Many of the Broas lessors were again contacted and induced to sign outright mineral conveyances by mere payment of the two-dollar-per-acre contingent consideration. These new conveyances were the notorious forms known synonymously as the Northern Coal and Coke form, the Mayo form, the broad form, or the long form; and the mineral grantees at this phase also picked up *all* minerals on the properties in addition to the coal and obtained the rights which the cooperating Court of Appeals said were tantamount to outright control of the surface. (In all honesty, no other factors of law being considered, this was essentially true.) But none of these acquisitions affected the basic title situation *which was*

*based on the ability of the original or the new grantors to give
sound titles.* However, in the next two decades, many of the
instruments became valid as some of the grantors perfected their
suface titles by fifteen years of various forms of *possession,*
validating the mineral conveyance by the same token. Various
means were used by the industry to aid and encourage specific
landowners to improve their titles, though the companies had to
work here in privacy for fear of exciting a public or an individual
interest in the possibility that the landowner had a better mineral
title than the operators themselves did. THIS IS STILL THE
BASIC FACT OF TITLE RESEARCH IN THIS REGION—
REGARDLESS OF ALL THE PURPORTED SEVERANCE OF
MINERALS FROM THE SURFACE, NO SEVERANCE IS
VALID UNLESS EXECUTED BY ONE WHO HAD A VALID
TITLE IN FEE. An invalid or false severance can be made valid
if the grantor in question later develops or obtains for himself
a good title to the property in question.

IN THE AREAS I HAVE MAPPED AND ABSTRACTED, I
WOULD ESTIMATE THAT THE MINERAL INDUSTRY HAS A
FIRM TITLE TO ABOUT SIXTY PERCENT OF THE TERRI-
TORY IT HAS MINED OR IS MINING. And this figure would
be less had there not been a continual program of shoring up
weak spots, obtaining various statute concessions, and an increasing percentage of buying in fee. I could cite incredible instances,
however, if space permitted, where large tracts are awaiting exploitation on title grounds which can reflect nothing but that
desperation in the thirty years after 1890 to get some sort of a
document from any sort of a person to cover the accretive surveys of Broas and his successors. In the head of Shelby Valley I
found a mineral deed to a large acreage, granted by an uncle of
mine to Consolidation Coal Company; the amazement of the
present "surface owners" equalled my own, for as I had sus-
pected and as they knew, his uncle, deceased for several years,
had never in life had the slightest claim on the property in question. And not only was he a good respected citizen, he was
certainly too sensible to have executed such a deed in the face of
his immediate neighbors. I can cite a variety of similar instances
in a radius of five miles, but I am trying to deal with trends
rather than examples. Incidentally, this acreage had already been
obtained as a Broas lease; the new or later document showed
clearly that Consolidation was foreseeing possible difficulty with
the leases.

So, while the Land and Property Departments at Jenkins, under the long chain of operating names of Consolidation Coal Company and Bethlehem Mines Corporation, schemed and drew and redrew its maps and watched over possible future sore spots, the industry maintained or tightened its grip on the state judiciary and the political systems. In the history of Kentucky mining, only one circuit judge has proven his integrity and openly fought for justice.[2] This is Courtney C. Wells of Hazard, Perry County, now in private practice. In BLUE DIAMOND COAL COMPANY v. NEACE, Perry Circuit Court, Judge Wells, having been already overruled by the Court of Appeals in a strip-mining case reversed for the operator, had to instruct a jury in a second one. Facing the fact that our honored appellate statesmen had ruled that only such stripping as was *"arbitrary, wanton, or malicious"* was forbidden or compensable, Wells gravely stayed inside their logic and told the jury:

> The Court instructs the jury that the plaintiff, Blue Diamond Coal Company, had the right to the use of the surface in the prosecution of its business of mining, for any purpose of necessity or convenience, unless this power was exercised oppressively, arbitrarily, wantonly, or maliciously, and if you believe from the evidence in the case that the plaintiff in the prosecution of its business of mining, exercised this right of power in an oppressive, arbitrary, wanton or malicious manner, and the defendant's property was damaged thereby, then the law is for the defendant and you should so find.

It was a foregone conclusion as to how a mountain jury would react to these instructions, and Wells, knowing that the Frankfort rogues would overrule him again, added a judicial opinion to the appeal record, flatly asking the Court to reverse its ruling and overturn the Buchanan v. Waton precedent upon which Kentucky stripping was based. Of course, all he established was his integrity, while that eminent jurist who was once promoted here for governor, the Right Honorable Judge Palmore, really put the appellate position in the proper perspective: "The mere exercise of a right to mine in a particular fashion cannot of itself be classified as arbitrary, wanton, or malicious. It is the manner of the mining operation, as distinguished from the fact of its being carried on, that determines liability for damages."[3]

And to show that he was capable of more than sophistry and that Kentucky law is what "this Court says it is—this week" (a direct quote from one of the seven Judases), he wrote some of the most astounding words seen in American jurisprudence:

> . . . .we are obliged to point out that Buchanan v. Watson does not upset any existing law, but applies the old principles to a new fact situation, AND RIGHT OR WRONG, *it would be a grave matter indeed for this court by overrulling it now to upset property interests which have since been invested in reliance upon it.* (Emphasis mine)

It would be hard to find plainer English to say that Kentucky's Court of Appeals would not overrule the mineral industry's prize precedent for any reason, and a franker confession that the Court is a base for the interests "relying upon it" could not be stated.

NOTES

[1]A few notable severances had been executed *earlier* than 1890 by Virginia Mining and Improvement Company. (Probably less than a half-dozen, in the late 1889's.)

[2]It would be well for me to note that two other judges have voiced opposition to the mineral-political-judicial combine. John Chris Cornett of Knott Circuit Court has twice denied the right of the operators to *destroy the surface without compensation* to the surface owner. Judge Edward Hill, formerly of Floyd County, now a Judge of the Court of Appeals, dissented in the latest appellate case which reversed Cornett in *Martin et ux V. Kentucky Oak Mining Company et al.* In the dozen or so mining counties with circuit judges having a four (six?) year term of office, these three legalists form a tiny and significant minority during a period spanning eighty years.

[3]Lateral and Subjacent support is required for the surface owners under Kentucky law. From the early days it has been illegal to remove *all* the coal under any area without leaving pillars (blocks) of coal to support the surface; the coal companies must expressly buy the right of total removal, i.e., breaking the surface.

This is from a state judiciary that later permitted the entire destruction of the surface.

THE LAND DEVELOPMENT RAG

by
Anita Parlow

This essay describes the economic, political, and social intrusions made by land developers in Watauga and Avery counties in North Carolina and outlines some tentative responses by farmers to halt the kinds of development which have made it nearly impossible for them to continue living on their own land. Avery and Watauga were among the first mountain counties to fall under the developers' shovels. The purpose of this essay is to document the effects of the corporate intruders and to warn mountain people in other counties that they might be next.

The Boom

For the past decade, North Carolina's mountains have endured the shock of rapid and uncontrolled development—development which is changing farming communities to "recreational shopping centers." Mountain and farm lands have been gobbled up and chopped away by developers who have transformed Watauga and Avery counties from farming valleys shield-

SOURCE: *Published by the Southern Appalachian Ministry in Higher Education, Knoxville, Tennessee, (c) 1976.*

AUTHOR: Anita Parlow *is a writer and contributor to* The Mountain Eagle, Southern Exposure, *and* Mountain Review. *She also produced a documentary for National Public Radio on Logan County, West Virginia.*

ed by gently sloped mountains to a cacaphony of strip-development/fast-food chains. The land grab has boosted land prices so that farmers can't afford farmland and has intruded a culture of affluence on farmers who are left to work as greens-keepers and domestics, to commute to industry towns, or to sell and move out.

Developers say North Carolina farmers are simply following a national pattern of leaving the farms since World War II. But the national decrease in farm acreage harvested was 10 percent during the past decade, while the decrease in Avery County was nearly 40 percent. In more developed Watauga, it was a whopping 50 percent. Farmers admit that it's been getting more difficult to stay on the farm every year because of rising prices, but the financial blow caused by tourist resorts makes farm life almost impossible.

The seasonal beauty of the Blue Ridge and Appalachian chains attracted corporate developers, many of whom had already splattered the Florida coast with beachfront resorts. They saw a quick profit to be made in an area with four tourist seasons, low tax rates, accessibility to the Appalachian Development Highways, and a 60-year history of exclusive, small resort communities. They came, they saw, they bought.

While the turnover of land to outsiders has been sizeable, the boom was initiated locally, in the early Sixties, by Hugh Morton and the Robbins brothers, who recognized the profit to be made in major land development. Morton, called a "conservationist before the word was invented" by one of his salesmen, subdivided a portion of the 7,000 acres of his family's land to create expensive resort subdivisions. Morton's and the Robbins' developments would have 6,000 people living on delicate mountain land. The Robbins' Hound Ears development charges $20,000 for a half-acre lot with covenants to build $50,000 homes; and the Morton family's Invershiel, a Scottish-deco community, charges $50,000 for two-acre lots with architectural covenants to build Scottish manor houses. The most exclusive and expensive development is Grandfather Mountain Golf and County Club. Morton and Oklahoma Oilman John Williams carved a suburban vacation complex into Grandfather Mountain and demand $20-30,000 per acre, $6,500 for country club membership, $600 annual dues, and $80,000 to $250,000 homes.

Corporate developers like Carolina Caribbean and Sugar Mountain, as well as a flock of smaller subdividers, have capitalized on Morton's cue and created a land grab to build moderately priced resorts modeled after his exclusive mountain retreats. The developers scalped the mountains from Avery County to Watauga's Boone to make room for a string of resort complexes, then pocked the roadsides with billboards which advertise "kicks in the sticks" images for urban tourists. The choice of a second home depends upon the size of your pocket-book. The most exclusive, like Hound Ears and Grandfather, are self-contained units which offer everything from golf, tennis, and skiing to restaurants and the requisite country store. Further down the road, Beech, Sugar, and Seven Devils hawk cheaper versions, and trapped in between are hurriedly-built places like Adam's Apple and Mill Ridge, with poorly built houses, some below the water flooding, and a single ski slope which runs virtually down onto the highway. The secluded and exclusive resort complexes appear to taunt the neighboring communities where some residents live in substandard housing with outdoor plumbing, no running water, and a per capita income of $1,500 for farming families.

Developers claim that their construction primed Watauga's and Avery's economic pump. But the facts speak differently. True, some people have profited from the spectacular land grab, but most people are hurt by the apparent and hidden costs of land speculation. And the buying was spectacular. Realtors turned land over three and four times in as many months, inflating the prices according to what other speculators or vacationers would pay. One realtor bought 300 acres at the base of Grandfather Mountain for $30,000 and sold less than of a third of the land the following month for $156,000. Land that once cost $250 an acre sold for $2,500 and up. Farmers couldn't resist the money and sold their land. Those who held out demanded prices they didn't dream possible and got them. "I asked $80,000 for my back 40 acres, and some fellow from Florida paid it," said one man who saved his farm by selling his mountain land. Other farmers were pressured to sell or swap their land, leaving the developers with huge tracts for subdivision. Beech Mountain quarter-acre lots cost 820 times the original buying price, and land prices in the rest of Avery County were boosted

401 percent in five years. (During the same period, farmland prices in the nation as a whole increased on the average from $115 to $194 per acre, or 60 percent.) According to a North Carolina Public Interest Research Group study, by 1975 outside speculators owned 164 percent more land in Watauga County and 47 percent more in Avery County than they did in 1970. Land boom threaded everybody's conversation, and realtors thought they'd never see the bottom of the money barrel.

Hard Times

But the recession hit the developers hard, and salesmen aren't showing anybody house lots anymore. "When the economy is strong people buy luxury items like second homes—in a recession we're the first item to go," said a developer. Most of the less exclusive resorts face bankruptcy, and several larger developers like Beech Mountain have gone under.

The history of bankrupt Beech Mountain challenges the assumption that the only reason for the failure of resort developments is that they've fallen victim to national recession. Beech's and Sugar's near bankruptcy demands an examination of the assumption that the development of recreation communities is a positive means for farming communities to sustain themselves. In her master's thesis, Robin Gottfried judged that "unless more and more homes are constructed in subdivisions, scattered lots or new recreation communities—the [economic] flow of benefits stemming from new construction will cease. If nothing else fills this gap, [the community] . . .could face a serious crisis."[1]

Beech owes $10 million more than its $25 million assets to a string of banks which includes North Carolina National Bank, Northwestern Bank, and Tri-South Mortgage Investors Trust of Atlanta. Former Beech President Roger Hard said Beech could have stayed afloat if the government had granted $8 million in tax-payer money to correct water and sewage violations and if bankers lent an extra $500,000 to prepare its ski slopes. But federal dollars cannot be used to build sewage plants for private industry, and the lenders said no.

Beech's collapse is also due to more than the recession.

According to court-appointed trustee Ralph O. Hutchinson, an investigation by the Securities and Exchange Commission (SEC) into Beech Mountain activities showed a "very relaxed attitude toward cost control, poor management and a complete lack of development and operational planning." He also said that the investigation uncovered some "irregularities in the use of corporate funds." Because of its financial and management shenanigans, Carolina Caribbean, Beech's corporate father, was suspended from the exchange.

Beech, like other resorts, "ran the financial numbers game to stay afloat," says President Hard, who was brought in by Carolina Caribbean to bail out Beech and is now attempting the same at neighboring Sugar Mountain. Hard says the resort developers put up tremendous amounts of front money to build ski slopes, lodges, and restaurants to attract people to the mountains in the first place. Then overhead costs for water, sewage, and operating expenses were borrowed on short term notes while the lots and houses were sold long term. "It's a cash flow problem," he said. "A purchaser buys a $10,000 lot but makes only a $1,000 down payment while it costs us $7,000 to prepare it."

"The $7,000 didn't include soft costs which added to our immediate obligations," said Hard. Nearly 75 percent of Beech's operating expenses were for salesmen, advertising, enormous salaries, and hefty expense accounts. "The original corporate owners should have put land sales money into escrow to build equity for land development; but they borrowed loans upon loans based on nothing but paper until the business operated only on financial device," said Hard. Banks and Real Estate Investment Trusts couldn't wait to press money into the developers' hands. They loaned 100 percent money at five and six points above prime for paper collateral. "It just didn't work," said Hard, who couldn't issue a 1975 annual report because of Beech's faulty bookkeeping.

Hard says he's a little more successful with his Sugar Mountain rescue, but he pays himself a month's salary in advance "just in case." Sugar is delinquent in all of its normal trade accounts. What Hard did was arrange with Sugar's lenders to defer payment on loans of $10 million which are currently secured by corporate real estate. The bank couldn't refuse to wink at Sugar's debts. Hard showed the lenders that they would lose $500,000 more by

foreclosing than by placing a moratorium on his old debts with
no principal or interest. He says if he stabilizes his credits, pays
current bills C.O.D., and borrows $2 million more, he'll make
money in five years.

"This time," says Hard, "we're going to change Sugar Mountain from a semi-private to a public resort." Hard plans to halt
land sales, push the ski lodge and convention business, and create
a weight-loss camp. Opening the doors to the public invites
criticism that local people who can afford to use the ski slopes
are caught in an economic ping-pong game. When times are bad
for the resorts, local residents are welcome. When times are
good, they're excluded. "We want to generate traffic through
the resort to sell houses," says Hard. "When the second home
business gets built out again, the slopes won't be able to handle
local people—there won't be room. So we'll have to close the
local people out."

Hard Sell

Developers say the resorts meet urban dwellers' recreational
demands. "Mountain retreats are what the people want," said a
realtor. But carnival marketing techniques of large resorts like
Beech and Sugar indicate that this particular form of recreational
demand is produced by the developers. "The whole thing is
created," admitted a former salesman for the Beech sales team.
"Developers create the value, the impression, the atmosphere—
and then sell it with emotional appeal." Professional sales teams
are trained to invent what people think owning mountain land is:
country living with suburban familiarity.

Beech's well-rehearsed dog-and-pony show tactics begin
with a deluge of telephone calls made to randomly-chosen
people in "prime target areas." When enough people agree to
participate in a free tour, chartered planes whisk the targeted
clients to a mind-boggling weekend of loose money and fast
talk which intimates that the last quarter-acre of Appalachia
might be sold before they got off the plane. The sequence of
well-controlled events leaves little room for thought. "If they
think twice about buying—they'll change their minds," said a
salesman who admitted that most people hadn't thought of
buying land before the sales team called. Free meals, free lodg-

ings, and the developers' idea of mountain culture are part of the package. "At Beech," said the salesman, "pretty little girls dressed up in Indian costumes drive buyers around the golf course and deposit them in briefing rooms where the benefits of purchasing a lot are described." Then they're released to the salesmen.

The salesman's job is to generate enthusiasm to sell land. "Salesmen drive people to the top of the mountain and literally cry about its beauty," said a man who did it. The procession to the mountain resembled an army convoy. Jeeps carried the buyers to pre-selected lots, the man in front and the woman in the rear. Two-way radios connected salesmen with each other and with general headquarters. Several jeeps would converge on a lot at a prearranged time. Sales were flashed onto the jeep radios. If a tourist wavered, the salesman radioed his indecision in code to headquarters who radioed the lot number of other jeeps. Bidders for the unclaimed lot would crowd the frequency. "What's important is to create a sense of urgency," said the salesman.

After paying $8,000 to $10,000, what does the client get? "Not much," according to a salesman. "The clients lose, too. Resort facilities aren't built to last. They're simply paste-up jobs to sell as much land as quickly as possible." Developers often build the minimum to sell lots and then leave the property owners to worry about maintenance and other problems like fire protection. Purchasers find themselves having to maintain security, water and sewage systems, golf courses, ski slopes, and roads not built to anyone's standards except the developers. "Nothing was built to last," repeated the salesman; "it was built to show that it had been done. We've butchered some of the prettiest mountains you've ever seen."

Fancy Doctors and Salty Roads

Resort developers say they're good for the county because they spend money locally and pay taxes. But laid off resort-construction workers are trying to revitalize their neglected farms, and female-oriented domestic jobs are seasonal and low-paying. "We've increased the tax base immeasurably," said the vice-president of Grandfather Mountain Company. If this were the case, then tax rates should have decreased or county services increased. In fact, not only have land values skyrocketed with each tax assessment, but Watauga's property rate increased by 46 percent last year. Also, high density resort communities overload a town's services and facilities. As for county-provided services for those increased tax dollars, local citizens say they get little and are second priority for the services that the county does provide.

County services have not increased since the resort boom. Road maintenance typifies an unequal provision of services. North Carolina's roads are state maintained. Snow removal is a primary maintenance function. Both Avery and Watauga counties are included in a "bare pavements program" which salts 165 of the 400 miles of paved roads at the first snowflake. Highway officials salt the most trafficked roads: All ski roads get first priority. Farm roads, often impassable in winter months, are not priority. Several Valle Crucis farmers said the school bus couldn't take their children to school during last winter's week-long storm because of the bad roads. But skiers could reach the slopes. Local maintenance workers, who once looked favorably on ski resorts, said they use one-third of the state's entire snow removal equipment to clear Avery and Watauga counties, but their own roads remain blocked.

Road salting is rotting cars and polluting people. The highway department dumps 6,000 tons of sodium and calcium chloride on the winter roads. Truck farmers say that since the salting began they've had to buy a new pick-up every two years because of corrosion. When the snow melts, salt percolates into the soil and drains into water systems. A district highway engineer said, "I daresay there's people who've got salt in their water systems right now." The reason the highway department uses salt instead of neutral sand is that "salt clears the roads cleaner and faster to the ski areas. We have to use so much of it anymore, it's cheaper."

The district engineer said he wished the state would put more money into road maintenance instead of expanding the highways to draw tourists, but he plans to build a $9 million expansion of the 5.3 mile tourist-used road from Boone to Blowing Rock, Watauga's only wet city. A coverall-clad realtor wondered why they "just don't move the liquor to Boone instead of building a $9 million four-lane."

Seasonally overcrowded hospitals force local people to bear the costs of new hospital-expansion bonds. The hospital at Banner Elk serves the resorts at Beech and Sugar Mountains, Seven Devils, and Grandfather Mountain, as well as Avery County residents. Hospital Administrator Juanita Shoemaker says, "It's simple to understand. We've had to expand the hospitals along with the developments." Mayor Charles Cannon agreed. "During ski season and hang-glider days, the emergency room is full." Shoemaker says the emergency room was a nightmare during Beech's first ski season. "Everyone worked weekends and nights to set broken legs and bones." A record 11,000 people used the emergency services that year while local residents complained that their children's illnesses often went unattended. Hospital administrators are unsure of the number of out-of-county patients because second home dwellers use local addresses for hospital admittance. Even so, nearly 30 percent of the patients at Cannon are not from Watauga or Avery Counties. When Beech Mountain collapsed, the total number of local patients at Cannon increased by 17 percent.

Boone's hospital is a highly specialized and expensive medical complex—a magnet which has tripled the number of its specialists in the past five years. Last year, the hospital board voted to purchase additional equipment and build a new wing to house the specialists. Local people judge they would be better served by community clinics engaged in preventive medicine and primary medical services instead of the highly specialized and expensive medicine available at the hospital. "We need regular doctors, not fancy medicine," said a woman who can't easily commute to the centralized hospital because she doesn't have a car and there's no public transportation.

Deeds and foreclosures descended like a paperwork avalanche on the county sheriff's office. The sheriff blames the rise in drug arrests and breaking and entering on second homes. "Robbers thrive on second home developments and tourists bring in drugs," he said. Some of the resorts maintain their own security, but the deputies routinely patrol the resorts and if there's an arrest to be made, "It's our baby." During the past 10 years, the sheriff has tripled his force and he says with the extra seasonal work, "It's not enough."

Volunteer fire departments suffer more than the police. With old and minimal equipment, the volunteers must douse fires in developments whose roads are sometimes so narrow that the truck can't squeeze through to the burning house. Rev. Campbell, who heads the Foscoe Fire Department, says the problem is more than firefighting, since the "closest thing we have to community action are the volunteers. Helping developers out cuts into our efforts to stop them from destroying our land." Some resorts, like Grandfather and Hound Ears, contributed money to local fire departments for extra equipment. "They've bought allegiance, round-the-clock protection, and lower insurance rates," said Campbell.

County officials agree that they spend proportionately more time meeting tourist demands than attending to local residents. "Tourists are a different class of people. They expect more service," said one official. The problem of service is both attitudinal and financial. Summer people pay taxes but aren't interested in specifically local issues like education. Therefore, their tax dollars become proxy votes to ensure that their interests are honored. Also, Watauga's government has invoked a spate of regulations to prevent future land abuse, which means more tax dollars must be spent on enforcement.

Cutting Up the Mountains

Developers have destroyed much of the ecologically fragile farm and mountain land. One of the worst problems is erosion caused by steeply graded subdivision roads. At Hound Ears the grades run as high as 20 percent—8 percent higher than the law allows. A county planner has said that some of the Hound Ears land as well as that of Seven Devils should never have been touched by a bulldozer. Not one lot has been sold in some smaller subdivisions, but hundreds of roads scrape through the mountains. The planner estimates that 11,000 recently subdivided lots sit on Watauga's roadripped mountains. At Beech Creek, a developer graded a zig-zag through the mountain's steep north face. Because the winter sun doesn't hit the north slope, the slick wet roads washed away after the first winter, leaving the developer with a several thousand dollar loss and the mountain with an eroded skin. The planner estimates that hundreds of road miles like Beech Creek were abandoned without the first

house ever being built. "There's no way to stop that road building—all we can do is require permits to keep the stone stabi-
lized."

Road erosion scrapes the mountain clean of its protective
vegetation, causing floods and runoff. When the slope is scalped,
rain water runs off without being absorbed by the streams and
lakes. In a monograph for the Economic Development Agency,
Ray Derrick estimates that after a one-inch rainfall, 28,000
gallons run off a one-acre dirt slope. This causes sedimentation,
flooding, and the lowering of the water table. Robin Gottfried,
in her master's thesis, says that sedimentation is a major effect
of resort construction which bares the mountains of their natural
vegetation for ski slopes, access roads and second homes. And
at developments like Hound Ears, more trees than necessary are
cleared so each lot owner can have a mountain view.

Bacterial pollution in the rivers and streams has increased
dramatically because the developments do not adequately provide for disposal of refuse and human wastes. Small developers
can't afford the expensive treatment plants, while larger resorts
like Beech were placed under a federal building moratorium because their sewage facilities are not adequate. Community
Planner Tom Foxx says that even if the waste is treated properly,
the effluents—treated chemical wastes—kill fish. "What we're
going to have around here is pure dead water." At Sugar, septic
tanks are on one-half acre lots. A local joke is that when Sugar
Mountain people flush their commodes, the water table rises in
the valley.

But the people living at the base of Sugar in the Norwood
Community aren't laughing. They resent the developers who
caused them to lose their farms and peaceful valley. Most of the
30 farming families left in the hollow depended upon prized
farmland for their food and clear streams for their water. All
that has changed now. Sugar Mountain Corporation built its golf
course adjacent to their land. Access roads to the resort traverse
the natural water flow and eliminated some streams. While the
remaining streams must absorb all of the water, Norwood people
are flooded each spring. The farmers say they can no longer harvest a garden since the water floods their crops and destroys
everything in its path. One farmer tried to sell his land, but nobody wants to buy property that is flooded each spring.

Another farmer said the streams won't hold a lizard now because they're polluted from Sugar's wastes. Every fish in the creek died, and the water became undrinkable even for the cows. Not only is sewage running down the stream beds, but the mountains themselves are crumbling into a mud and rock mixture which dams the streams.

Sugar contractors laid tiling on the access roads to keep them from washing away. The tiling reroutes storm water directly onto Norwood gardens. "Before Sugar Mountain came here," said one woman, "we didn't have a drop of floodwater. Now it runs into my living room, kills the vegetables, and rises as high as the top of the pick-up's wheel base."

But Sugar executives refuse to respond to the Norwood people. The woman whose garden was flooded called Sugar's executives to explain what was happening to her community as a result of Sugar's development. The executives did not assist Norwood, but Sugar's maintenance people did throw old wood, junk tires, and metal scraps against her fence which sits about 20 feet from the resort's golf course. "Early on," said the woman, "they tried to buy us out—now I reckon they're going to try and run us out."

Noise from the snowmaking machines crashes into the valley late at night. "When they're making the snow you can't sleep. I never heard such a racket in all my life," said one woman. The ski-doos and trail bikes add to the racket and scare the animals. "It's not so peaceful any more." she said.

Invading the Culture

Like the problems at Norwood, the effects of tourism and resort development cannot all be measured by cost-efficiency analyses. Mountain living is packaged and huckstered so that business-filtered remnants of mountain culture can be purchased at tourist shops which capitalize on Al Capp myths of corn pone, white lightnin', and geehaw whimmeydiddles. "The new shops make you think hillbillies are old-withered-up people who just sit and make those whimmeydiddles all day long," said a young man who returned home to Watauga after completing college. "We aren't someone's vacation fantasy. What the Florida people and developers don't understand or care about is that their actions keep us from living the way we want."

Shopkeepers who long served their communities with food, farming equipment, and such have learned they can make more money by catering to free-spending tourists and second home dwellers. Richard Mast, county precinct captain and son of the former owner of Mast's General Store, described the changes in his family's recently sold store. "The new owners raised the prices so that local people can't afford to shop there any more and now what was once a community supply store and meeting place is a curio shop which sells pottery made from organic dirt and three-dollar baloney sandwiches which you have to make yourself." The new owners of Mast's store, also the oldest Exxon station in the United States, plan to build an 85-seat delicatessen, with funds provided by Exxon, to commemorate the Bicentennial. One burley tobacco grower wondered what use a high-priced restaurant would be to working farmers.

Local community associations have been taken over by second-home dwellers. In Mast's Valle Crucis community, monthly get-togethers and pot luck dinners once provided a forum for community discussions. Second-home people flooded the summer meetings, elected one of their own as chairman, and cancelled winter meetings because they wouldn't be able to attend. Angry farmers labeled them the "Valle Crucis Cut-up," boycotted the meetings, and are forming a new community group. Mast says Valle Crucis is being torn apart.

Local landmarks are also being torn apart. Dutch Creek Falls has been a Valle Crucis playground for as long as anyone can remember. Two years ago, the falls were bought by an attorney who is building a house on a platform he erected directly over the water. To make room for the house and equipment, the attorney scraped the area clean of its trees and brush. He also hung a no trespassing sign on the land.

"The first thing those outsiders do is hang up a no trespassing sign," said a woman whose grandmother's name is carved on the Dutch Creek Elm. "Land that was used for hunting and shortcuts isn't ours to use anymore, and there are so many signs you need a plat to tell where you can go," she said. "I used to love this land, but now I'm ready to move out."

Politics As Usual

Despite any evidence to the contrary, development agencies like the Appalachian Regional Commission (ARC), which are supposed to assist communities like Valle Crucis, actually pave the way for the current brand of tourism and recreation development. During the past nine years, the ARC has sunk a half million dollars in studies to evaluate the economic and social benefits of tourism and resort trade in Appalachia. Most of the studies warned the Commission to stay away from investments in tourism. ARC's preliminary study on the impact of tourism in Appalachia warned the ARC that the resort industry is one of "low pay and seasonal in nature." Later, a Spindletop Research Project confirmed the earlier conclusions and added that the tourist business creates a "service class of an entire body of people." The single study which supported tourism was sponsored by the Department of the Interior, whose primary concern was to alleviate urban congestion.

The conclusions of ARC's own studies describe resort investment as a "poor financial risk and deterrent to mountain life." In 1974, the ARC released a film documenting bulldozed mountains sprayed with resort developments and quick-snack shops. Its public relations director said the film was made to "sensitize the region's people to abuses of tourism and resort development."

But the bankrupt developers found the way to their governor's ear, and ARC's sensitizer was filed with the rest of their mountain of tourism studies. A new $100,000 study was called a "significant document making the case for public assistance to the troubled resort industry" by North Carolina's Secretary of Natural and Economic Resources, James Harrington, a former Sugar Mountain executive. The *Twin Sentinel* flatly disagreed with Harrington in an editorial which called "the ARC attempt to reinflate the resort balloon at public expense, the height of folly."

Some critics call the problem of resort development more a matter of structure than of judgment. One observer said, "The ARC serves the narrow interests of specific industrialists under the guise of community development." The ARC implements its development programs through its development district, called

Lead Regional Organizations (LRO). The LRO Board consists of mayors and county commissioners—no directly elected members. In the overall economic development program for Watauga and Avery counties, LRO Director Carl Tuttle wrote that the "tourism industry should be the single sector of the economy to make the largest gain." To make sure the prophecy is fulfilled, the LRO does not court small factories which would employ farmers during off-season because such development might interfere with the "scenic quality" required by resort developers. Even though Watauga's factories are generally cut-and-sew, low wage, labor-intensive, predominantly employing women, farming families agree that they provide a steady income which allows them to keep their land. Tuttle's new development plans support tourism and resort interests at farmers' expense. In his 34 recommendations for community development, Tuttle directly supported resorts while making not a single recommendation to assist the 950 farmers who live in Watauga.

H. C. Moretz, director of the five-county community action program (WAMY), suggests that the reason the LRO pays no attention to farmers is that there are no farmers represented on the multi-county planning body. "Oh, they'll tell you that elected officials who sit on the LRO board represent all the people but the fact is that farmers and poor people have no direct access to it. Elected officials who sit on the Board are either small businessmen who financially gain by tourist trade or they're politically tied to realtors and developers."

Farming is pretty well written off by the chamber of commerce and county commissioners. When asked about the demise of farming in Watauga County, the chamber of commerce director—who works for Tweetsie Railroad—said, "Don't get hung up on agriculture."

But farmers and some planners are hung up on agriculture. Tom Foxx, chief planner with the North Carolina Department of Natural Resources & Community Development, says, "We must scrutinize whether public taxpayer dollars should be further used to subsidize the resort business." Foxx, paid by the state to provide local planning and management services, is at odds with LRO planners who ignore farmers. "The initial impact of resorts on tax revenues was positive," said Foxx. "Now the services required to sustain the developments, higher taxes, and land prices are not worth the additional dollars collected." Foxx says resorts will increase their demand for services. "What we're doing is providing an inordinate amount of services to attract skiers and don't have money left for people who've lived here all their lives."

Foxx has his first opportunity to stop taxpayer assistance to resort developments in a current thrust by Sugar and Beech Mountains to win federal-state-ARC financing of a water and sewage treatment plant. Sugar's President Hard figures that a government bailout is the only thing that will save the resorts from certain bankruptcy. Hard wants an area-wide $10 million waste treatment plant to serve Sugar, Beech, and the town of Banner Elk. Without Banner Elk's participation, the resorts are not eligible for federal largesse. Banner Elk's mayor says, "We need a sanitary district to relieve developers from having to operate their own sewer and water facilities." But the mayor privately fears that a sanitary district consolidation might be the first step toward resort rule.

He's right. To obtain the necessary federal money, 51 percent of the property owners must sign a petition. Two categories of property owners live in the farming-resort communities: one is a freeholder—property owner, and the other is a resident freeholder—resident property owner. Since Beech and Sugar's resort owners greatly outnumber permanent Banner Elk citizens, freeholder voting status would plunge long-time residents into an automatic minority.

The developers are looking down the road and want to incorporate the sanitary district into a township. Then they would be eligible for federal funds, revenue sharing, and state aid. "What we're planning is incorporation but it's not good to publicize the fact; it's too political," admits Sugar's publicity director. Since the developers want legalized liquor in dry Banner Elk, the first confrontation is likely to force a difficult change on the community. Hard says he doesn't want to lose control of sewage facilities or a power base. "If we create a city and give up control, we'd be creating a monster in Banner Elk that could kill us."

Farmers near Banner Elk say their farms are more likely to be killed than the resort business. Valle Crucis and Matney residents, who live in the shadow of the resorts, approached Foxx and his planning board to stop developers from encroaching on their communities. They asked the zoning board to prohibit resort-type developments in their townships. But Foxx couldn't do much. "We could zone them residential—that allows golf courses and subdivisions—or industrial." North Carolina state law makes no provision for agricultural zoning.

Foxx says alternatives for agricultural developments do exist, but the state never passed enabling legislation and officials aren't interested in lobbying for farm legislation. "The destruction of farming is a self-fulfilling prophecy. Officials read statistics of declining farm land and decide that farmers don't want to work the land any more. Then they assist developers which increases the farmers' problems, and go back and read the statistics," said Foxx. The county could provide incentives to maintain farmland as farmland and commit non-farm land to non-urban types of development. "If a 100 acre tract of land was not used for 20 years, it doesn't have to be taxed. Five-acre conservancy zones could be designated to prevent large developers from tearing up farmland and ecologically fragile wood-land. Nearly 50 percent of the county would fit into this type of zone," explained Foxx. But developers and county officials aren't interested in land preservation because high growth development brings in money. After the tourism boom, said Foxx, "Farmers lost the right to decide how they will use their land."

Land Use Planning and the Small Farm

Foxx believes the county can stop unchecked growth with the tools of land-use planning and regulatory ordinances. The Watauga County Planning Board recently imposed regulations to stop the developers' worst abuses: excessive subdivisions, building violations, erosion, and flooding. But regulations must be enforced to be effective, and even then they don't halt development—at best they slow it down.

Government-controlled land-use planning has its own set of problems. Who will control land-use decisions? Will land planning create more uncontrolled growth or will it be structured to encourage cooperative development? Resort developers are against government intervention and call the free enterprise system "its own plan." "The value and use of land will be determined, rightfully, by the open market," said realtor Randy Phillips, who tripled his land investments in one year. Phillips says government control and planning raise the costs of development. County planners say strict government control will inhibit destructive growth and direct future land development so that it will benefit all county residents. Farmers generally want nothing to do with government control because, as one farmer said, "The right to private property is inviolate." But the developers' easy money gives them a higher right than the farmers. Whether government control or *laissez-faire,* farmers are locked out of the decision-making process and excluded from growth plans. "Maybe we ought to build land and market cooperatives which would benefit our kind of people instead of those scalawags who cross state lines to destroy our land," said a Watauga County farmer. "Maybe," he said, "we ought to ask ourselves if this growth thing is good for us."

"Whither growth?" is a question never asked by developers or government planners. Developers think of land as a commodity and not as a resource. The government says the land resource should be developed for its optimum use. While the private developers and government planners appear to be at odds over what generally amounts to environmental issues, both eliminate farmers with their growth plans. The only real question is "how fast the elimination." The contradiction of specialized growth is implicit in the system of development. While the federal government does not have an overall land use and growth policy, grants for highway construction, sewer lines, water systems, and the like define land use. Government-paid definition is encouraged by some developers who, like Hard at Sugar, define land's highest use by its highest profit. Since growth agencies like the Appalachian Regional Commission only invest in projects with the greatest dollar return, private developers and government policy complement each other. Senator Morris Udall agrees when he says the politics of land use has given special interests "the upper hand."

State planning is little better than federal planning. Special interests are acutely evident in North Carolina's defeated Mountain Area Management Act which was introduced in the 1974 N. C. Legislature. The act called for a 15-member mountain commission to oversee a comprehensive state-local plan which

would designate specific areas of environmental concern and enforce orderly development through a system of permits.   The
political nature of the bill is evident; timber and utilities are
exempted from regulation.   The opposition, according to an
article by Joy Lamm in *Southern Exposure,* called the bill
"politically tied."   "The state government is mistrusted by past
action, condemnation powers would destroy an already weak tax
base, lack of local input ensures that development would be tied
to a small group of individuals and there is no provision for class
action suits."

County-controlled zoning fares no better in the test of
planning by special interests.   Zoning defines land use by the
dollar.   Foxx says the LRO planners predicted that "between
1970 and 2020 agriculture will drop from the present level of
approximately 6,000 people to about 3,000 and then will stabilize at this reduced level."   "What planners don't understand
is that implementing policies like zoning for special interests will
cause their statistics to come true," said Foxx.   But many farmers don't intend to bow to statistics. "The land is our frontier,"
said a farmer, "and we're planning to get up a posse."   The posse
is forming slowly and deliberately.   "To survive we need a
cheaper way to buy supplies, and markets to sell our produce,"
explained a farmer whose wife took a cut-and-sew job and whose
children help cut their burley tobacco.   "What we've done is
organize a Farmer's Market to sell some of our extra crops."
The market was created as an economic alternative for farmers
who don't have outlets for their vegetables.   Most of the 80
farmers who sell their produce through the market own small
farms worked primarily for family consumption.   Now the
market allows them to sell their excess and plant additional crops
in anticipation of a cash market. "Last year," said one market
regular, "I made $3,000 during the selling season. It certainly
helped out."

The market costs $2 to join and a flat 50 cents fee per
selling day.   Food stamps are accepted by sellers who undercut
supermarket prices by ten cents per item.   Quality control is
sometimes a problem since the group doesn't set standards, but
most of the vegetables are graded by the growers.   "We can't
let bad quality vegetables slip in because we'll lose our customers.
We're still in the organizing stages about things like that," said
one of the planners of the market.

One farmer thought organizational problems stemmed from the fact that the market was conceived and implemented by non-farmers and picked up by the New River Resources Conservation Development Committee. "It may never have gotten started without outside help, but we must make decisions about the market's future." The consensus is that farmers must have an outlet for their crops and access to equipment.

Market members say they should be more tightly organized and focus on one issue at a time. "The first thing we need is a permanent facility so the vegetables won't wilt in the sun and we can sell refrigerated cheese and meat," commented one market organizer. "Then we should buy a truck to deliver produce regularly to shops." Cutting production costs is high on the issue list. Common purchases of grading or spraying machines would reduce expenses and create greater purchasing power for the entire community. "After that we can think about farming-support industry like canneries, mills, and supply stores," said a farmer who has been nearly wiped out by the tax increases and the rapidly increasing prices of equipment. "We've got the problems of all small farmers in the country and the added affection of resort developers," he said.

Agricultural extension agents could be helpful, with the organizational experience they've gained from the 20-year-old cooperatives which sell specific items like sheep and cattle to large eastern markets. Their wool and cattle cooperatives generally involve larger farms, but the county agent said, "If a man has one cow and it meets our standards, he can sell it through us for a better market price than on the open market." The cooperatives, like the Farmer's Market, return more money per pound to the farmers than the open market while saving customers money.

Looking down the road, market organizers see several phases of action which must occur simultaneously. The first is a transition to high yield, not so labor-intensive specialty crops. "The problem is that we're not competitive with mid-western farms. Our mountain land is not suitable for mechanized farming, so we have to go with things like cabbage or burley tobacco." Second, a combination of crops would prevent farmers from being wiped out if one crop didn't make it. Third, a more tightly organized Farmer's Market, with capital and equipment shared by the participants, would free money for other things. Fourth, outlets must be found for the produce. "Community Development Corporations like Chicago's Fedco and the Cooperative League in Washington, D.C. would be direct connections for our produce." Fifth, farming-support industries like cooperative canneries, supply stores, and mills would increase the markets, return money to the community, and allow farmers to grow more. "If we get this underway, we wouldn't have to work for the resorts or cut-and-sew places," said a woman who works as a maid for Sugar. And finally, the resort developers must be forced through community organization and county government to halt their farmland gobbling and ensure a more equitable use of tax dollars. "The Farmer's Market is a way to get a handle on all these problems, but we've a long way to go," said a market member.

Some tax and land plans could be implemented through the Farmer's Market. The "circuit breaker" system rebates taxes to farmers if property taxes exceed a fixed percentage of income. If no taxes are paid, a rebate is paid by the state treasury. In Michigan, the circuit breaker is tied to state and local planning.

The Internal Revenue Code, in occasional cases, is used to preserve farmland. Section 501(a)(3) governs the rights and responsibilities of certain non-profit corporations. Groups have incorporated themselves, gained non-profit status from the Internal Revenue Service, and donated land or money to an incorporated land trust. The trust is committed to maintaining the land as farmland and leases the land back to farmers. Because of the non-profit aspects of the trust, the land is not taxed and the donor receives tax advantages from the transaction. The problem, of course, is giving up the land to the corporation. In California, the Northern California Land Trust intends to use its land base as a vehicle to help migrant farmers live and produce on their own land—land owned by the trust but theirs to work and pass on to their children.

Land banks are another land planning device. In British Columbia and on Prince Edward Island, the land bank system allows the state to purchase farm land. Instead of a retiring farmer selling his land to a corporation, the state buys his land and leases (or sells) it to another farmer.

The problems caused by corporate developers are not new to the mountains. Company towns used to mean coal towns which served the interests of the coal operators. Now a new set of corporate strip miners are disturbing the land and organizing labor around their resort-oriented needs. Mountain people are again going to be forced to fight for the right to decide how to use theor own land. County officials say that planned land-use regulations will block future over-development. They have hired professional planners to carry out what they perceive the public will to be. Who decides what that will is, and how conflicting demands on land-use will be accommodated in a rational land-use policy are decisions which cannot remain in the hands of the owners of the company towns if farming is to survive.

NOTE

[1]Yolande DeB. McCurdy (Robin Gottfried), "An Ecosystematic Analysis of the Vegetation of Hanging Rock State Park, Danbury, North Carolina," MA in Ecology, University of North Carolina at Chapel Hill, 1976.

EDUCATION AND EXPLOITATION

by
Mike Clark

> "You need an educated class willing to run the local businesses, set up schools and other institutions which train people to do the job and keep their minds and mouths shut. You need an educated class to keep poor people in their 'place.' "

It's always a mixed blessing for me when I return to Berea. On the one hand, I can always visit with old friends. On the other hand, I usually get the depressing feeling that the school goes its old ways without really being influenced by outside forces which affect all of us. As you are already learning, it's a hard and difficult process to change things, here on this campus or in our larger society, for change only comes in response to pressures from people who are determined to obtain their goals.

I work in the hills and hollers of Southern Appalachia—an area many of you now know as home—West Virginia, Virginia, Ohio, Kentucky, Tennessee, and North Carolina. Most of my work is with poor people's community groups who are actively trying to change things in the mountains. Today I want to share with you some experiences, ideas, and events which I have seen,

SOURCE: *Speech given at Berea College, March 1971, and later published in* Mountain Life and Work.

AUTHOR: Mike Clark, *who was raised in the Smokey Mountains, is a Berea College graduate and a former newspaper reporter and photographer. He is currently the director of Highlander Research and Education Center, New Market, Tennessee.*

heard, and felt, over the past four years. Tremendous changes are coming to the mountains—whether we want those changes or not. I hope some of you are already aware of these changes and I hope you are determined to participate in these events so we can all begin to influence the people who rule this country; for I came here today to talk about taking political and economic control of our country.

Before I talk about how people might begin to take power, I want to say a few words about Berea College and about the changes which I feel sure all of you are experiencing as you spend time at this place.

For those who are from Appalachia, who love it, and who want to remain, I'm sure each trip back home is a hard one; for the more formal education we get the more we tend to be isolated from the old ways and from our own people. Perhaps we need to examine why this isolation takes place, for I don't believe it is an accidental thing.

If I understand Berea's aims today, you students before me are the cream of this year's crop. You are the best-read, most likely to succeed in the Berea Way, of those thousands who applied to come to this lonely and sometimes barren ridge. Those of you who stay here for four years and obtain a degree can be expected to go out and become teachers, doctors, scientists, engineers—the people who help to keep this country prosperous. Those of you who have successful careers and stay in the mountains can be expected to become leaders of Appalachia. I hope not, for I believe we have too many leaders in Appalachia already. There are too many now who believe they know what is best for the area and for the people. Most of these so-called leaders or experts are trained as I am trained, and as you will be trained, to think only as middle class people with middle class values and middle class ways. Because of this, I would say that many of Appalachia's problems result from the fact that its leaders are middle class and formally educated. Let me explain further.

Back home, wherever that is, and probably within sight of this building, an older culture is dying before our eyes. The physical changes are the most obvious; the old cabins, nestled in a quiet cove with surrounding chicken coop and barn, are almost gone. For the expanding middle class their way of life differs little from that of middle America. The differences which still exist are mental ones: nostalgic memories stirred by church hymns or traditional music, the old friendships built before mills and roads brought a new way of dealing with one's neighbors. But for the working class, the unemployed, the subsistence farmer, the people who barely get by, the old ways and values are still a living thing; and the relationships based on an agrarian society are not so easily discarded despite the invasion of roads and schools and TV sets.

Our real problem in Appalachia is not whether the old culture will die—only time will decide that now—but whether mountain people can begin to find ways to deal directly with the political and economic forces which are at work in Appalachia and in the rest of the country. If Appalachia's problems are to be solved, it will be done because we understand our past and because we begin to find out who really controls this country. We need to know who really has economic and political power in Appalachia.

America began to move away from Appalachia with the utilization of the steam engine, the building of the railroad, the opening of the West, and the coming of the automobile. Because the terrain was rugged and difficult to penetrate by modern means of transportation, it was easier for businessmen and speculators to go west, to gain their tremendous profits in the drive toward western seashores. But Appalachia was not forgotten for long. It was too rich, too valuable, and too close to the existing centers of industry in the Northeast.

By the late 1890's the robber barons who made their fortunes in rails, steel, textiles, and coal began to turn their attention to new areas in their search for raw materials and cheap labor. Appalachia, in all its unspoiled splendor, was close at hand, for the area had huge attractive reserves of coal, timber, and water. Rail lines, which had paralleled the major ranges and opened up the broad river valleys years before, began to penetrate the deeper regions of the mountains. In these rugged hills, the oldest in the world, the robber barons found tremendous riches. In eastern Kentucky alone, thirty-three billion tons of coal would eventually be surveyed. Over the steep slopes from New York to southern Georgia were stands of magnificent virgin timber, perhaps the most luxuriant growth of hardwood timber on the American continent. It was a land of great beauty, a wilderness island in the midst of America's industrial push west. And just as the early pioneers and land speculators devised ways to steal this land from the Indians, the northern industrialists began to devise ways to steal it from our ancestors.

The opening up of Appalachia in the quest for raw materials and cheap labor was not unique. Across the Atlantic in their corporate offices European businessmen began to look for more markets for their wares. The targets they chose were Asia, Africa, and Indochina. The race was on across the world. For as industrial production rose to new heights, new markets were needed to supply raw materials, cheap labor, and more profits.

The first industrial incursions into this region were tenuous ones, but over a period of time they were successful. My family, and yours, helped to make them that way. In the coal mines, lumber camps, paper mills, and textile sweat shops of the Southern mountains, our ancestors helped to develop this region with their labor and their lives. My folks worked for the paper mills and textile plants. Your families may have worked in the mines or mills. No matter. The results are the same. They worked for it, but we don't own it. Today, if we look across the region, we can see the process still going on. The names may differ from the past—U.S. Steel, Ford Motor Company, Standard Oil, Mead Corporation, American Enka, Eastman Kodak; the names may differ, but the process remains the same. The people who labored to build this country do not own it. Neither do their descendants. We are a people with some material benefits, but we are still at the beck and call of the rich 10 percent of our population who still control 90 percent of the capital wealth. And one percent of that 10 percent actually controls how all the wealth is spent. Impossible in a democracy? Yes, it would be impossible if we lived in a democracy. But we don't.

Much of this is probably not new to you. I didn't come here to bore you with facts but to ask some questions which I think you will all face very soon. My questions have to do with what we can do to change these facts, if you think they need to be changed.

Historically, people who wanted change in this country have

worked with the people who are most obviously oppressed: with the union movement, with Black people, and with other oppressed minorities around the country. But so far all of these attempts to build a national movement have failed because people have been bought off, leaders have been killed, or the present system has found a way to meet the immediate needs raised by the protestors. Let's look briefly at some of these attempts.

In the late 1800's the labor movement in this country developed along two radically different lines. The first branch was the traditionally-oriented trade unions or guilds, established along authoritarian lines and interested in obtaining immediate material benefits for their members. They wanted a larger piece of the pie, and they were willing to live alongside the bosses if they could get some pie. Out of this group came the American Federation of Labor and the Congress of Industrial Organizations.

The other branch was quite different. The best known was the Industrial Workers of the World, popularly known as the "Wobblies." It was the most militant union industrial America had ever seen. It called for one big union of working people and for the workers to control and own all phases of production. It wanted no bosses. "This land is ours," the union said. "We built it, we should control it, lock, stock and barrel." Its tactics were the boycott, the strike, the lock-out, and, if necessary, industrial sabotage. "If we can't have it, it won't exist," was the cry. And as the union chapters spread across the land, they became a threat which could not be ignored. Eventually the strikes were defeated, the leaders jailed or killed, and the members blacklisted from any jobs. By the early 1920's the Wobblies were finished as an industrial power. Yet today many of their ideas are echoed in the demands for community control of police and schools and industry. The Wobblies failed and they were destroyed, but their ideas live on.

In the 1930's with the Great Depression, a militant mood began to build again in the country. Big business and the federal government were forced to take action to overhaul a collapsing system. With the reorganization of the federal government and the reforms pushed through by Roosevelt, the last militant drive of the labor unions ended in defeat. The reforms were just enough to satisfy people and to keep them from tearing the whole thing down. With the National Labor Relations Act and the right to collective bargaining given to the unions, the last attempt to build militant unions ended. FDR's recognition of labor's right to organize was a short-term boom for the unions; but in the long run it meant that the unions could be controlled, channeled, and directed by big business through the courts and through arbitration and contracts. FDR's ploy to save the system by changing a little part of it succeeded. The American trade unions, already rigid and authoritarian, bought a larger piece of the pie and none of the action.

Mountain people—in Detroit, Cabin Creek, Blair Mountain, Gastonia, Elizabethton—fought for their unions during this time. Yet today these unions have sold them out.

In the 1950's and 1960's Black people began to build a movement which had potential for a national coalition of poor people. Instead of just calling for more material benefits, Black people called for liberation from psychological oppression and then for economic equality. Organizations such as the NAACP, CORE, and SCLC began the fight. It was brought to a new level by the demands of SNCC and later the Black Panthers and other Black groups. And just as the Wobblies were attacked, so were Black leaders. Over the past few years we have seen Black leaders killed, jailed, or driven into political exile because of their beliefs and because they were willing to stand up for their beliefs.

In the mountains things were no different. In the early 1960's a group of poor mountain people was formed in eastern Kentucky known as the Appalachian Committee for Full Employment. It was composed of unemployed miners who were trying to force their union and the coal operators to pay them full union wages. During the same time that Black people were demanding social and economic equality, poor mountain whites were making many of these same demands of the federal government. The methods chosen by the government to deal with both groups were the same—the War on Poverty. For in the same way the government bought off militant people in the 1930's, the War on Poverty was established to keep this country's poor quiet.

The results can be seen around the country where federally-funded projects have attempted to check, channel, and thwart the drive of America's poor for political and economic rights. Where the government has been unwilling or unable to step in, the large private foundations have provided financial backing, knowledge, and, most importantly, guidance.

But while these programs have often diverted people's attention from some basic needs to the more easily controlled tasks of grants, paperwork, red tape, surveys, etc., the basic alienation of the American poor remains—along with their desire for drastic change.

The reasons the poverty programs failed could be held to faulty reasoning: It's not really possible to save this system by reforming it. It might have failed because of a lack of will power on the part of most Americans. But I would say the program failed because of lack of trust. No government in history has paid its own people to overthrow it. Many poor people, either instinctively or consciously, realized this and never trusted the motives and designs of the federal bureaucrats and politicians who run the program. This has been especially true in the mountains where people are traditionally distrustful of any government. Part of this distrust is based on years of being on the bottom and seeing all kinds of promises but very little action. Poor people, because of their economic experiences, look for action—not talk. In order to survive they must become experts in judging people's motives and designs. They may not always make the best decision for themselves in the long run; but they are usually accurate in judging who has the power and who will use the axe, if and when it falls.

What does all this mean to you people as students at Berea College? I think it has a lot to do with you, for many of you will probably end up being the people who will attempt to control the lives of Appalachia's poor folks.

Earlier I talked of how the northern industrialists came into Appalachia and began to exploit its natural wealth and cheap labor. That trend continues, and it will continue for the foreseeable future unless there is an abrupt shift in how people act in the mountains.

It's not enough to simply own a region if you cannot control it and then exploit it. In order to do this, you need people in the middle who will do the dirty work. You need an educated class willing to run the local businesses, set up schools and other institutions which train people to do the job and keep their minds and mouths shut. You need an educated class to keep poor people in their "place."

Around the world wherever empires are built, you can see the same process at work. An educated class is built from the native people—a class whose loyalties are not to their own people but to the people who own the region. These educated people, the middle men, are paid well with material benefits, money, status, and power. And they rule with an iron fist. Once such a system is established, it's not necessary for the rich folks to pass down orders to their stooges. The stooges already know what their self interests are and they will protect them at all costs.

But where do you recruit an educated class and how do you train them? It's my belief that Berea College and other colleges in Appalachia have fulfilled this function since they were established.

Berea College was founded by missionaries who believed they had a divine purpose to bring enlightenment and education to this rugged land. But education in our society means control, not freedom. It means a way of transferring values from one group to another so that the first group can keep the second under control. The missionaries, or their supporters, ended up by controlling the people they were trying to save from eternal damnation. This was true in India with the British, in Latin America with the Spanish, and in Appalachia with our own missionaries. By setting up an educated class of native people who are trained to be doctors, lawyers, teachers, and social workers, a larger society can control a smaller one or one without political power.

How does Berea help in all of this? I think it's fairly evident. By training the people who have functioned best in mountain schools, Berea helps to insure a steady supply of people who will take over the reins of power when the existing local leadership dies. By teaching students a new set of values, values based on the dominant middle-class American society, this college insures that people can be co-opted and bought off like most other people in this society who are formally educated and middle class.

This system will always allow a few people to fight their way to the top, for those few are needed to control those who are on the bottom. Remember this fact, and remember it well, fellow Bereans: We got where we are by climbing over the backs and bodies of our brothers and sisters who now work in the mills, mines, and factories, who fight in Vietnam, or who sit jobless at home and wonder what tomorrow will bring.

I don't know what your reaction is to these thoughts. I don't mind anger. I hope you do have some kind of reaction. I also hope you don't feel guilty if you find some truth in what I say. Guilt is the traditional means of escape for the American liberal who rushes out into the cold world to help poor folks, whether poor folks want help or not.

The problem is not with poor folks. The problem is with the rich folks in this country who control the wealth and then control us. And part of the problem is with the middle class who help to perpetuate this evil, racist system which we now have.

We have the potential as a people to build a democratic society in this country. If we want to build a democratic society we must begin to figure out how the present system works. Then we must begin to build a new society which will serve people, not exploit them.

THE MAINTENANCE OF CONTROL

Section IV: The Maintenance of Control

The seven articles which follow demonstrate a variety of ways in which control over the colony is maintained socially, culturally, and politically through the various institutions, commercial control of music, the development of stereotypes through literature, maintenance of economic dependency, control over state and local government, and regional planning and control agencies such as the Tennessee Valley Authority and the Appalachian Regional Commission.

Jim Branscome in "Annihilating the Hillbilly" points to ways institutions working in the area: the media, ARC, education, health care, governmental agencies, the corporate structure, and the church denigrate native culture and exploit the native. They act to destroy mountain culture which is antithetical to exploitative, technological society.

Rich Kirby in "Our Own Music" describes the process whereby commercialization of mountain music serves to control, limit, censor and change the style of the art. Topical, industrial, protest music which challenges the system is eliminated or repressed.

Don Askins in "John Fox, Jr., A Re-Appraisal. . .". analyzes Fox's depiction of mountain people which produced a stereotype and shaped the nation's view of the mountaineer and his homeland and legitimized the exploitation and colonization of a "backward" and "inferior" people. Fox consistently views both the area and the people in contrast with the Bluegrass and denigrates the former while lauding the latter.

Tom Bethell and Davitt McAteer in "The Pittston Mentality" describe and analyze the disaster at Buffalo Creek and show the failure of state and federal authorities to assess Pittston's responsibility and impose sanctions. Corporate power in Appalachia controls people's lives and keeps them economically and politically dependent and powerless.

Two excerpts from "Coal Government of Appalachia" show corporate control over the state government of West Virginia. One article reviews the corporate connections of a former governor, and another points to influence in the building of roads.

James Branscome in the TVA Story reviews the history of what began as a progressive program to develop the Tennessee Valley and how it has become an exploiter and unresponsive governmental "corporation."

Phil Primack in the "Hidden Traps of Regionalism" points to the ways in which the federal government and programs to assist the area serve corporate interests and further control Appalachian people.

ANNIHILATING THE HILLBILLY:
THE APPALACHIANS' STRUGGLE WITH
AMERICA'S INSTITUTIONS

by
James G. Branscome

Not too long ago, CBS television featured, back-to-back on Tuesday nights, three of America's most popular TV programs: "The Beverly Hillbillies," "Green Acres," and "Hee-Haw." This combination has to be the most intensive effort ever exerted by a nation to belittle, demean, and otherwise destroy a minority people within its boundaries. Within the three shows on the one night, hillbillies were shown being conned into buying the White House, coddling a talking pig, and rising from a cornpatch to crack the sickest jokes on TV. All of this occurred on the same channel, all only a short while after Eric Sevareid completed his nightly lecture to the American public on decency, integrity, dignity, and the other great American virtues to which he and his network supposedly adhere.

If similar programs even approaching the maliciousness of these were broadcast on Blacks, Indians, or Chicanos, there would be an immediate public outcry from every liberal organization and politician in the country and a scathing editorial in the *New York Times* about the programs' "lack of taste." The new culture people would organize marches and prime-time

SOURCE: *Published by* Katallagete: Journal of the Committee of Southern Churchmen *(Winter 1971), (c) 1970, 1972, The Committee of Southern Churchmen, Inc.*

AUTHOR: James Branscome, *a native of Hillsville, Virginia, is a free lance writer who writes for* The Mountain Eagle.

boycotts and perhaps even throw dog dung at Eva Gabor as she emerged from her studio. They might even go a step further and deal with that hillbilly maligning patriot, Al Capp. But with this, as all things Appalachian, *silence*. America is allowed to continue laughing at this minority group, because on this America agrees: Hillbilly ain't beautiful.

The treatment given by the media to Appalachia is only one example of the massive failure of America's institutions for over a century to meet the needs of the people of the region. From government at all levels to churches, private welfare agencies, schools, colleges, labor unions, foundations, newspapers, corporations, *ad infinitum,* the region has received an unequal share of exploitation, neglect, unfulfilled promises, and misguided assistance. This is not to deny that America is interested in Appalachia. It has been interested for some time, in the peculiar American way, in Appalachia's worth to industry, of course; only erratically has it been interested in the plight of the people. General Howard of the Freedman's Bureau is said to have convinced Lincoln that he ought to try to do something for the poor mountaineers after the Civil War. The New Deal brought the then rather progressive Tennessee Valley Authority to one part of the region, but TVA's recently developed capacity to burn lower-grade strip-mine coal brought the hellish human and material waste of that process to Central Appalachia. John Kennedy and his brother Robert both professed an interest in the hillbilly and his vote; and eventually, under Lyndon Johnson, their interest was translated into the Appalachian Regional Commission, a unique political and economic development agency. But, as Harry Caudill remarked, its assignment was "one of the most awesome tasks since Hercules cleaned the Augean stables."

It is especially Herculean when one applies some good American economic analysis: The agency was given about *one-twentieth* of the amount of money it takes to fight the Vietnam war *for one year* and told to use the amount over a *six-year period* to correct almost two hundred years of abuse to areas of a thirteen-state region! Now, for the riddle: If 80 percent of that money was spent on highway construction, how interested is America in the nineteen million people who occupy the territory the Commission described in 1964 as "an island of poverty in a sea of affluence"? This is not to deny that the Commission has had a positive influence on the region. Given the parameters in which it had to work, it has made many investments in public facilities and increased the accountability of state governments to their Appalachian sections. If Congress extends the program and significantly increases its funding for human resource programs, the Commission may be able to bring to the Appalachian poor some of the services even ghetto residents have come to accept as normal. There are some big *ifs* in this, not the least of which is the critical question today about the relationship between institutions and people: *If* an institution today had unlimited funding and unlimited maneuverability, could it bring to people the services they need without destroying the kind of life they want to live?

If the ability of institutions to respond to people's needs is judged on the basis of the Federal government's enforcement of the Mine Health and Safety Act of 1969, then the answer to this question is *NO!* Loud and Clear. The death of 78 coal miners in Farmington, West Virginia, in November, 1968, led to the passage of that act, which is the strictest mine safety legislation ever to get through Congress and be signed by a President. The public outrage over Farmington gave government one of its few opportunities to wrestle successfully with the powerful American coal-oil conglomerates. But something did not work: Either there is no will or there is no desire by the bureaucracies (*the institutions*) of the Federal government to go to the mat with the conglomerates. Perhaps their interests are so inseparable that no contest is ever possible. In any case, since the disaster more than 700 miners have been killed *in the mines,* and more than 10,000 have been crippled or injured. There has been no public outcry to avenge the deaths of these men.

Moreover, the Social Security Administrations's own Bureau of Disability Insurance provides some statistics to indicate how the bureaucracy of one fundamental institution—government— deals with one crisis that the 1969 Act sought to meet: compensation for miners disabled by "black lung" contracted after long years and long hours inside the mines. The national average of claims under the black lung provisions of the act processed by the Bureau of Disability Insurance is 43 percent. However, only 22 percent of the claims from eastern Kentucky and 24 percent of those from West Virginia had been processed by early November, 1970. And 52 percent of the processed claims of West

Virginia miners have been denied; 71 percent of Kentucky miners
have been denied. The figure for claims denied for the rest of
the nation is only 20 percent.

If one reflects on the fact that in the past seventy years
there have been 101,000 mine deaths, a number larger than the
total of miners now working in Appalachia, and double the number of Vietnam deaths, then an inability of the government to
enforce regulations, which are mild by international comparison,
strikes one as not speaking well for the capacity of political institutions to use the very arena of action which is theirs by
democracy's mandate, or for the American public's capacity to
care for anything more than the dramatic, never the substantial.

And with the death of thirty-eight men in the Finley mines
near Hyden, Kentucky, on December 30, 1970, the nation was
once again reminded about the plight of miners in Appalachian
coal pits. The President of the United States himself announced
that he would have visited the scene of the disaster—if it had not
been for "the bad weather." (Yet no airports in the region were
closed.) The more important visits (those of inspectors from the
Bureau of Mines) had not been made on schedule some few days
before the disaster in order to check correction of violations of
the 1969 act cited on earlier visits. It was the same old refrain:
New priority guidelines for violations under the new act had just
come down from Washington to the bureau's regional office in
eastern Kentucky, necessitating a new schedule of visits; the
office itself was short-handed because some of the inspectors had
taken "Christmas leave"; the mine operators complained that
some provisions of the act were a peril to the safety of miners
and mines; no one, not even the inspectors, understood all of the
provisions of the act, etc., etc. In any event, the Finley mines
were permitted to operate up to the disaster on December 30.
They did so in large part because an inspection required under
the 1969 act was subjected to the administration of a bureaucracy which, perhaps unwittingly but in fact, vetoed the will and intention of the Congress and the President and—if representative
government is still taken seriously—the will of the people. Thirty-
eight men were dead. And the litany of charges: Families of the
dead miners were exploited by funeral operators, insurance
claim men, and government officials; cover-ups and double-
dealings and politics were involved in the "hearings" to inquire
into the disaster; illegal "prime-cord" and "dynamite" had (had

not) been used in the mines; an inspector "who didn't want his name used" said a simultaneous explosion ten times the legal limit was set off when the men were killed.

The complete failure of the American corporate structure to accept even a charitable responsibility for the region that it has raped so successfully is hardly arguable. Since men like General Imboden in the late nineteenth century went before the state legislatures to argue that "within the imperial domain of Virginia, lie, almost unknown to the outside world and not fully appreciated by their owners, vaster fields of coal and iron than in all England, maybe, than all Europe," the American corporate community has wrenched resources estimated at a worth of nearly one trillion dollars from the mountains. While these companies pay some of the highest dividends of any company in the world to their already wealthy shareholders, the *communities* in Appalachia where those resources originated survive on a subsistence economy, if "survive" is the proper verb here. Often more than half of the money in circulation comes from state and federal welfare coffers. This fact alone tells us something about the American Way, if not the American Dream. Three months after the June 30, 1970, deadline for reducing the amount of hazardous dust in the mines as required by the 1969 legislation, 2800 of the 3000 underground mine operators had not complied. These same companies have continually opposed severance taxes on coal and medical benefits for the more than 100,000 disabled miners who suffer permanent lung damage from poorly maintained mines. Apparently when these corporate institutions of American free enterprise become incredibly wealthy, they cannot be expected to have the conscience even to allow *government* to pay for the damage they have caused. Somewhere that "pursuit of selfish interest accruing benefits to all" went astray in Appalachia.

It has always been asserted with pride that America takes great interest in its children. "Dr. Spock" has been a best-seller for over a decade. But his "child-dominated" society has interest only in certain children. Of the more than 925,000 poor children under six in Appalachia, as estimated by the office of Economic Opportunity, only about 100,000 receive cash benefits in their homes from Aid to Dependent Children or other similar welfare programs. The national participation rate of children in Head Start programs decreased three percent between 1967 and

1969; the Appalachian participation decreased 15 percent. The greatest decrease in Appalachia, significantly, was in full-year programs, those regarded as most beneficial to poor children. What other group in the country received the benefits from the cutbacks in Appalachia is unimportant here; that "hillbillies" were not on the priority list is obvious.

In the area of prenatal and infant care, the situation in Appalachia is even more alarming. Examinations of children in several areas of the region have shown that as many as 70 percent have "parasitic infestation" (the euphemism for "worms"), one of the causes contributing to Appalachia's unusually large number of retarded and "slow" children. "Worms" abound in the miserable shacks and grassless yards American free enterprise has put aside for the hillbillies. If the Appalachian infant mortality rate were reduced at the same rate as East Germany's in a five-year period (as reported by the World Health Organization), the lives of more than 1,000 children a year could be preserved. In certain areas of the region, as a matter of fact, the situation worsened over a decade. In Lamar County, Alabama, for example, the infant mortality rate rose from 32.5 percent to 40.9 percent in ten years. The rate in Hancock County, Tennessee, rose from 21.4 percent to 42.2 percent in the same time period. While increased attention to child development at the national and regional level promises to better the situation, for many the help comes too late. Perhaps if it were possible to estimate the number of mountain children who would be alive and healthy if Appalachia had received and retained a more equitable share of the nation's wealth, certain institutions could be persuaded more easily to invest in saving children. Until the case is made, however, we all labor under the curse of the prophets and the admonitions of the poets (increasingly, it seems, the only sane people) that the final judgement on civilizations and their institutions rests on how well they treat their children, who are—in appeal at least—the "least of these."

The Appalachian child who makes it to school does not find the institution America has charged with equipping youth with basic "survival" skills any better prepared to meet his needs. The inability and unwillingness of local government to tax the property and extractive resources of large corporations have resulted in an educational system in Appalachia that can only be compared with that in the so-called "underdeveloped" nations. Add to this the fundamental resistance of middle-class teachers to acknowledge the unique cultural heritage of the Appalachian youth, and you have a laboratory for studying one of the classic historical struggles between a nation intent on erasing a minority from its midst and a people intent on preserving their identity and lifestyle at any cost to themselves. In an Appalachian school, the middle-class aspiring teacher is just as insistent that the student be aggressive, obedient, and joyless—in short, everything that his culture tells him he is not—as is the teacher in the Bureau of Indian Affairs school on a reservation. No wonder, then, that as many as 65 percent of the students drop out of school before graduation, a figure 25 percent higher than the national average.

Responding to the fiscal needs of the Appalachian educational system alone is overwhelmingly beyond the capacity of government agencies as they are presently funded. In 1967, for example, the Office of Education estimated that the construction needs of the thirteen Appalachian states represented over 42 percent of the total school construction needs of the entire country. It would require the additional expenditure of $363 million annually just to raise the per pupil expenditures of Appalachian schools to the national average. Title I of the Elementary and Secondary Education Act, designed to increase the amount of funds available for the teaching of disadvantaged students, will spend more money on an equal number of students in the schools of Westchester, New York, where the number of poor students is about three percent of the student body, than it will in a county in Appalachia where more than half of the student body is poor. Talent Search, a special college recruitment and placement program funded by Congress for high-risk students, spends only 3.8 percent of its money in Appalachia as compared to the 10 percent the region deserves. Simply to make the Appalachian educational system equal in educational resources to the nation would require a political miracle at a time when no miracle workers are to be found.

While Appalachia is heavily populated with institutions of higher learning supported by various religious denominations and state governments, the region's students are no better served than in the secondary institutions. Neither is the region's need for professional and para-professional manpower. No institution of American society, in fact, is more divorced from Appalachia than the higher educational system residing within it.

Forced by accrediting agencies, visiting boards, and hundreds of other pressures to maintain a facade of "academic excellence" and "a sound liberal arts education," usually with Christ thrown in somewhere, the church-supported schools spend little time thinking about the community below their own mountainside. Their emphasis on admitting Appalachian students is so small, their tuition so high, and pressure so intense from church supporters outside the region to admit their sons and daughters, that most of these colleges have an inordinately high percentage of students from states like New Jersey. Certainly to these colleges, "Christian" education has nothing to do with serving the victims of Caesar's educational system.

The "open door" policies of state universities are often, in actuality, "revolving doors" for the Appalachian student. Once the student is admitted and the fees collected (either from him or the state), the more aggressive and well-trained student from another section of the state or nation, and the freshman composition teacher, can be expected to send the Appalachian student scurrying home. In January, 1968, the National Association of State Universities and Land Grant Colleges summed up the record of their members in the region as follows: "To maintain quality they raised student charges substantially, turned away qualified students, limited enrollments, and refused urgently needed public services."

The regional universities and colleges place little emphasis on promoting a regional consciousness on the part of their students. In fact, there is not at present a single Appalachian studies program in the region which could begin to rival the offerings in Far Eastern studies or astronomy. One, Eastern Kentucky University in Richmond (which in reality is in "Blue Grass," not "eastern," Kentucky), prides itself on its training and research in law enforcement and police work. All this continues and intensifies a channeling process begun by the elementary teacher to send the Appalachian student—ashamed of his background and ill-equipped to meet the needs of his region—into middle-class society outside the region. The sixteen-year process of credentializing that the student has been subjected to, becomes finally a ticket to the world of Dick and Jane, Support-Your-Local-Police, and the affluence of America built at Appalachia's expense. So a region that needs more than 200,000 college graduates—a minimum of 5,000 physicians, many thousands of nurses, teachers, businessmen, government leaders, *ad infinitum*—finds no help in another of America's institutions.

◄◆►

The young Appalachian left behind by the higher educational system is destined to be the object of a number of complicated channeling devices. The male youth, if he can pass the examinations, is eligible for one of the more obvious youth channeling programs in the country, the Army. Selective Service does not maintain records on Appalachians as a group, but the number in the service is estimated to be higher than their percentage in the population because the armed forces represent the only opportunity available to many young mountain men to be assimilated into mainline America. Recent Department of Defense figures report that West Virginia led the nation in per capita Vietnam deaths. *Twenty-five* West Virginians per 100,000 population had been killed, compared to *seventeen* per 100,000 nationally.

For the youth who seeks opportunity and training in some special opportunity program, such as the Job Corps, the fate may not be a great deal more encouraging. Because of the Job Corps' resistance to establishing a center especially for Appalachian youth, the mountain youth are sent to camps, both within and outside the region, where the population may be largely urban and black. Combining his unfamiliarity with urban life and blacks with his affinity for home and family, one can easily understand why the Appalachian youth drops out of the program in equal frequency with his Indian counterpart. Even if he lasts the program out, according to Joint Action in Community Service (the agency that contracts with the Job Corps to place and counsel graduates), it is very difficult to find him a job or to locate a person or agency willing to assist him in the mountains.

For the youth who has not dropped out of school by the ninth grade and who has no prospect of attending college, vocational training represents the only channel open to him. Many find it a wicked channel indeed. Three years ago the Education Advisory Committee of the Appalachian Regional Commission reported that half of all vocational training programs in the region consisted of agriculture and home economics—areas in which there were almost no job openings. Since that report the Commission and the states have required all 235 vocational programs which they have funded to teach job-relevant skills. While only half of the schools are now open and no thorough evaluation has been reported, it is expected that the schools will be better than their predecessors.

As late as 1968, however, the West Virginia Commission on Higher Education reported that only about 18 percent of the students in that state had access to vocational training. Given the fact that post-high school vocational training is still not available to the majority of Appalachian youth, this major channel of supposed opportunity still has a long way to go to overcome the serious handicaps it has represented in the past. And with improvement, vocational education's role may be to channel all the so-called disadvantaged students into neat slots, thereby diminishing not only the student but vocational education as well. Additionally, so long as vocational school graduates must leave the mountains to find jobs, the region will remain a loser. It is already estimated that 900,000 high school graduates will have to leave the region to find jobs in the 1970's. They will thus become the people the cities do not want and the people the region cannot afford to lose.

The fact that a mountain youth takes advantage of the opportunity to finish high school and apply to college does not guarantee that the tentacles of the system will let him go. For instance, one of the high-risk students I taught in the Upward Bound program at Berea College applied and was accepted in the fall at that college. During the preceding spring he was approached by a recruiter for the FBI who gave him a hard sell on the benefits of working for the Bureau in Washington. He dropped the idea of college and is now a low-paid clerk at FBI headquarters. Since this incident I have checked with school personnel in other areas of the region and found that intensive recruitment of high school graduates in rural areas is now carried out by the FBI and other government agencies which are not finding recruits for their clerk and typist posts in urban high schools. The law, it seems, has a long arm and no qualms about modern forms of impressment.

Most high school dropouts (except those who marry and somehow find work or welfare payments) and unemployed high school graduates eventually end up being forced to migrate to find work. In West Virginia, for instance, 70 percent of the young people leave before they reach the age of 24. Usually referred to as "migrants" instead of more accurately as economic refugees, these youth join the more than 3,000,000 other mountaineers who have preceded them to northern cities such as Cincinnati, Chicago, Indianapolis, and Detroit since World War II. If they have a skill and happen to move during a period of relative economic prosperity or are willing to accept a job run by the stopwatch and a minimum-wage employer, as many do, their chances for survival are good. If, on the other hand, they have to move in with kin in the "back home" ghetto, the situation is different.

The unemployed and unassimilated mountain youth finds himself in a bewildering ghetto that defies description and usually comparison with the ghetto life of other minorities. He also finds that in the city there is one thing more unacceptable than a black man—a hillbilly, a ridgerunner, a briarhopper. For the first time in its history America has recognized him as a cultural minority. If he ends up in juvenile court for stealing hubcaps, he is offered leniency with his promise to go "back home." Judges make this offer to youth whose families may have been in the city for three generations and can only consider themselves Cincinnatians or Chicagoans. If the mountain youth enters school, studies show that its foreign nature drives him out faster both psychologically and physically than it does his black migrant counterpart. For the mountain youth who is unable or unwilling to assimilate into the life of the city, there is little help from the social service agencies which understand much more about blacks than they do about him. He is thus not only without help, but, perhaps more appallingly, he is without an advocate in a city that he does not understand and that does not understand him.

One group of Appalachians who are consistently overlooked and underserved by the institutions of the region is the blacks. As a matter of fact, both government and the so-called "private" welfare agencies refuse to acknowledge the existence of blacks in Appalachia. While the percentage of blacks in the region as a whole is low, about eight percent, they make up the entire population of many small isolated hollows and ghost coal towns abandoned by the corporations and welfare and poverty

agencies. Because the backbreaking jobs that brought black imports into the region are gone and because of the discrimination
and competition with the majority of poor white people for
jobs and welfare funds, their existence is a poor one indeed. As
yet no agency report or journalist has documented the presence
and needs of these people, let alone described the culture of a
minority group in the midst of another cultural minority.

—◆►—

America's unwillingness to deal with the Appalachian as he
asks to be dealt with is probably no more baffling than America's
seeming obsession with studying and understanding his unusual
life-style and values. Even before the Russell Sage Foundation
published John Campbell's *The Southern Highlander and His
Homeland* in 1921, writers and sociologists were making forays
into the mountains alternately to praise, condemn, and collect
the mountain culture. The studies are still being made today
in the midst of the technological revolution that is, for all practical purposes, making "Middle Americans" all alike. The conclusions of modern studies do not differ from those made in the last
century. The Appalachian is different: He is existence oriented
and independent, has close family ties, is fatalistic, cares for his
elderly, *ad nauseam.* If, as Robert Coles and others have written
of late, the Appalachian has a life-style and a culture that America would do well to listen to, if not opt for, why has America
failed so miserably at times to meet his needs?

Part of the answer is obviously that Appalachia has been
in the main a colonial territory for America within her own
boundaries. The life-style of the region served well the need of
the mining and lumbering corporations for a subjugated people
willing to be peasants in their own land. Even after the bloody
struggles to unionize the mines, the capacity of America's institutions (including its labor unions) to contain the people's struggle
remained intact. What on the surface appear to be quaint people
whose character can be explained away by their isolation and
independence may, in fact, be more accurately described as the
historical reaction of the people to colonialism.

What on the surface may strike Jack Weller, author of
Yesterday's People (published jointly by the University of Kentucky and the Council of the Southern Mountains), as ignorance,

that keeps people from taking polio shots even when they are offered free transportation, may, in fact, be better explained by Frantz Fanon, a physician himself, who argues (in *The Wretched of the Earth*) that the Algerians resisted "modern medical techniques" as long as the French were in control of them but adopted the new practices immediately when they felt themselves to be in control. I have seen parents who had refused to have their children vaccinated at the public health clinic willingly have them vaccinated when it was "our" medical students who were giving the shots.

One has to understand how the medical profession in Appalachia operates to appreciate fully this phenomenon. He has to sit with a young father in the mountains and hear the story of how his pregnant (now deceased) wife was turned away from the hospital because he did not have the hundred dollars that the doctors demand as a down payment for those who do not have medical insurance. It is these same compassionate physicians who, rather than reform their own practices to meet the needs of people, have turned the Medicaid program into a thriving business. The potential earnings from the health support programs is so great that a recent government report on physician manpower in Appalachia suggests that it is one of the most lucrative enticements to get doctors into the region—another colonial characteristic. A largely overlooked article in the Louisville *Courier-Journal* in the spring of 1970 describes how doctors and pharmacists have turned Medicaid recipients in eastern Kentucky into addicts and junkies. It repeats reports from law officers and nurses who had seen "whole families lying around in a stupor" and "glassy-eyed teenagers and small children wobbling or passed out along the roadside" because they took narcotics prescribed by their physicians. One eastern Kentucky pharmacist admitted that 65 percent of his business came from Medicaid dues. "The poor people are substituting pills for faith," he explained. He went on to describe why the abuses are allowed to continue: "It would cost the pharmacist a great deal in time away from work to keep a check on abuses. They are just too busy."

By and large, American institutions can be said then to have held no respect for the mountaineer other than for his use as an object. Richard Davis notes in his recent book, *The Man Who Moved a Mountain* (Fortress Press), that large metropolitan newspapers used the notorious Allen feud of the second decade of this century in Hillsville, Virginia, to interpret the Appalachian to their urban readers. Said one:

> The majority of mountain people are unprincipled ruffians. They make moonshine, 500 horsepower, and swill it down; they carry on generous and gentle feuds in which little children are not spared, and deliberately plan a wholesale assassination, and when captured either assert they shot in self-defense, or with true coward streak deny the crime. There are two remedies only— education or extermination. Mountaineers, like the red Indian, must learn this lesson.

Another editorial in a northern newspaper on the same event went on to conclude:

> The Scotch-Irish mountaineers are more ignorant than vicious, victims of heredity and alcohol, and now that their isolated region has been invaded, must change or perish.

One of the often overlooked aspects of the outsiders' fetish for Appalachia has been the premises that underlie their own prescriptions for the people's future. One finds in Jack Weller's influential writing, for instance, comments such as these:

> There is little in the mountain child's training that would help him develop self-control, discipline, resolution, or steadfastness. Thus the way is prepared for future difficulties in the army or at work.

> Since the culture inadequately prepares its members to relate to "outsiders," there is a great need for "bridge" persons, who can help the suspicious and fearful to respond more positively to persons and institutions which will increasingly be of help and resource—doctors, psychiatrists, clinics, hospitals, government in the form of agency officials, policemen, public health nurses, welfare workers, and recreation leaders. The mountaineer's suspicion of these persons limits his use of them in crisis occasions, when, in fact, their purpose is to be of assistance in many ways at other times. He needs help in

understanding that government and other institutions
cannot be run in person-oriented ways but must be conducted in great measure on an impersonal objective basis.
He needs help in seeing that a certain amount of bureaucratic organization is a necessary thing, and that a government does not exist for an individual person's benefit
(*Yesterday's People*, pp. 157-158).

Responding to the Appalachian culture, outsiders are
sometimes incapable of interpreting the evidence because of their
own training in research procedures. One (while, of course, re-
peatedly enjoining his readers that he is passing no judgment on
the culture) describes mountain music and literature as "regres-
sive looking," "nostalgic and melancholy," over all, "repressive."
Thomas Merton, on the other hand, after hearing some mountain music for the first time at the Abbey of Gethsemani, gave
the correct interpretation and exclaimed, "It's apocalyptic!"
Perhaps the only fair hearing the culture of the people of Appalachia will receive is from persons like mystics and contempla-
tives who do not assign ultimate importance to the things that
the modern state and today's seminarians have blessed as divine.

The churchmen, educators, welfare agents, independent do-
gooders, journalists, and novelists, and the institutions which
pay their salaries—that is, those who have made an extraordinari-
ly good living trying to "understand" the mountain man—have
studied the Appalachian not to learn from him but rather to
"teach" him, to "school" him, to "doctor" and "save" him by
making him into what they already are: Middle America, assimilated into the America of the television and Holiday Inn—the
America which Tocqueville and Faulkner warned was founded
by those who sought not to escape from tyranny but to establish one in their own image and likeness.

Only in Appalachia, for example, have the mainline churches come upon a "Christian" religious expression which stands
four-square against what they expect religion in America to
"do." The rejection of the *Christian Century* by Appalachia has
baffled and annoyed the mainline churches, their agencies,
theologians, and sociologists. And because the church in mainline America is unable to understand the church in Appalachia, it
has so far been unable to assimilate it. It has failed, in other
words, to make it over into another of the agencies of social

welfare alongside HEW, Social Security, the Council of the Southern Mountains, the Commission of Religion in Appalachia, the Home Mission Board, etc. The mainline churches have tried to obliterate the Appalachian churches with demands for expressions which are "progressive," "rational," "contemporary," and "relevant." What more haunting and, in many instances, disgusting examples of the philosopher's ambiguity of "reason" or the theologian's "original sin" could be asked for? The liberal churchmen, Catholic and Protestant, insist that the snake handling of the mountain man must come to an end (as must the "emotionalism" and "irrelevance" of the black church). And all the while the mainline, liberal church ignores the more dangerous "snake handling" which defines their efforts to "save" "yesterday's people"—a phenomenon described precisely by Thomas Merton in "Events and Pseudo-Events: Letter to a Southern Churchman."

The answer to the question of why mountain culture must be destroyed is to be found in the fundamental truth about the technological society: The techniques which undergird all our institutions are assimilating all of us into, as Jacques Ellul puts it, "a society of objects, run by objects." Institutions in the technological society—and this means not only those of the state and its welfare bureaus, but the do-good agencies which include churches, schools, and colleges—can respond only by and with the techniques of the impersonalized, bureaucratic means, procedures, and formulas. Technique cannot discriminate between right and wrong, justice and injustice. That is why the same technique that gives (and takes away) the health card to an ailing miner assimilates the pious mountaineer into the five-point grading system and the Uniform Sunday School Lesson.

The meaning is clear. Institutions working in Appalachia today can work for only *one* end: the extinction of the Appalachian people. The extent to which these institutions have so far failed in the venture is the extent to which this people and culture have successfully resisted the formidable pressures of the institutions of contemporary technological society. Why institutions—political and private, church and business, industrial and charitable—have responded and can respond to the Appalachian the way they have tells us something very important about power and powerlessness in the technological society.

For those of us who believe that the struggle is for the soul of man in the technological society, the resistance of Appalachian culture against assimilation into middle America demands earnest, indeed prayerful, attention. The struggle of the mountain man against the institutions of the technological society is the struggle to deny his right to define any man by his relationship to Middle America. The struggle—whether one believes that it comes out of resistance informed by left-wing Protestantism or opposition to colonialism and genocide—has implications for all who question not only the possibility but the quality and character of any resistance to the totalitarianism of the technological society.

OUR OWN MUSIC

by
Rich Kirby

In 1916 an English scholar travelled through the Southern mountains hunting for folk songs from England, and he found them—so many, in fact, that his book, *English Folksongs of the Southern Appalachians,* has become a classic. Cecil Sharp found more than just songs; he found a culture alive with music. In England, he recalled, only the old people remembered folk songs, but in the mountains:

> I found myself for the first time in a community in which singing was as common and almost as universal practice as speaking. With us of course [in England] singing is an entertainment, something done by others for our enjoyment. The fact has been forgotten that singing is the one form of artistic expression that can be practiced without any preliminary study and that it is consequently just as ridiculous to restrict the practice of singing to a chosen few as it would be to limit the art of speaking to orators. . . .In an ideal society every child in his earliest years would as a matter of course develop this innate capacity, and learn to sing the songs of his forefathers in the same natural unselfconscious way in which he now learns his mother tongue.

SOURCE: *A revised and enlarged version of an article of the same name which has appeared in* Mountain Life and Work *and* Sing Out! *among other places.*

AUTHOR: Rich Kirby *plays old time mountain music and lives on a farm in Dungannon, Virginia.*

> And it was precisely this ideal state of things that I
> found existing in the mountain communities. So closely
> indeed is the practice of this particular art interwoven
> with the avocations of everyday life that the singers,
> unable to remember a song I had asked for, would often
> make some such remarks as "Oh, if only I were driving
> the cows home I could sing it at once."[1]

Sharp's book contains hundreds of beautiful tunes and
poetic texts, but there was more. He looked only for English
material and so passed over the vast amount of fiddle music
brought from Scotland and Ireland, the banjo learned from
Negro slaves, and the powerful Regular Baptist church singing,
which apparently originated in the mountains and may have
come from the Cherokee.

The people who made this music were, like their music, in-
dividualistic, democratic, and self-sufficient. We don't need to
be romantics to see in the mountains of 1916 a free and independent people to whom this stable culture gave the strength
and vitality to stay that way. Today, living in the ruins of that
culture with that independence only a memory, it would be good
to try to analyze what happened to it.

People's culture comes from the way they live and in turn
feeds back into that way of life. If you change one, the other
must change with it. So as Appalachia was turned into a colony—as people stopped being independent farmers and started
working for wages—the old music was cut loose from its place
and quickly began to decay. Cecil Sharp's co-worker Maud
Karpeles observed:

> It is surprising and sad to find how quickly the instinctive
> culture of the people will seem to disappear once they
> have been brought into touch with modern civilization
> . . .and the singing of traditional songs is relegated almost
> immediately to that past life which has not only been
> outgrown, but which has no apparent bearing on the
> present existence.

What is not as obvious, though, is that our mountain culture was exploited in its own right, picked apart and ruined just
as surely as our forests and coal seams. Old time music was

removed from its roots and nearly destroyed. It had been free—made by many and shared by all. Now it was put in packages and sold. It is striking how this process went hand in hand with the opening of the coalfields.

Coal brought cash and jobs to a region that had seen little of them before, and it also brought goods that the cash could be spent on. Why is it that the new drives out the old? Why did people move off the farms to the coal camps? Why did they begin to buy clothes rather than make them? or buy phonographs instead of fiddles? I can't answer that—but these things happen.

> The modern era of folk music recording began shortly after World War I when Ralph Peer of Okeh Records went to Atlanta with portable equipment. A record dealer there offered to buy 1000 copies if Peer would record the singing circus barker "Fiddling John" Carson. "The Little Old Log Cabin in the Lane" and "The Old Hen Cackled and the Rooster's Going to Crow" were cut. According to Peer, "It was so bad we didn't even put a serial number on the record, thinking that when the local dealer got his records that would be the end of it. We sent him 1000 records. That night he called New York on the phone and ordered 5000 more sent by express and 10,000 by freight. When the national sale got to 500,000 we were so ashamed we had Fiddling John come up to New York and do a re-recording of the numbers." (From folklorist Harry Smith in an introduction to a collection of early recordings)[2]

Soon many mountain musicians began to make records. Commercial music was not so exclusive then as now. A company might record and press 1000 records and sell them in the singer's home area. Much rare and beautiful music of varied style and good quality was recorded in this way.[3] One variety in particular, the string band style, for instance, of Gid Tanner and the Skillet Lickers,[4] gained quite a following; and instrumental music began to crowd out quiet unaccompanied singing.

As time went on, musicians began to tailor their songs to records, and in some ways this music seemed more fitting than that transplanted from barns and living rooms. The Carter

Family from Scott County, Virginia, became the first recording "stars" in the area. Their "Wildwood Flower" is today the most widely known instrumental piece in the Southern mountains. Other stars followed: Mainer's Mountaineers, Charlie Poole, eventually Jimmie Rodgers, "the Singing Brakeman." In 1925 the Grand Ole Opry went on the air, certainly the best-loved radio show in history.[5] Week after week superb entertainers like Uncle Dave Macon and Arthur Smith came into thousands of homes, entertaining families that ten years earlier might have been at barn dances or telling ghost stories around the fireplace. And aspiring musicians now had an opportunity. Ten years earlier they had looked no further than the barn dance for an audience.

The lives of the listeners were changing profoundly too. As many people moved into the coal camps, country traditions like square dances and husking bees began to wither. Working in the mines left little leisure for fiddling. Musicians by the hundreds quit playing and fell out of practice. A few became professionals and worked at radio stations (still today the first step up for professional musicians). Food was bought, not made, and so was music, and gradually the record came to define *where* music was and *what* it was.

For the first time young musicians imitated new styles while older ones began to feel awkward and old-fashioned. Then came the Depression with desperate poverty and brutal oppression that smothered most of the mountain music.

Traditional culture—the wholeness of mountain life—was gone. The old music had no context, little meaning or social place. Traditional songs died by the thousands; record companies and promoters controlled popular taste, and hungry musicians tried desperately to please them. Mountain people's music, like their labor, was bought and sold in the market.

II.

By the 1920's the mountains had, for better or worse, become part of the American economic system. In 1929 the system went abruptly from better to worse, and in the mountains worse was only the beginning. FDR saw "a third of a nation ill-fed, ill-housed, ill-clad"; in the mountains it was a third of a third of a third that was not so destitute.

Social and cultural life, like economic life, went to pieces in this crisis. In some places miners, their families, and neighbors turned to militant labor organizations; and outside organizers who arrived in these communities found people singing about their situation.

Topical singing is not new in the Southern mountains. Indeed, almost all mountain folk music was "topical" in that it related directly to everyday life. When economic or political forces were felt, they too were reflected in songs. An early 19th century song describes unemployment:

> They've got a brand new machine
> Prettiest thing you've ever seen
> Hand me down my peg, my peg, my peg and awl
>
> Peg a hundred shoes to my one
> My shoe pegging days is done
> Put up my peg, my peg, my peg and awl[6]

The Civil War, which deeply split the mountains, produced a large number of songs. Here is a white abolitionist song from east Kentucky that I learned from my grandmother:

We're Stolen Souls From Africa[7]

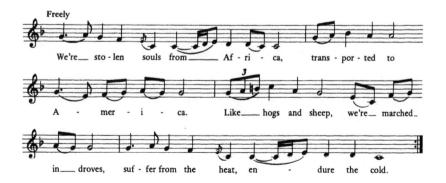

Similarly when coal mining arrived, singers responded with a large body of music. One of the most widespread was the following:

Dream of the Miner's Child[8]

And one of many songs to come from Claiborne County, Tennessee, in the 1890's was this one:

Buddy Won't You Roll Down the Line[9]

la - bor re-belled a - gainst it, to win it took some time, But while the lease was in ef - fect they made 'em rise and shine. Bud-dy won't you roll down the line, bud dy won't you roll down the line. Yon-der comes my dar - lin' com-ing down the line. Bud-dy won't you come down the line, bud-dy won't you roll down the line, Yon-der comes my dar - lin' com-ing down the line.

My opinion is that just as coal mining subtly forced people off their land, commercial recordings and radio forced them away from their music. But for two generations or so, mountain musicians commented extensively on the changing society around them, leaving us with a lot of good music and a good example.[10]

Two songs, both composed by Kentucky miners' families in the depth of the Depression are the following:

Which Side Are You On

Come all of you good work - ers, good news to you I'll
tell,____ Of how the good old un - ion has come in here to
dwell. Which side are you on, which side are you on?

The Allais Song

Get up in the mor - ning,____ hear the whis - tle blow,____ Get up in the
morn - ing,____ hear the whis - tle blow, Grab my po - ta - to can and a - way I go.

Which Side Are You On was written by Florence Reese, a miner's wife in Harlan County, while her husband, an organizer for the National Miner's Union, was hiding from the gun thugs who would have killed him if they could. *The Allais Song* was written by my cousin Bill Maloney who worked in the Allais Brothers' mines near Hazard. Mrs. Reese's song was learned by NMU organizers who taught it to people in New York and elsewhere. The song took on a life of its own and popped up in the deep South in the 1960's as a freedom song. It is sung widely by people who have no idea it originated in Kentucky.[11] My cousin's song was posted at the Allais mines (Allais would have fired the author had he known who it was), but it has not gone much beyond the family. I happened onto it at a family gathering near Jackson.

This brings up an interesting question: What was the function of topical music in this period? Were such songs sung only in living rooms? At rallies? By men at work or on strike? On marches and picket lines? The question needs to be studied some more, to say the least. My own idea is that if the miners did not sing as much as the civil rights fighters of the 60's, they still had a musical time of it. A lot of their movement was in small isolated fights in remote areas not visited by outsiders, and most of the musicians were not professionals. But I think that if research were done, a large number of mining songs would be found, many in the nature of protest.

Two more examples include *The Coal Black Mining Blues,* which was written in 1932 by Nimrod Workman of Chattaroy, West Virginia, and was more or less unknown until Nimrod issued a record in 1972. *How Can A Poor Man Stand Such Times and Live* was recorded in 1931 by Blind Alfred Reed of Pipestem, West Virginia, and has become somewhat widespread through recordings by the New Lost City Ramblers. The last two stanzas were added quite recently by Hazel Dickens and Alice Foster.

Coal Black Mining Blues

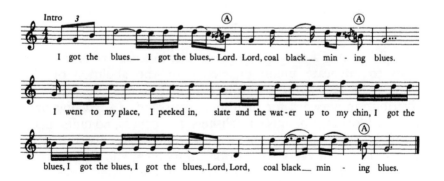

I got the blues___ I got the blues,__ Lord. Lord, coal black___ min - ing blues.

I went to my place, I peeked in, slate and the wat-er up to my chin, I got the

blues, I got the blues, I got the blues,_Lord, Lord, coal black__ min - ing blues.

How Can A Poor Man Stand Such Times And Live

There once was a time when ev-ery-thing was cheap, But now pri-ces near-ly

puts a man to____ sleep; When we pay___ our gro-cer-y bill, we just

feel__ like ma-king our will, Tell me how can a   poor_man stand such times and live?

How did it happen that one song was recorded and the other not? How many more like these have been lost?

It is worth stopping at this point to look at the ways songs are learned and spread around. Most of the well-known songs from the coalfield struggle of the 1930's come from one east Kentucky family—Sarah Ogan Gunning, her sister Aunt Molly Jackson, and their brother Jim Garland. All three were active in the NMU and worked closely with outside organizers for that body. And it was through these organizers that the songs were spread to people who felt they were important. In 1937 and 1938, researchers from the Library of Congress "collected" the family's music and from then on it has been part of our heritage.

So getting a song around is a risky business if the song happens to advocate union organizing or the abolition of strip mining, or some other controversial matter. In the 1930's the distribution network for such songs consisted of a few organizers and folklorists—no music publishers, no records, no radio, magazines, or newspapers. None of these things had existed in 1890 either; but then every song stood on its own, and a piece could travel if it was its nature to do so. But when radio came along and *excluded* industrial music, a powerful form of censorship was established.[12]   And it's still with us, to be broken only by already famous singers of exceptional ability like Merle Travis (*Sixteen Tons*) or Loretta Lynn (*Coal Miner's Daughter*).

I think that situation can and should be challenged. Music is too important to be left to the businessmen.

III.

Most music heard in the Southern mountains today comes via radio, records, and TV from commercial musicians in Nashville. It's good music. It ought to be: The best musicians in the South have left home and gone to Music City to make it. And it really is the people's music now, widely known and loved. Alone among major forms of entertainment, country music is made by working people of the mountains and the South, the same people who listen to the music. Alone among entertainment forms, it talks directly about people's lives, often about the singer's own background. Dolly Parton must have been speaking for a lot of people when she wrote:

> No amount of money could buy back from me
> The memories I have of then
> No amount of money could pay me
> To go back and live through it again
> The good old days when times were bad[13]

But after saying this, I want to bring up some criticisms I have of the music industry, since they bear on the question of people making music. Mostly, I resent its turning music into a commodity, made in Nashville much as cars are made in Detroit. In other words, production and distribution are controlled by a relatively small group of people who try to make money from it. This has bad results:

1. One style (the "Nashville sound") is made dominant over all others, like fiddle music, old ballads, or children's game songs. People should choose their favorite style, true, and should have a choice. The extreme diversity of musical styles heard in the mountains fifty years ago was a very good thing, and I wish it hadn't been lost.

2. Only professional musicians are heard. Nashville's musical standards are so high (and its equipment so expensive) that most people feel like musical idiots next to them; so they shut up and listen.

3.   The flood of material overwhelms most institutions that provide for face-to-face music-making. Square dances are all but gone; only the churches have been able to shelter a large amount of handmade music. Records and radio are where it's at. Amateurs almost always imitate professionals; original songs are rarely heard.

4.   A few (a very few) people decide what music is going to sound like. The producer, not the singer, decides whether to put trombones in a love song or when to change keys. I think some producers are tone-deaf. Only a real superstar will have artistic control over what his/her records will sound like. It depends, in most cases, on what the producer thinks will sell. So while the music talks about average people, it is many steps removed from belonging to them.

5.   It perpetuates a form of control over people. There is a kind of sameness to most C & W music, especially in subject matter. It says that love, marriage, divorce, religion, and beer are important; it says by implication that strip mining, black lung, boring or dangerous work, cruddy schools and health care are not so important. There are exceptions (see below), but when it comes to politics, C & W is mostly pretty conservative: endorsing the flag, the war, and women who know their place. People's history and their past and present struggles are mostly ignored.[15] Since C & W largely dominates what people hear, it helps define how they look at themselves and their lives. I think it encourages them to be placid, which I think is bad.

IV.

Country music was always a stepchild of the music industry; its writers and artists, often underpaid, were not in the trade association (ASCAP) which controlled most material. So when ASCAP went on strike in 1941, industry executives latched onto country music as programming. It immediately went nationwide and, to everyone's surprise, proved quite popular. A war story relates that Japanese soldiers, trying to insult Americans during battle, shouted "To hell with Roosevelt, to hell with Babe Ruth, to hell with Roy Acuff." In the boom years following 1945, commercial country music got to be truly bigtime.[16]

Homemade music continued to decay. It carries on among old singers, particularly in the Blue Ridge and in eastern West Virginia. But most often people sing material that has already been recorded and standardized (if not written) by an established musician. Some songs of Jimmie Rodgers or Roy Acuff, in fact, are so widespread they are practically "folk music." For a while, anyway, it looked as though old-time music was headed for the museum. As late as 1964, a group called Friends of Old-Time Music was arranging New York concerts for musicians unknown in their own communities.

Why this decay? I wish we could figure it out. Maybe with some study, we could. Part of the answer, I think, is in a conversation I had with two old fiddlers in Pike County who haven't played in twenty years. The reason, they said, was "all this fighting"—the well-known fact that you can't have a social event in east Kentucky without twelve fights, three arrests, and considerable property damage. The mountain have always been a rough place (my grandfather died minus two fingers and plus several bullets and uncounted scars), but it seems that what we experience now is different—so disruptive and self-destructive that a lot of social life is simply impossible. This may have something to do with our political and economic history. Frantz Fannon, writing of black communities, detailed how oppressed people can turn their violence on each other; it seems to me that the mountains have experienced this. Where our own music has survived, it has been in very private settings (living rooms) or in very structured ones (churches, bluegrass festivals). And the form that has most flourished, bluegrass, is very structured and set in a strict audience-performer pattern.

In the last ten years, however, something has happened that has led large numbers of young people into old-time music. Today you can hear thirty or forty at a time playing *Old Joe Clark* or *Flint Hill Special,* 50,000 people come to the Old Time Fiddler's Convention in Union Grove, N.C., and even more go to Galax in August. Bluegrass festivals (like Ralph Stanley's annual at McClure, Va., on Memorial Day) are crowded. Magazines like *Sing Out!* and *Bluegrass Unlimited* carry music and articles to thousands of enthusiasts. County, Rounder, Folkways and other record companies offer old-time music from old recordings and present-day pickers. Guitars and banjo sales are at an all-time high as picking and singing spreads like wildfire.

Just one thing. A good many of the folks now enjoying mountain music have never even seen a cow, let alone a mountain. The "folk revival" of the 60's, plus the general frustration of life in America, has made the music of the mountain past seem extremely inviting to people (mostly young) from both the flatlands and hills who haven't seen much of it before.

What does this mean? A fair number of kids have decided (not unreasonably) that the Appalachian Region is Paradise Lost; this fact has given West Virginia a fair number of communes and short-lived organic restaurants.[17] The "revival" has meant some income for good musicians, including former recording artists like Clarence Ashley and Dock Boggs. And it has meant some truly wonderful music made by people ("authentic" hillbillies as well as outsiders) who have bothered to seek out old-timers and learn from them. The Fuzzy Mountain String Band, for example, started playing hoedown music in college in North Carolina, and now they make what I call some of the best music anywhere.

There is a good and a bad side to all this. The kind of exploitation of "quaint" mountain people that gives us Gatlinburg can also destroy old-time music. Fiddlers' conventions aren't meant to hold 50,000 people. It brings hero-worship and "stardom" to music that wasn't designed for it. The majority (colonialist) culture has largely absorbed and nearly destroyed our subculture ("L'il Abner" and "Beverly Hillbillies"[18]), and even their dropouts can be a tidal wave. They have no culture of their own and don't adopt mountain culture (even if they could); therefore, they offer mountain music no context or place. So they too may be mining the mountains, taking what they want, and leaving wreckage behind; or they may be here just in time to keep the old music alive and growing. Or both.

So mountain people deserve to ask: Which side are you on? How deep does (or can, or will) this revival go in the mountains? It is hard to say. But we can see that musicians face the same questions of insiders-outsiders or us-them, that organizers, politicians, and everyone else has to deal with. Like earlier adventurers I guess we will see some musicians who go one way, some another, and some who try to stay in the middle.

Despite the music industry's takeover, there is one small but important area where mountain people keep control of their own music: topical music made by people who feel the need for songs to comment on some immediate aspect of their lives. A lot of it has been written in the last ten years or so; it goes along with the many movements that have stirred the mountains recently. Much has been "hidden" by being known only to a few people near the singer. Gradually, however, an increasing number of songs are getting passed around, some even recorded. A superb collection of them is to be published soon, edited by Guy and Candie Carawan.

Music like this seems to do two things: comment on social forces, struggles, and so on; and to be in some way part of the struggle. Songs that describe or comment on things are the easiest and most common. Composed and sung by individuals (though they may express the feelings of thousands), they can be extremely powerful in poetry and music. Here is Hazel Dickens' black lung song:

Black Lung

He's had more hard luck than most men could stand,
The mines was his first love but never his friend.
He's lived a hard life and hard he'll die,
Black lung's done got him, his time is nigh.

Songs that are directly part of a struggle are not as common in the mountains as in, say, the civil rights movement. This is partly because there is not much tradition of large groups singing together except in church. Union struggles and picket lines, however, have inspired some good singing. A popular union song inspired by an old spiritual, with some new verses from the Pikeville, Kentucky, hospital strike of 1972-74 is the following:

We Shall Not Be Moved

And a song by Michael Kline that has been sung at many anti-stripping rallies is this one:

Strip Away, Big D-9 Dozer

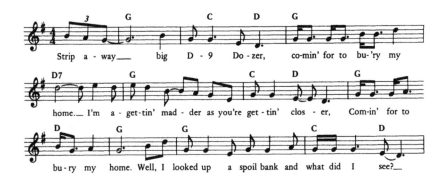

We are all so used to judging music by commercial standards that it is worth looking briefly at what this kind of music can do that Nashville doesn't. It can spread and popularize ideas and information and counter propaganda. If well grounded in people's culture (new words to an old tune, for example), it can break through the censorship of the media and travel everywhere. In the South the "freedom songs" became a part of many people's lives, an important source of strength for their hard fights. I hope we can manage to call on some of the same forces. In the past, "topical" songs contained practical instructions for resistance, as in songs that told slaves how to escape or miners to "keep your eye upon the scale." And finally is the simple fact that *people singing* is a very moving experience, a powerful force that needs to be turned loose again.

A song that tries to do some of these things must be really well based in people's lives. The singers of the IWW made it a point to use only familiar tunes (since they couldn't make records and most folks can't read music). Some modern writers (like Hazel Dickens) are making new tunes that sound old and familiar. A song won't travel unless it says what folks want it to and in their own language. I think it should also remind people of the surroundings that they associate with music, like churches or beer joints. A song that sounds like an old gospel tune is easier to listen to than one that sounds like an art song.

One more song, one that covers a lot of territory, including a practical lesson in songwriting is this one:

Fountain Filled With Blood

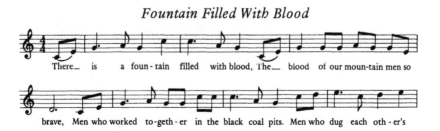

graves. Men who dug each oth-er's graves, Oh, God, men who dug each oth - er's graves.

Men who worked to-geth-er in the black coal pits, men who dug each oth-er's grave.

Anyone interested in this kind of music should also consider a little about ways of spreading it. Long-play records can cost as little as a dollar each (at least before the energy crisis); songbooks are cheaper still. Music festivals have become established in some communities, and smaller local gatherings are happening also. Books are appearing and a magazine is being talked about. Local radio stations are occasionally open to local musicians if approached personally. Cable TV is a largely unexplored area, with local programming already being made in some areas. Who knows? If enough pressure is brought, maybe even Nashville would open up a little.

The old traditional way of life in the mountains is gone. What is important now is not to try to bring back an old-time culture with old music and the old ways of doing things but to build on the old to make new ways of doing things, ways that we control. We need to preserve what old-time music is left so people can go on enjoying it. We need to have our own music which we make and control ourselves, instead of taking everything Nashville sends us. We need to encourage each other to make music, to sing, write, and play songs. We need our own ways of distributing music—including record companies, radio and TV stations that respond to all kinds of local music instead of trying to discover stars.

Old-time mountain music belongs to everyone. So should new-time music.

NOTES

[1]A beautiful and moving picture of this sort of thing is Jean Ritchie's autobiography, *Singing Family of the Cumberlands* (1955).

[2]*Anthology of American Folk Music*, a six-record set issued by Folkways. It consists of an astonishing variety of traditional music originally recorded on 78 rpm records from 1925-30, with such legendary musicians as Dock Boggs, Mississippi John Hurt, Uncle Dave Macon, Blind Lemon Jefferson, the Carter Family, and dozens of "unknowns." One session with this set is worth several thousand pages of description of our musical heritage.

[3]Without trying to be scholarly, I can distinguish seven distinct styles of traditional mountain music, most of them now going if not gone:

1. Fiddle tunes. Hundreds of tunes came from Scotland and Ireland; hundreds more were made here. The fiddle was the first and the most widespread country instrument, its music with endless regional and personal variations. Dozens of "fiddlers' conventions" are held each year in the mountains, primarily outside the coalfield. Most of the best fiddlers, however, are old now.

2. Banjo music, which deserves an article to itself, as do banjo players like Dock Boggs and Roscoe Holcomb (who Bob Dylan says influenced him greatly).

3. Shape-note hymn singing, now almost extinct except in northern Alabama and western Kentucky.

4. Gospel music, both the quartet style and the "holiness" style of congregational singing like "I'll Fly Away."

5. Regular Baptist singing in the "lining-out" manner, a powerful, stirring music that seems to be absolutely unique to the South-

ern mountains.

6. Ballad singing, both accompanied and unaccompanied. Many ballads were preserved in the mountains long after disappearing from England and Scotland. Many more were made here.

7. "Social music"—songs and lyrics for parties, dances or whatever ("Old Joe Clark").

Not to mention stories, dances, and games, and children's songs.

[4]Other string bands included such as Dr. Smith's Champion Horsehair Pullers, the Henpecked Husbands, the Moatsville String Ticklers, and the Fruit Jar Drinkers (who still play on the Grand Ole Opry).

[5]The first performer on the Grand Ole Opry was Uncle Jimmy Thompson, 80, who fiddled while his niece played piano. After an hour George D. Hay (the Opry's founder) asked if Uncle Jimmy was tired. "Why shucks," he said, "a man don't get warmed up in an hour. I just won an eight-day fiddling contest down in Dallas, Texas, and here's my blue ribbon to prove it." See George D. Hay, *A Story of the Grand Ole Opry* (1953).

[6]From Hobart Smith of Saltville, Virginia, who has been called "America's greatest folk instrumentalist."

[7]From Mrs. A. R. Graham of Cynthiana, Kentucky, who learned it as a girl in Magoffin County, Kentucky.

[8]Treated at length in Archie Green's book *Only A Miner* (1972).

[9]Also discussed in Green's book. The story of the Coal Creek Rebellion is worth at least a footnote. In the 1880's Tennessee miners tried to organize in the Knights of Labor. To block this, Tennessee allowed coal operators to lease the labor of convicts as scabs. The miners organized, and in 1891 fought a series of battles in which they burned stockades and helped the prisoners (mostly black) to freedom. Tennessee sent militia and quelled the "disturbance" but the convict labor system was soon abolished and the miners organized the mines under the UMW.
   Other songs from Coal Creek (now called Lake City) are on Hedy West's record *Old Times and Hard Times*.

[10]Besides Green's book, coal mining music (up to 1945) is the subject

of two excellent books by George Korson, *Coal Dust on the Fiddle* (covering the bituminous industry) and *Minstrels of the Mine Patch* (covering the anthracite field). Both books were commissioned by the UMW.

[11]Mrs. Reece has lately been singing this song at the UMW strike of Duke Power Company's mine at Brookside in Harlan County. The miners there think it is still quite relevant.

[12]In the 30's record companies did issue some records of protest music. In those hard times no one ignored anything that would sell. The New Lost City Ramblers have issued on LP of recorded industrial music, called *Modern Times.*

[13]Maybe the reason so many stars sing of being poor but happy is a nostalgia for their own past. It takes a strong person to become a star and stay common—not many can.

[14]A country-western song is indeed lucky to last ten years; some old tunes and ballads have already made it past 400.
   I think a lot of young mountain musicians, feeling oppressed by the closed, competitive aspect of C&W, turned to the relative freedom of rock—at some cost, I suspect, of cutting away from their own roots. "Country rock," at any rate, is popular now, and Goose Creek Symphony is the favorite band of many people I know.

[15]There is only one black star in Nashville, Charley Pride, though "country music" is shot through with things derived from black music. DeFord Bailey, a harmonica player who may have been the first musician ever recorded in Nashville, was the only black star of the earlier days.

[16]See Bill C. Malone, *Country Music USA* (1968), 186-88, 206, 208-38.
   A note on terminology. When record companies started producing music for rural audiences they didn't know what to call it. In 1925 Ralph Peer recorded a nameless string band from the Blue Ridge who called themselves "hillbillies." He named them the "Original Hillbillies" and the music became "hillbilly music." (Similarly, black singers were marketed on "race records.") Later, after World War II, as commercial hillbilly became popular and respectable, the industry looked for a more dignified name and settled on "country music"—a little odd, since by then it was all made in the city. The term "country and western" and the cowboy suits Porter Waggoner *et al.* wear onstage stem from the work of "western" singers like Tex Ritter and Gene Autry, who sang popular "cowboy" songs in the 30's and

40's.

When traditional music was discovered by city musicians of the 60's, the "hillbilly" music of the twenties received still another name and became "folk music."

[17]The same feeling among their elders leads to long-lived developments and National Forest land grabs.

[18]The original Beverly Hillbillies were a group of "cowboy" singers who broadcast from Hollywood from 1928-32 and were quite popular.

JOHN FOX, JR.
A RE-APPRAISAL; OR,
WITH FRIENDS LIKE THAT, WHO NEEDS ENEMIES?

by
Donald Askins

> He was always kindly in what he wrote about the mountain people and it has been said [that he] was the best friend these people ever had.
>
> —William Cabell Moore

Half a century after his death, John Fox, Jr. still dominates the "cultural" activities of the little town in southwestern Virginia to which he came in the 1890's hoping to make his fortune in land and coal speculation. Although he failed as an industrial entrepreneur, he stumbled upon another natural resource ripe for development and proceeded to exploit his discovery with a vigor that has preserved his name as one of the very few readily recognizable in any list of Appalachian authors. Both at home and abroad, Fox achieved a great popular success in his novels and stories depicting mountain people; and today, in Big Stone Gap, his memory is cultivated with an ardor Americans rarely accord a mere writer of fiction. The atmosphere of sanctity in which *The Trail of the Lonesome Pine* is produced invests the annual dramatization more with the quality of ritual than that of outdoor drama.

SOURCE: The Mountain Review (c) 1976.

AUTHOR: Don Askins *heads the Appalachian COALition Against Strip Mining. He is a former professor of English at Clinch Valley College and lives on Marshall's Branch in Kentucky.*

Fox's national popularity (his books are readily available in paperback editions while those of James Still are out of print) and the general consensus that would agree with William Cabell Moore call for a reappraisal of his depiction of the mountain people to whom he is supposed to have been such a good friend. Undoubtedly, Fox's novels and stories have influenced the nation's view of its Appalachian minority, so we turn to his fiction to evaluate the cast of that view.

Fox's first bestselling novel, *The Little Shepherd of Kingdom Come,* is structured on a set of contrasts that characterize his work: the Mountains vs. the Bluegrass, Melissa Turner (mountain girl) vs. Margaret Dean (bluegrass relative), Chad in the mountains vs. Chad in the bluegrass, and so on *ad infinitum.* Without exception, the thrust of these contrasts is denigratory in relation to mountaineers and laudatory in relation to the bluegrass aristocracy.

In *The Little Shepherd of Kingdom Come* Fox characterizes mountain society as pyramidal in structure and divided into three classes. At the top he locates "the valley-aristocrat"—those farmers of the rich river bottoms who occasionally own slaves and are "perhaps of *gentle blood*" (italics mine). In the middle are the free-settlers, "usually of Scotch-Irish descent, often English, but sometimes German or sometimes even Huguenot," who dwell in "rude" log cabins along tributary creeks. At the bottom are the poor white trash, "worthless descendants of the servile and sometimes criminal class who might have traced their origin back to the slums of London"; these last exist in "wretched cabins at the head of the creek or on the washed spur of the mountain above" and function as "hand-to-mouth tenants of the valley-aristocrats." Although the typography of the region conceivably could have resulted in some such economic stratification as Fox indicates, one must demur at his essentially racial classifications. Surely there were some Scotch-Irish and Germans among those "valley-aristocrats," and perhaps now and then one could have traced his ancestry back to the London slums.

In Fox's social theorizing, however, man is a product of the interaction of "blood" and environment; hence, in order to account for the "semi-barbarous" condition of life he discovers in the mountains, Fox posits an inferiority of blood-line which is compounded by the rigors of the environment. Even those "valley-aristocrats" like Joel Turner or Judd Tolliver, who had perhaps the initial advantage of "gentle blood," are little more than genial barbarians, notable primarily for their physical prowess and characterized mentally and culturally as possessed of an ignorance and child-like simplicity that reduces them to the level of clowns. The less fortunate, in terms of blood-line, may be either well-meaning or villainous, but they invariably lack the mental capacity to rise above their environmental limitations. The physical destitution in which they exist mirrors a corresponding mental, spiritual, and cultural destitution.

The children of such people, "thin, undersized, underfed, and with weak, dispirited eyes and yellow tousled hair" or "round-faced, round-eyed, dark, and sturdy" grow "large-waisted and round shouldered. . .from work in the fields." They sit uninterested and restless through the "blab schools" and quit, their minds untouched and unenlightened, to take their place in the generations of degeneration. Rare indeed is the mountain child who shows himself "erect, agile, spirited, intelligent." Chad, one of these rarities who eventually takes his rightful place among the bluegrass aristocracy, derives his superior qualities apparently from the twin advantages of his mother's having been "a lawful wife" and his grandfather's having worn a "wig and peruke." Melissa, the true mountain waif of unknown parentage, must perish because her mother was so uncircumspect as to get herself bedded before she was wedded.

Fox's bias against mountain people is underscored when he comes to speak of the Bluegrass as it is with his curious blend of romantic mysticism and naturalistic determinism. Chad is introduced to the Bluegrass by an itinerant cattle dealer and the schoolmaster, who tell him of a "faraway, curious country"

> where the land was level and there were no mountains at all; where on one farm might be more sheep, cattle, and slaves than Chad had seen in all his life; where the people lived in big houses of stone and brick—what brick was Chad could not imagine—and rode along hard, white roads in shiny covered wagons, with two "niggers" on a high seat in front and one little "nigger" behind to open gates, and were proud and very high-heeled indeed; where there were towns that had more people than a whole county in the mountains, with rock roads running through

them in every direction and narrow rock paths along these roads—like rows of hearthstones—for the people to walk on—the land of the bluegrass—the "settlements of old Kaintuck."

And there were churches everywhere as tall as trees and schoolhouses a-plenty; and big schools, called colleges, to which the boys went when they were through with the little schools.

The contrast here, although couched in language comprehensible to a child's mind, suggests the materialistic and racist value-base on which Fox's attitudes and judgments are founded, attitudes which preclude any sympathetic understanding of the mountain culture he found in Jellico and Big Stone Gap. This bias is much more explicitly stated in a chapter of *The Little Shepherd of Kingdom Come* entitled "The Bluegrass." Fox begins the description with the epithet "God's Country!" and continues to characterize Bluegrass Kentucky as the land that seems "to have been the pet shrine of the Great Mother herself."

She fashioned it with loving hands. She shut it in with a mighty barrier of mighty mountains to *keep the mob out*. She gave it the loving clasp of a mighty river, and spread broad, level prairies beyond that *the mob* might glide by or be tempted to the other side. . . .

In the beginning, such was her clear purpose to the Kentuckian's eye, she filled it with flowers and grass and trees, and fish and bird and wild beast, just as she made Eden for Adam and Eve. . .And when *the chosen people*— such, too served her purpose—the Mother went to the race that obstacle but strengthens, that thrives best under an alien effort to kill, that has ever conquered its conquerors, and that seems bent on the task of carrying the best ideas any age has ever known back to the Old World from which it sprang. The Great Mother knows!. . .And how she has followed close when *this Saxon race*—her youngest born—seemed likely to stray too far—gathering its sons to her arms in virgin lands that they might suckle again and keep *the old blood* fresh and strong. (My italics throughout)

The aristocratic and racist elitism manifested in this passage explains easily enough Fox's lack of sympathy for the mountaineers he wrote of. The mountaineer, it is implied here, is one of that inferior breed which has succumbed to the mighty barrier Mother Nature erected "to keep the mob out"; hence, he is hardly worthy of serious consideration, for the true bearers of the living heritage are "the chosen," whose manifest destiny it is to "plant their kind across a continent from sea to sea" and move on "through the opening eastern gates of the earth."

When Fox descends from the heights of such mystic racism to describe the state of civilization in the Bluegrass, his idealization of circumstances contrasts markedly with his comments on mountain society:

> The land was a great series of wooded parks such as one might have found in Merry England, except that worm fence and stone wall took the place of hedge along the highways. It was a land of peace and of a plenty that was close to easy luxury—for all. Poor whites were few, the beggar was unknown, and throughout the region there was no man, woman, or child, perhaps, who did not have enough to eat and to wear and a roof to cover his head, whether it was his own roof or not. If slavery had to be— then the fetters were forged light and hung loosely.

This Edenic vision reveals clearly where Fox's sympathies lie, if not his understanding.

One can understand why Fox, imbued with such romantic illusions about his birthplace, consistently depicted mountain people as incapable of developing to a state of civilization. When civilization comes to the moutains, it is imposed forcibly upon the native populace, as was the case of the Big Stone Gap Guard, a group of Harvard and Yale graduates self-appointed to bring "law and order" to the rude savages in their mountain fastness; or it is achieved by the exceptionally gifted native who leaves the region for one of the national cultural centers, as June Tolliver does in *The Trail of the Lonesome Pine*. In either instance, an outside influence provides the catalyst which the mountaineer is unable to initiate for himself or his society.

The mountaineer's debility, in Fox's critical view, is attributable in part to inferior ancestral stock, and in part to the malign effects of the mountain environment. Fox holds firmly to the degeneration theory of mountain societal development, as is evidenced in the history of Chad Buford. The original Buford was a "fine old gentleman in a wig and peruke"; after three generations of mountain isolation, the Buford line has eventuated in Chad, a supposed "woods-colt," orphaned and at the mercy of the viciousness or generosity of whomever he meets. Although the potential inherent in his blood-line raises him head and shoulders above his peers, the disadvantages of his environment prevent the full realization of that potential. In comparison with his counterparts in the Bluegrass, his achievements are inferior indeed. However, when Chad is exposed to the cultural and material advantages of the Bluegrass, his progress is amazingly rapid, soon equalling or surpassing his counterparts in level of attainment.

The same theme is more explicitly developed in *The Trail of the Lonesome Pine* through the characters Jack Hale and June Tolliver. Through years of exposure to the mountain environment, Hale, who comes to the mountains as the representative and harbinger of approaching civilization, gradually loses his civilized refinements and takes on many of the brutish qualities of Fox's mountain inhabitants. June, the little mountain lass who loves him, in the meantime undergoes the opposite process of development as a result of her exposure to the civilizing influence of New York society. In Fox's view, environment is the ultimate determinant of character, and the *status quo* of mountain society as he describes it precludes any progress toward what he recognizes as civilization, i.e., the cultured societies of New York and the Bluegrass.

In spite of much that has been written to the contrary, John Fox, Jr., who achieved a degree of fame and fortune through the literary exploitation of the Appalachian mountaineer, reveals in his fiction little love for either the mountain people or the mountain milieu. His view was always that of an outsider who was examining a quaintly curious but inferior breed with whom he could scarcely sympathize, much less empathize. The potential viciousness of such a view has since become concretely demonstrable in the sacrifice of the people and the area he so befriended to the rapacious progression of

"Saxon" civilization.

THE PITTSTON MENTALITY:
MANSLAUGHTER ON BUFFALO CREEK

by
Thomas N. Bethell
and
Davitt McAteer

Buffalo Creek, in Logan County, is reasonably typical for the southern part of West Virginia—a long, winding hollow, snaking between steep ridges on both sides for more than 20 miles from the town of Saunders at its headwaters to the town of Man, where the creek empties into the Guyandotte River, which flows north to join the Ohio River at Huntington. The narrow valley is just wide enough for the creek, the railroad, and an almost unending line of company-built houses stretching along both sides of the tracks. There are occasional wide places in the valley where tributaries flow into Buffalo Creek, and in the wide places there used to be towns—small towns that nobody ever heard of: places like Kistler, Crown, Accoville, Braeholm, Fanco, Becco, Amherstdale, Robinette, Latrobe, Crites, Stowe, Lundale, Craneco, Lorado, and Pardee. Some of the names come from coal companies that no longer exist. As coal towns go, these are

SOURCE: The Washington Monthly, c May 1972.

AUTHORS: Tom Bethell, of Brophy Associates, researches and writes on coal related issues. He is the former director of research for the United Mine Workers of America and a former contributor to The Washington Monthly.
Davitt McAteer is the author of numerous books and articles on coal mine health and safety. He is a former staff member of the United Mine Workers of America and a native of the West Virginia coalfields.

old, most of them built before World War I. They are in varying stages of decline. Some of them are not much more than post-office addresses. The old frame two-family houses are settling unevenly. Some have collapsed altogether. Others, considering their age and the haste with which they had been built, are in surprisingly good shape. As a general rule, if a house is freshly painted you can assume that a working miner lives there.

The population of Buffalo Creek has fluctuated with the times, declining when the industry declined, recovering when the industry recovered. In 1970, coal had its best year since 1947, and a rosy glow of optimism suffused National Coal Association predictions for the future. Big companies opened new mines along Buffalo Creek and stepped up production in their old ones.

When coal comes up out of the ground, the impurities that come with it are separated out in preparation plants—tipples, as they are more commonly called. The coal rolls away in long, black trains; the impurities stay behind, and something has to be done with them. They have a way of accumulating with staggering speed: A ton of raw coal generally contains up to 25 per cent of extraneous material, and a good-sized tipple, handling the production of several mines at once, will separate out thousands of tons of waste every day. Miners have different names for it—"gob" or "slag" or "culm"; but whatever you call it, it still has to be piled somewhere. In the crowded hollows of West Virginia, finding places to pile slag is a problem of major proportions. As a general rule, no engineer is ever called in to consult on the best and safest locations. Instead, the company superintendent simply hunts around for some vacant space convenient to his tipple, and the slag is dumped there, either by trucks climbing up a mountainside and dumping down the slope, or by an aerial tramway strung between peaks and dumping in the middle. Whatever system is used, the slag is piled up until it is higher than the dumping spot, and then a new pile is started.

FACING THE GOB

Since 1946 a tipple has been in operation at the head of Buffalo Creek. The plant was built by the Lorado Coal Mining Company, a mostly local outfit that sold out to the Buffalo Mining Company in 1964. Buffalo Mining, in turn, sold out in

1970 to the Pittston Company, which is headquartered in New York and is the largest independent producer of coal in the United States. All this time the tipple continued in operation. And all this time it grew. Originally designed to process coal from a single mine, it was expanded periodically as new mines were opened nearby. By 1972 Pittston was operating a total of eight mines in the Buffalo Creek vicinity—five of them underground, three of them stripping jobs. The coal from all eight was processed in the single tipple. On an average, the tipple operated six days a week, two shifts a day; it handled about 5,200 tons of raw coal daily, and shipped out about 4,200 tons of cleaned coal on the long Chesapeake and Ohio trains. That meant that every day a thousand tons of gob, more or less, had to be dumped.

Three tributaries run into Buffalo Creek near the Pittston tipple. From 1947 until about 1955, the refuse was dumped along the hillside a few hundred yards upstream from the tipple, but by 1955 the available space was mostly exhausted and the tipple began dumping a little farther away, across the mouth of a small hollow where the Middle Fork tributary meets the creek. At first the gob pile grew slowly. It had to, because most of the hollow behind it was occupied by miners living in company houses. But when production at the tipple increased, the growing gob pile began to menace the houses, and the miners were forced out. The houses were abandoned (some of them were knocked down for the lumber), and the gob was dumped where they had stood. The families moved away, some of them out of West Virginia entirely, some of them only a few hundred yards to vacant houses in the small community of Saunders, which stood facing the gob pile at the intersection of Middle Fork and Buffalo Creek.

SAUNDERS WAS GONE

The gob pile grew, and grew, and grew more swiftly as the tipple kept expanding production. At first this grotesque black mountain was only an eyesore. Later, it became a source of air pollution and a fire hazard. Gob piles may be nothing but waste; but much of that waste is flammable, and a combination of compaction and oxidation can result in spontaneous combustion. Once a fire gets going deep within a gob pile, extinguishing it is nearly impossible. The fire smoulders, sometimes bursts into open flame, fouls the sky with acrid smoke, and occasionally produces an explosion. The Federal Bureau of Mines has spent millions of dollars in research on the problem, but the end result is that hundreds of gob piles are smouldering in the Appalachian coalfields right now, and nothing is being done about them. The gob pile at Middle Fork began burning years ago and kept on smouldering.

As the dumping continued, another problem arose. Tipples require vast quantities of water in the cleaning-separating process, but water can be a scarce commodity at times in West Virginia. Partly to provide itself with a reliable year-round supply of water, and partly to comply with new state regulations governing stream pollution, Buffalo Mining began to build a series of settling ponds in 1964. Previously the contaminated wash water had simply been sluiced directly into Buffalo Creek, despite the objections of people who liked to fish there. The ponds were created by building retaining dams in the most immediately convenient location: on top of the huge Middle Fork gob pile. By that time the pile had reached stupefying proportions: as high as a 10-story office building, 600 feet across, stretching back into the hollow more than a quarter of a mile. Sweeping down through the pile and wandering across the top, the waters of Middle Fork ran sluggishly to join the main stream of Buffalo Creek. Damming the water was a relatively easy task, using the material closest at hand: mine waste. No civil engineer in his right mind would permit the construction of a dam from such materials (as many a civil engineer would later confirm), but no engineer, it now appears, was consulted.

In operation, the settling ponds not only contained runoff water from the hills but refuse-filled water piped from the tipple. The solid refuse would settle out and clear water could be piped back to the tipple. The first of the ponds impounded a relatively small volume of water, however, and it silted up within a couple of years. A second dam was built in 1967 slightly farther upstream. When the tipple was operating full blast, it required 500,000 gallons of water a day, pumping back between 400 and 500 gallons of waste-filled water every minute. Some of the water would seep out through the porous dam, but the waste settling to the bottom—500 tons every day—rapidly filled the pond, and a third dam was built in 1970. Again, no engineering was involved—just truckloads of mine waste, a bulldozer to push them around, and *presto*! A dam grew across the hollow, built of nothing but junk and standing on a foundation of slime and silt and dead trees. The trees were there because nobody had bothered to cut them down. It was simpler and faster just to dump on top of them.

In West Virginia, February means snow and rain. February meant it this year, as always. In Logan County, there were heavy snows and flash floods; but they were, as the state meteorologist would later point out, "nothing uncommon." At the head of Buffalo Creek, the waters rose behind Pittston's makeshift dam. Early on the morning of February 26, Pittston's local mine boss, Steve Dasovich, sent a bulldozer operator up the access road to the dam with instructions to cut a drainage ditch to relieve the pressure from the swollen lake. The access road winds around a mountainside with the dam out of sight much of the way. When the bulldozer operator finally came around the last bend and looked through the rain at the dam, he saw with a sudden, terrible shock that it wasn't there.

The dam was gone, and 21 million cubic feet of water and an immeasurable mass of mud and rock and coal wastes were charging through the narrow valley of Buffalo Creek. From where he sat on his suddenly useless machine, the bulldozer operator could look down toward the little town of Saunders—a town consisting of nothing more than a church and some two dozen houses. Now it consisted of nothing at all. Saunders was gone, eradicated completely. Beyond Saunders, the valley curved away out of sight, but the air was filled with the terrifying sound of the flood bearing down on the 15 communities in its path.

FATHER OF STRIP-MINING

There are no slag heaps on Park Avenue, and no floods will ever wash through the offices of Joseph P. Routh unless the island of Manhattan sinks into the sea. Thirty-five floors up in the Pan American building, the chairman of the Pittston Company has a commanding view. When he looks down to the street below, he can see Brinks armored trucks moving the wealth of America from place to place. The trucks belong to Joe Routh. A good deal of the money does, too.

Routh is 79 now, and he has been making money longer than most men have been alive. He was already a power to be reckoned with when the Pittston Company, which then operated a dozen anthracite mines in Pennsylvania, stumbled into bankruptcy during the Depression. A friend at Manufacturers Trust suggested to Routh that he take over the company and lead it out of the wilderness. The bank sweetened the offer with a $10-million loan—essentially unsecured, since there would be no way to recoup the loss if Pittston went under—and Routh moved in. Anthracite, he concluded, was a dying industry. The future lay in the vast bituminous fields of Virginia and West Virginia. He unloaded most of Pittston's properties in Pennsylvania and began buying up tracts of coal in central Appalachia.

At a time when coal prices fluctuated wildly, he had discovered that the best way to tear loose a chunk of coal in time to take advantage of favorable trends was to strip it from the mountainsides rather than go through the difficult, two-year-or-more process of engineering and constructing a deep mine. By 1950, when strip-mining was still an infant industry in Appalachia and conservationists hadn't the foggiest notion of the plague to come, one of Routh's companies, Compass Coal, was profitably tearing the hills of Harrison County, West Virginia, to shreds. Since there were no state or federal reclamation requirements, no money had to be spent on binding up the wounds. It must have been the best of all possible worlds, unless you lived near one of Routh's mines. He, of course, didn't.

Routh kept himself busy with other conquests, picking up coal companies in Kentucky, West Virginia, and Virginia, buying up trucking companies and warehouses in New York, enlarging his oil-distributing operations, hatching long-range plans for a giant refinery on the Maine coast. Money flowed from Routh's various holdings into his Manhattan office in a never-ending stream, and Routh bought Brinks, Inc., to carry the cash in his own armored cars.

AN ACT OF GOD

Despite abundant evidence that he was in no danger of going soft, Routh decided in 1969 to bring in a new president. He looked around for a man to match his own toughness and found one—a 53-year-old native of West Virginia named Nicholas T. Camicia who had already made a mark in the industry as a notable scrambler. "The coal industry is run by men who got where they are by not being nice," says one former federal official in a position to know, "and when Camicia smiles, you can hear his jaws making a special effort." Routh liked him fine.

But Camicia already had a good job when Routh approached him about taking over Pittston. Routh reportedly told him to write his own ticket, possibly remembering his own reluctance to sign on until Manufacturers Trust gave him the $10 million to play with. Camicia did, in fact, write his own ticket, putting his signature to a contract that has never been publicized but makes fascinating reading in the archives of the Securities and Exchange Commission. The contract runs until 1976 and guarantees Camicia not only a minimum salary of $100,000 (increased now to $134,000), but it stipulates that a deferred salary of $25,000 will be set aside each year, compounded, and paid out to him in 120 monthly installments whenever he quits or gets fired; if he reaches retirement age before that happens, he also qualifies for a hefty pension. The contract also appears to have included some highly attractive stock options; SEC records show, for example, that Camicia picked up 7,200 shares, worth approximately $270,000, for a price of $78,000—less than a third of their market value. That wasn't all. Camicia was living comfortably in an exclusive Chicago suburb when Routh signed him up; in return for agreeing to move to New York, Camicia got Pittston to buy his house for $90,000 and furnish him, cost free, an equivalent home within commuting distance of Manhatten. He went to work for Joe Routh, reportedly satisfied with the terms of his employment.

If ever there was any doubt that Routh and Camicia were a pair of industry touchdown-twins, it was dispelled early in 1970 when Pittston signed a contract with the Japanese steel industry. The Japanese wanted a long-term contract and were willing to make concessions to get a reliable supply of American coking coal. By 1970 Pittston had gained control of a third of all the available commercial metallurgical coal in the United States, and no one could offer more reliability than Routh and Camicia. They would not offer it without certain stipulations, however. The contract they signed with the Japanese called for Pittston to deliver 140 million tons of coal over the next 10 years at a reported average of $15 per ton, which is about twice the going rate elsewhere.

Pittston's directors were so happy last year that they boosted dividends twice and voted themselves a three-for-one stock split to boot. The company now has more than 50 mines working with nine more under development, and there is no end to the good times in sight.

Is everybody happy? No. Federal mine inspectors in Appalachia are not pleased with Pittston's safety record; they never have been particularly pleased with it, but the past couple of years have been especially bad. Nine miners lost their lives in 1971 in Pittston mines (two of them in the newly acquired Buffalo Mining division), another 743 were seriously hurt, and the company's accident frequency rate was one of the highest in the coal industry. The record in 1970 was even worse: 18 dead. Investigators found that in a solid majority of the fatal accidents bad management practices (rather than personal carelessness) were to blame. "The company appears to be sincere in its desire for health and safety throughout its mines," one inspector wrote. "This desire," he added drily, "is not always fulfilled." Not always. All told, some 98 men have been killed in Pittston's mines in the past decade, and a 1963 explosion in which 22 men died still ranks as one of the worst of recent disasters. Three or four thousand men have been seriously injured or maimed in the company's mines since 1962, and the U.S. Public Health Service estimates that as many as 5,000 Pittston miners may have developed pneumoconiosis during that time. The profit margin of the new Japanese contract is a reported 24 per cent, almost three times the normal profit margin in the coal industry; you can't help marveling at how much of that money will be going back to the disabled derelicts living out their lives in Appalachia after destroying themselves to help make Joe Routh a millionaire for the third or fourth time.

Pittston's stockholders don't have to concern themselves with such things, because they don't hear about them. The company's handsome four-color annual reports talk about money, not about people. There are pictures of freshly painted oil storage tanks, spotless armored trucks, gleaming computer banks—and aerial pictures of the long, black coal trains winding their way through seemingly virgin Appalachian valleys. The pictures are taken with care: On the inside back cover of the 1971 report there is a color shot of lovely hills and hollows with a sturdy complex of mine buildings prominent in the foreground. "Aerial view of the Lorado Mine of newly acquired Buffalo Mining Company," the caption reads. Beyond the mine, railroad tracks stretch away, disappearing behind a hill. If you could see beyond that hill, you would see the massive, smouldering gob pile that stood at the head of Buffalo Creek and on top of it the jerry-built dams that Pittston used with its preparation plant. But those things are not part of the picture, not part of the annual report. As far as Pittston's stockholders are concerned, they never existed—not until the morning of February 26, when suddenly the dams collapsed and the burning gob pile erupted and all hell broke loose.

Helicopters were still thrashing back and forth between Buffalo Creek and the nearest hospitals when reporters began calling Pittston's New York headquarters to find out what the company had been doing to cause such a monstrous disaster. Camicia and Routh weren't available, wouldn't answer the telephones, wouldn't return calls. Finally, Mary Walton of the Charleston *Gazette* flushed out a Pittston lawyer who insisted on remaining anonymous but was willing to give the company's point of view. "It was an act of God," he said.

DASOVICH'S YARDSTICK

" 'Act of God' is a legal term," Robert Weedfall remarked when he heard about Pittston's explanation of the flood. "There are other legal terms—terms like 'involuntary manslaughter because of stupidity' and 'criminal negligence.' " Weedfall is the West Virginia state climatologist, the man who keeps track of basic acts of God such as rain and snow. He was in a better position than anyone else to know whether there could be any possibility that Pittston's dam had collapsed from natural causes, and he was convinced that it had not—could not have—not by any stretch of the imagination. There had been heavy rainfall in Logan County during the week of February 26 and considerable flooding. But it was nothing uncommon for February, Weedfall said, and he had the statistics to prove it. When reporters called him they were impressed with his conviction. Pittston officials had called, too, looking for ways to document their private theory of divine intervention. Weedfall wasn't much help.

Nor were the technical specialists of the Department of the Interior who arrived from Washington and, in the aftermath of the disaster, poked and probed among the ruins in search of clues. The U.S. Geological Survey sent a crew, as did the Bureau of Mines; the Bureau of Reclamation summoned a former chief of its Earth Dams Section from retirement. The investigators examined the remains of the dam in microscopic detail, interviewed Pittston workers and company officials (who would not talk to reporters), and pieced together a convincing account of what had happened and why. None of the investigators showed any doubt that the dams had been badly engineered. Fred Walker, the retired Bureau of Reclamation expert, went further and refused to use the word "dam" to describe the structures. "Locally these barriers are called dams, but to me this is unacceptable nomenclature," he wrote. "These structures were created by persons completely unfamiliar with dam design, construction, and materials, and by construction methods they are completely unacceptable to engineers specializing in dam design."

West Virginia law, Walker noted, "requires permits, approval of plans, and inspection during construction for impoundments more than 10 feet deep. I was unable to find that such requirements had ever been complied with." Suggesting that similar potentially disastrous situations could be found elsewhere in the coalfields, Walker commented scathingly that "fortunately most of these barriers are built in valleys that have small watersheds above them, as apparently little if any consideration is given to the flood hazard involved."

Pittston's consideration of the flood hazard at Buffalo Creek seems to have begun at 4 p.m. on Feburary 24—exactly 40 hours before the so-called dam collapsed—when Jack Kent and Steve Dasovich drove up to survey the situation. Kent was superintendent of Pittston's stripping operations in its Buffalo Mining division; Dasovich was superintendent of the tipple. The water was rising behind the newest of the three dams. A federal mine inspector had driven past on the previous day and recalled later that the water seemed to be about 15 feet below the top; now it was within five or six feet. According to the Bureau of

Mines report, Kent and Dasovich "agreed that neither the dam nor the rising water presented danger of collapse or flooding at that time." The report makes clear that they were concerned only with the possibility of water overflowing the dam; they seem to have been untroubled by the possibility that the dam might simply give way, even though it was settling visibly in places—and even though part of it had given way almost exactly a year earlier during the rains of February, 1971. (It had been under construction then, with not much water backed up behind it, and there was little damage.) Kent stuck a measuring stick into the sludgy surface of the dam, with the top of the stick about a foot below the top of the dam. It was raining; Dasovich and Kent decided to keep an eye on things.

Kent was back at the dam 24 hours later to check his measuring stick. The water was up about a foot and a half. Rain was still falling. Kent, who lives in an imposing home a few miles below the dam, decided to start checking the water level every two hours. He found that it was rising about an inch an hour. At 3:30 a.m. on February 26, peering at the stick with the aid of a flashlight, Kent saw to his alarm that the water was rising faster—two inches an hour, maybe more. An hour later the level was up three inches more and the measuring stick was almost covered. Kent telephoned Dasovich and asked him to come take a look. By the time Dasovich arrived the stick had disappeared entirely and the water was only about a foot below the top of the dam.

According to the Bureau of Mines investigators, Dasovich decided to cut a ditch across the dam; he had some drainage pipe on hand and intended to use it to relieve the pressure. He called some of Jack Kent's strip-mine bulldozer operators at home and told them to go to the stripping operation—some three or four miles away—and bring their machines to the dam. Kent, meanwhile, made some calls, too: "He telephoned several families in the Lorado and Saunders area after his 4:30 a.m. examination," Bureau investigators reported, "and advised them of the rising water and the possibility of the dam overflowing." Three hours before the dam broke, in other words, the disaster had been foreseen by someone in a position to do something about it. A telephone call to the state police—who could have traveled the entire length of Buffalo Creek by 7 a.m. ordering a general evacuation—might have saved more than a hundred lives. But the call was never made. And the drainage ditch was never dug, because the dam had given way before the bulldozers arrived.

WALKING IN SOUP

You can find Jack Kent at home—his house is on high ground and survived the flood untouched—but he doesn't like to talk to reporters. His eyes tell everything; there is no need for words. Dasovich seems to have disappeared entirely. He was in a nearby hospital after the flood, being treated for shock, and nurses said later that he was hysterical and blamed himself for the tragedy. Still later he was reported to have been admitted to a private psychiatric clinic—still later, released. The Federal investigators have not yet talked to him and some of them, knowing now what they do about the dam, see no need. "He knows what was up there," one of them said. "He'll always know what was up there."

Other men knew, too. In the community of Saunders there was general concern about the safety of the dam; and on the night of February 25, most of the families who lived nearby decided, on their own, to take refuge in a schoolhouse five miles down the creek at Lorado. The decision saved their lives; the schoolhouse survived the flood, but when the families returned to Saunders to look for their homes, there was nothing to be found. No homes, not even the foundations; everything was gone, everything except an appalling sea of slowly settling, black, foul-smelling sludge.

Off and on during the night, in the last few hours before the dam broke, miners went up to have a look at it. There were rumors spreading that it was going to go, but no one really seemed to know. Dasovich reportedly was telling people that things were under control. About 6:30 a.m., according to the federal reports, a miner saw ominous signs of what was coming. "The dam was moving like a bridge moves under heavy traffic," he remembered later. "Water was coming through the dam. . . not much, but it was causing the lower lake to fill up fast." By 7:30, according to another eyewitness account, "The top of the dam was moving back and forth. . . .the dam was settling down and shoving forward." Trying to walk anywhere in the vicinity of the dam was "like walking in soup—it had gotten real, real juicy, buddy, all the way down. I got in the car and got the hell out of there."

The top of the dam was lower on one side than on the other, apparently from foundation settling, and now the top was slumping still further with a momentum that could not have been stopped by an army of bulldozers. One of the several federal reports theorizes that the water level rose quickly during the night, not just because rain was falling, but because the dam had been collapsing slowly into the lake for several hours. But even while the rain continued, the tipple went on pumping its 500 gallons a minute into the sludgy lake behind the dam.

30-FOOT FLOOD

Whatever happened in the night, it was morning now, and there was enough light to see what was happening. Apparently no one saw the actual moment when the dam finally gave way. It seems to have happened very fast—the dam settling until water was running across the top, the water cutting a cleft into the dam, more water hurrying through, and then complete and total collapse, and millions of gallons of water and hundreds of thousands of tons of sludge streaming across the top of the slag pile at the beginning of catastrophe.

The water cascaded into the burning section of the slag heap and erupted in a volcanic explosion. Men were coming off shift at the tipple and saw what was happening; they saw a mushroom cloud burst into the air from the explosion, saw mud and rock thrown 300 feet into the sky, saw the windshields of their pickup trucks covered with steaming mud. They raced back up the road and tried to use the telephone at the tipple to send out a warning, but the line was already dead. The tipple was safe—it was upstream, up another fork of the creek, out of the path of the destruction—but the men were cut off from the main stream of Buffalo Creek and there was no way they could help anyone. They could only watch as the water and sludge crested over the top of the exploding gob pile and burst into the valley, "boiling up like dry flour when you pour water on it."

The flood traveled at first at a speed of at least 30 miles an hour—in a solid wall 20 or 30 feet high. People who saw it coming as they headed up the Buffalo Creek road barely had time to throw their cars into reverse, turn around wherever there was room, and head back downstream, leaning on their horns, flashing their lights, trying to warn other people who had heard the explosions but still did not know what was happening. There was very little time to do anything. It takes a few seconds to collect your wits when you see a wall of water bearing down on you, especially when you live in a valley where there are only a few exits—hollows running at right angles to the main valley. For most of the people who died, it was like being in the barrel of a gun and seeing the bullet coming. There was nowhere to go.

That so many people did escape is something of a miracle. Nearly 5,000 people lived in the path of the flood. Probably a thousand were caught up in it, battered, left shaken, and sometimes badly hurt, but alive. From the wreckage of 16 communities, the bodies of 118 people have been found. There are others still missing; the final toll may be close to 150.

THE ONLY LIFE THEY KNEW

What happens after a disaster of such magnitude? There are inquiries, of course, and inquiries are under way in West Virginia. But in Appalachian affairs, the official response tends to have a common theme. After the Farmington mine disaster killed 78 miners, it was an Interior Department assistant secretary who said brightly: "We don't know why these things happen, but they do." After the 1970 mine explosion that killed 38 men in Kentucky, it was a newly installed director of the Bureau of Mines who said: "We can almost expect one of these every year." While the search for bodies was still continuing in Logan County, West Virginia's Governor Arch Moore was already defending the Pittston Company: The sludge-built dam had served a "logical and constructive" use by filtering mine wastes that would otherwise have gone unfiltered into Buffalo Creek. It didn't seem to matter much how the thing was built. The state legislature chose not to investigate, instead leaving to the gov-ernor the selection of an official commission which would be told to report back by the end of summer. "It's easy to say that the dam shouldn't have been there," Moore said at one point. "But it had been there for 25 years." He was technically wrong, of course, but the inference seemed to be that if a hazard simply exists long enough, it has a right to be left alone. And by the same token, the Governor made it painfully clear that he would ask the same treatment for the problems of West Virginia. The real tragedy, he said, a tragedy greater even than what had befallen the people of Buffalo Creek, was the unflattering coverage of West Virginia in the national press.

In fact there had been precious little of that. The flood had been on page one for two or three days, but it was eclipsed by the President's tour through China (from Shanghai, where he learned of the flood, Nixon sent an expression of regret, concluding from a distance of many thousands of miles that it was a terrible "natural disaster" and promising speedy federal aid); and within a week it would be forgotten, dismissed as one of those things. *Time,* for example, observed that the people of Buffalo Creek would have been well advised to live elsewhere, but they had stayed on in the shadow of the smouldering gob pile presumably because "that was the only life they knew."

PASSING THE BUCK TO GOD

The Interior Department, meanwhile, explained through Assistant Secretary Hollis Dole that there was, in its opinion, no federal responsibility in the matter, despite the fact that regulations within the 1969 Federal Coal Mine Health and Safety Act specifically cover the construction and use of gob piles and retaining dams. There were no indications that the government would move to take action against Pittston unless it was prodded by an outraged Congress; on Capital Hill there was no outraged Congress to be found.

There would be room for doubt, in any event, about the kind of action that the Department of the Interior would take even if it were forced to do something. The department is reluctant to think of itself as a regulatory agency, or as a federal cop, and among all of the subordinate agencies within the department, the Bureau of Mines is a standout example of one that has refused to grasp the idea of representing the public interest. The problem might not be serious if a system of countervailing power were in operation—if, for example, the people of Buffalo Creek could have counted on the United Mine Workers to represent them against the overwhelming resources and indifference of the Pittston Company. There had been scattered efforts along Buffalo Creek to protest the slag heaps and the sludge dams—petitions had been circulated, attention had been demanded. But the effort never went anywhere, and it never went anywhere partly because no powerful organization, like the union, chose to push it. The union hasn't pushed much of anything in some time except perhaps the fringe benefits available to its ranking officers. The result is that on one side of the equation there is a powerful industry deeply dedicated to its own interests; on the other side there is, most of the time, nothing at all. And in the middle, where there should be an even-handed government agency, there is instead the Bureau of Mines, an organization so encrusted with age and bureaucracy that it will not even support its own inspectors when they try to do their jobs.

They had, for example, been trying to do their jobs at Pittston's mines, trying to cut down the number of men killed in needless accidents. Over the past year they had slapped thousands of violation notices on the company. The idea is that the notices will cost money; get fined often enough and hard enough, the theory goes, and you will become safety-conscious in the extreme. It hasn't worked that way. Thanks to a highly complex assessment system set up in Washington by a former lobbyist who is now in charge of the Bureau's fines-collection operation, Pittston has been able to defer, seemingly indefinitely, any payment for its sins. Specifically, over the past year inspectors had fined Pittston a total of $1,303,315 for safety violations. As of April 1, the company had appealed every one of the notices it had received and had paid a grand total of $275 to the government.

Meanwhile, on Buffalo Creek, the investigations continue, the reports are compiled, the survivors try to plan a future; the mines, only briefly disrupted by the raging flood, are back at work, and the long trains roll. One month after the disaster, Pittston set up an office to process claims—without, however, accepting liability. The company's official view is still that God did it—and if, by any chance, God should pass the buck back down: "We believe that the investigations of the tragedy have not progressed to the point where it is possible to assess responsibility." It's possible that such a point will never be reached. Who was responsible, for example, for deciding to spend $90,000 to buy Nicholas Camicia's house, but *not* to spend the $50,000 that it might have cost—according to one of the federal reports—to build a safe dam at the head of Buffalo Creek? There are sticky questions like that rising in the aftermath of the disaster, questions that will be hard to answer. "There is never peace in West Virginia because there is never justice," said Mother Jones, the fiery hell-raiser of West Virginia's early labor wars. On Buffalo Creek these days there is a strange kind of quiet, a peacefulness of sorts, but it is not the kind that comes with justice.

This article was published by *The Washington Monthly*, May 1972. Reprinted by permission.

COAL GOVERNMENT OF APPALACHIA

Compiled By A Student Task Force
For Appalachian Research and Defense Fund
1116-B Kanawha Boulevard E.
Charleston, West Virginia

. . . GOVERNORS

Prior to his election as governor, Arch Moore represented West Virginia as a Congressman. Prior to his election to Congress, however, Governor Moore began his career in the corporate structure as an attorney serving Allied Chemicals, Mobay Chemicals (which he continued to serve while he was a member of Congress), Columbia Southern Chemicals, and Texas Eastern Transmission Company. His predecessor in office, Hulette Smith, had previously served as president of Investment Securities, Inc., vice president of the First Beckley Corporation, director of the Bank of Raleigh, vice president of Beckley College, director and treasurer of Beckley and Oak Hill hospitals; he also helped organize the Beckley Area Rural Development Council and the Beckley Business Development Corporation. Since leaving office, Mr. Smith has continued his many-faceted career in banking and hospitals. Cecil Underwood rose from humble beginnings as a school teacher, but he apparently attracted corporate attention while he was governor. He went on to serve as vice president of

SOURCE: *Published by the Appalachian Research and Defense Fund, August, 1971.*

AUTHORS: *Report compiled by a Student Task Force for the Appalachian Research and Defense Fund in cooperation with the American Friends Service Committee and Law Students Civil Rights Research Council.*

278 *Colonialism in Modern America*

Island Creek Coal Co., Director of Civic Affairs for Monsanto, Director of West Virginia Life Insurance Company, director of Huntington Federal Savings and Loan Associates, and President of Cecil H. Underwood Associates, in which venture he was joined by David Francis, president of Princess Coal Company.

By contrast, William Marland forgot whom the governor commonly serves. During his term he made the error of recommending a severance tax on coal; he finished life as an alcoholic cab driver in Chicago.

. . . CASE STUDY: THE BUILDING OF STATE ROUTE 99

Route 99 cuts a swath through the tops of the beautiful high mountains which mark the southern edge of the Coal River Watershed. The road is only 10.016 miles in length and runs from a junction with State Route 85 in Boone County, slightly north of Kopperston (an Eastern Gas and Fuel Company town in Wyoming Co.), and east to Bolt in Raleigh County. At some unspecified future date there is supposed to be an extension of the road which will turn Route 99 into a major east-west artery connecting Logan and Beckley. The road is made of six inches of asphalt poured over 12 inches of crushed rock—extremely sturdy construction, even for a mountain road. Both firms which built the road obtain more of their money from strip mining than they do from construction. They gouged a tremendous cut for the road with explosives and heavy equipment. This left towering high walls, often on both sides, of bleak rock. Driving over the road, one is not surprised that it cost over $5,200,000 to build initially. However, it is surprising to find that there is almost no traffic on the road, since the State Department of Highways insists that the first criterion used in the building of a road is whether the road will pay for itself in terms of the gas tax taken in by vehicles using the road. A quick check of the state road map shows no sizable town on or around the road and almost no one who will be served by the road as a through route.

Why then was this particular road built? The highway department and other officials have offered various reasons. Former Governor Smith suggested that the entire area was going to be a scenic recreation area, but both sides of the road are lined with some of the most devastated countryside imaginable, scarred by the stark slashes of the 40 strip mines in the area.

The central office of the Department of Highways offered a different and far more plausible explanation. Although unsure who it was that made the decision, one high ranking official did point out that the road has "opened that area up." Acknowledging that almost no one lived in an area to use the road as a through highway connecting any urban centers, he nonetheless allowed as how it was important to open areas up to people to live in and industries to develop. Just which people and which industries the area has been opened up for becomes obvious when the history of the road and the surrounding area is examined.

Kopperston is a model company town built near the mouths of many large underground mines by the Koppers Company; it is now operated by Eastern Gas and Fuel Associates, one of the giants of the coal industry. Building such towns is expensive, however, and no such plans were made in connection with the development of the Harris mine, another giant underground operation which opened near the current junction of Route 99 and Route 85 about the same time the road was built. Eastern's new mine employs over three hundred miners, a quarter of whom live in the eastern part of Boone County and Raleigh County. Before Route 99 was built, the only way for these miners to get to work was to drive far north of their homes to Seth and then across or far south along Route 1 through Glenfork and Oceana, then north again. The more than eighty miners who lived east of Bolt live on a road pattern designed for access to Beckley, the seat of Raleigh County. Near Beckley, Eastern was in the process of closing down several worked-out deep mines. In order to keep its miners, it had to find some way to get them to the new mining site. Route 99 provides a perfect connection for people in eastern Boone County and the Beckley region to get to the Harris Mine and back. It serves almost nothing else, or nothing else which existed before it opened that part of Boone County up. Now it serves more than 40 strip mines which are in operation along its length and at one end of the road.

At the same time the plans were finalized for building the road, Eastern Coal and Appalachian Power Company jointly indicated an interest in building, with Federal assistance, a rural New Town at what is now the eastern end of Route 99 near

Bolt.   As work on the plans for the new city at Fairdale advanced, it became clear that the type town Eastern had in mind was not the type that would obtain federal approval.   Initial inquiries were discouraging enough to prevent formal application from ever being made, and the idea of the city was put silently to rest.   The major problem was Eastern's nervousness whenever mention was made of attracting other industries into the town. Eastern wanted the town to be housing for its workers. Eastern had been seeking a company town which would not cost Eastern anything, one for which the state and the federal governments would pay.

Officials then serving in the highway department were delighted when they first heard that a new city was under consideration for Fairdale. Their joy stemmed from the fact that the plan to build that city (of which they had known nothing when Route 99 was laid out) would serve as an excellent justification for a previously unjustifiable project. They were no doubt even more disappointed than Eastern when the plans never advanced beyond the talking stage.

Since the owners of the land over which Route 99 was built are large land companies which hold the land until it can be profitably mined, it is not surprising that they were quite willing to grant the state permission to enter their land and construct the road—even before the price of the land was negotiated and the land bought. As of late 1970, the land (upon which the road lay) had still not been purchased, and the case was slated for adjudication. Their willingness to allow the state on the land becomes understandable when maps of the area are examined. State road maps of the region before the route was completed show no mines along Route 99. The area, now stripped so completely, was almost inaccessible before it could be reached by 99. The highway department personnel who reported on the use of the road always mentioned the semi-trailers carrying explosives and equipment to the strip mines' cutting face in addition to the miners going to and from those sites and the large underground sites further to the west. Most of the land being stripped and most of road right-of-way were owned initially by Eastern Gas and Fuel Associates. It is now owned by Pennva, a giant land-holding subsidiary of another giant coal producer, Pittston Corp.

Another major beneficiary of Route 99 was stripper and road builder Leo Vecillio of Beckley. Vecillio and Grogan, Inc. is the construction firm which built most of Route 99. Ranger Fuel (Leo Vecillio, President) operated 21 strip mines along the road and also 20 mines in Pond Fork now made accessible to them by Route 99. Ranger Fuel marketed its coal through Eastern Gas and Fuel Associates. In 1970, Ranger was also sold to the Pittston Corporation.

Nor have expenditures stopped after 1966-1967, when the road was cut and graded through the mountains. In 1970, another contract was awarded to Black Rock Contracting, Inc. of Charleston to pave the road, which theretofore had not received a permanent blacktopping. That added an additional 1.4 million dollars to the figure of 5 million previously spent.

The original 5,000,000 dollars used to build this impressive stretch of two-lane road came from a bond issue passed initially to be used on the federal interstate system. If the money had been used for that purpose, it would have been matched by $45,000,000 in federal dollars and could have built over 30 miles of four-lane interstate.

The use of the funds on a project which could not qualify for any federal matching money (the Appalachian Regional Commission's money at the time would not go to roads serving only mines) was not illegal. The legislature had provided that the money could also be used for the public roads of the state (a provision intended for any excess of funds after spending on interstates), but it was at least improvident to spend it on a solely state-financed road which in reality cost the state not 5 but 50 million dollars in lost road-building ability. Shortly after the road was contracted for, the federal government, stung by the cost of its military adventures in Southeast Asia, ordered a freeze on interstate building. This freeze was based on the amount of money which the states had previously spent on the program. Thus the Route 99 fiasco continued to hurt the state over the next few years.

A delegate from Wyoming County bemoaning the costly construction of Route 99 for special interests pointed out that the policy still continues. In his county one road was being built from Pineville to a new Bethlehem Steel Mine five miles away.

Another road from Pineville to Baileysville was being widened to better serve the Keppler mines. "It's certainly sad that the only way we can get any roads in southern West Virginia is when it benefits the coal operators," the delegate observed. "The people can cry for roads, but the only time they ever seem to be built is when the coal companies need them." ("Roads for Coal Firms Only Pattern Ripped by McGraw" *Sunday Gazette-Mail*, 28 June 1970.)

THE FEDERAL GOVERNMENT IN APPALACHIA:
TVA

by
James Branscome

INTRODUCTION

On May 18, 1933, President Franklin D. Roosevelt leaned back in his chair and handed Senator George Norris the pen with which he had just signed the Tennessee Valley Authority Act. While Roosevelt was an enthusiastic supporter of the TVA idea, he could hardly have guessed that this act of signing a bill, previously vetoed in 1928 by President Coolidge and in 1931 by President Hoover, would result in the creation of one of the most enduringly controversial and also saluted projects to emerge from the famous "hundred days."

Roosevelt believed the crucial compromises had already been made. In his signing the bill he hoped he had laid the "socialism" and "regional favoritism" criticisms to rest with his promise that TVA would be a "corporation clothed with the power of government but possessed of the flexibility and initiative of a private enterprise." The President, who had fought high utility rates as the governor of New York, hoped that the agency would be a "yardstick" of true power production costs; but he wanted more. TVA was to be more than dams and water and power lines. It was to be more than a Washington-based bureaucracy mired in the competing jealousies of tired and face-

SOURCE: *The Field Foundation, (c) 1977.*

AUTHOR: James Branscome *is a free lance writer who writes for* The Mountain Eagle.

less federal agencies.   It was, the president said, to be a near
contradiction as a federal agency: "a return to the spirit and
vision of the pioneer," based in the region it was to serve, concerned with the complexities of national development, but also
an agency that "touches and gives life to all forms of human
concern."   It was, in short, a mere first step in a national experiment where—if it succeeded—"we can march on, step by step,
in the like development of other great national territorial units
within our borders."

Even though it was favored several times by the Supreme
Court, and beat government-inspired conspiracies like Dixon-
Yates of the early 50's, even though it successfully defeated one
of the toughest onslaughts ever organized by private power
trusts, and even though it made a remarkable record of achievement imitated world-wide, the TVA idea never sprouted successfully in any other area of the country.

A. *The Early Record of TVA*

Few people who have had a course in modern American
history need a recitation of the good deeds by the agency in the
early days.   It tamed the nation's fifth largest river, turning the
once flood-prone 650 mile giant into the world's most controlled
river.   It planted eroded land and invented fertilizers and gave
them away.   It turned poor farmers into skilled workers, employing at the height of World War II 40,000 people, most of
them trained by the agency.   Unique even today among federal
agencies, it allowed its employees to join unions.   When the
companies defeated the United Mine Workers' first large organizing drive in the southern coalfields in Fentress County, Tennessee, and then blacklisted the miners, the agency hired more
than 200 *en masse* in 1934.   It sold its power only to cooperatives organized and controlled by the people.   It did other
things, and, importantly, it won the confidence of the people.
When the private power companies built "spite lines" into TVA
territory, the farmers chopped down the poles.

In 20 years the agency built 20 dams.   In 1953 the total
dam system had cost $24.5 million and averted potential flood
damage estimated at more than $51 million.   In 1952 alone the
navigation system had saved barge shippers probably $10 million,

at an expense of $3.5 million. Since 1933 it had reforested 212,000 acres of land and produced 295 million seedlings in its nursery. Over the same period 68,000 farmers had allowed their farms to be TVA test demonstration areas to educate them and their neighbors about new farming techniques. Per capita income had risen from 44% of the national average in 1929 to 60% in 1952. Manufacturing employment opportunities had increased 20% faster in the valley than in the nation.

As impressive as the statistics are, they fail to convey the sheer magnitude of the project in a seven state area of 201 counties, the size of New England. The concrete, rock, and earth laid in the path of the river and its tributaries were 12 times the bulk of the Great Pyramids. The volume of water behind its dams would cover the entire state of Illinois to a depth of eight inches. But more important, and surprising, an agency that had a vague mandate to "sell the surplus power not used in its operations" had by its twentieth year become the nation's largest utility, selling power at the lowest prices to a people who in 1933 had almost no knowledge of the electric age. By 1953 the agency's customers—one in 28 farms in the valley had power in 1933—were consuming twice as much power as their national counterparts.

TVA's wonders were not accomplished without sacrifices, however, and there were many less than admirable aspects to the agency even in the early days.

To build its dams the agency forced the removal of 125,480 people. It has bought or condemned two million acres of land, creating in the place of occasional flooding a giant permanent flood. In the early days, board member Harcourt Morgan, a former president of the University of Tennessee, turned the agency's farm program into little more than mimicry of the policies of the land grant colleges and the extension services. The agency made its peace with the Farm Bureau, even though that organization had advocated that instead of a TVA, the government should sell its $90 million investment in the Wilson Dam at Muscle Shoals to Henry Ford for $5 million. Ignoring its reputed commitment to civil rights, the agency built separate facilities at its dam sites for blacks and whites. (Even today, among the top 37 staffers who meet regularly with the board, only one is a black and one a woman. In the memory of reporters who have attended the meetings since they were forced open in 1975 in response to press pressure, the black has never spoken at a meeting and the woman has spoken up only once, when the agency was moving to abolish the home economics division of which she is a part.)

But despite the scars, most people agreed with Henry Steele Commager in 1950 that the agency was "the greatest peacetime achievement of twentieth century America."

B. *The Turning Point*

From almost the first meeting of the three board members in 1933, the agency was torn over its direction. Arthur Morgan's "human engineering," his seeming willingness to compromise with Wendell Willkie (then head of the southern power trusts), and his undocumented charges of "evasion, intrigue, and sharp strategy" against Lilienthal and H. A. Morgan, led to his dismissal by Roosevelt in 1938. With Morgan gone, Lilienthal, who believed the agency would live or die by the power program, was victor. His successor as chairman, Gordon Clapp, launched the agency in 1949-53 into building seven coal fired plants—the largest in the world—to meet the power demands on the system. Had it not been for the cold war and the Atomic Energy Commission, which by 1955 was consuming a full half of TVA's output at its Oak Ridge and Paducah uranium enrichment plants, the agency would have had the largest surplus capacity of any utility in the world. To stave off the Eisenhower administration's Dixon-Yates conspiracy and other efforts to reduce its effectiveness, the agency began saluting its contribution to defense above all its other efforts. In that climate, a new generation of leadership—far more cautious, technically oriented, and politically conservative—moved in to make policy at TVA. This new generation saw cheap power as the means to trump all opposition.

By the middle 1950's TVA had set a pattern for its future coal purchases, concentrating them in western Kentucky where low grade, high sulfur coal fields were being developed by independent coal firms. Armed with long term contract offers, technical equipment at its plants that would allow the burning of low quality coal, and no hesitancy in purchasing non-union coal, TVA's coal buyers, with direction from then General Manager Aubrey J. Wagner and Board Chairman Herbert D. Vogel, set out to guarantee that fuel prices would remain low. Operating against a slumped coal market and a rapidly declining United Mine Workers (UMW) union, the TVA revolutionized the steam coal market. As the nation's largest buyer and with skillful use and re-use of competitive bidding to lower the price of coal proffered to the agency, TVA helped to bankrupt operators in the southern Tennessee, east Kentucky, and other central Appalachian coal fields. Union-organized deep mines, especially those with strong locals that deprived operators of sweetheart contracts from the increasingly corrupt UMW, found themselves unable to remain in business.

Not so Appalachian and western Kentucky strip mines. Small strip mine companies like Kentucky Oak Mining of Hazard, Kentucky, found TVA a willing accomplice in granting long term contracts and providing technical assistance in machinery design and mining procedures. In the early 1960's when the "Roving Pickets" movement was shutting down the eastern Kentucky coal fields and violence was causing concern even at the White House, few coal miners realized that the reason for the sweetheart contracts, the withdrawal of the UMW hospital cards, and the starvation economy was in part the steam coal policies that TVA was pursuing quietly in Knoxville. With Kentucky Oak Mining bringing strip mining, a process little practiced until then, to eastern Kentucky on a vast scale, no deep mine could possibly compete with its prices, which were frequently as low as $3 a ton.

Meanwhile, in western Kentucky and eastern Tennessee, TVA was building mine mouth steam plants on or near strip mines and signing long term contracts for millions of tons of coal. The prices for the western Kentucky coal, albeit of lower quality, were far below what it cost Appalachian producers to mine coal. With the long term contracts, which amounted to loan guarantees at most financial institutions, the western Kentucky producers opened mines in thick seams, mined with shovels that dwarfed anything ever seen before on the American landscape, and sealed the doom of the independent Appalachian deep mine companies. In the name of cheap fuel, the agency was laying the groundwork for the horrors that now haunt it and its region.

C. A Bitter Harvest

When President Kennedy called together his advisers in the
early days of his administration to determine how to deal with
the disturbing reports that were coming from Appalachia, especially eastern Kentucky, he found them ill-prepared to come
up with solutions or, in fact, able to comprehend that what was
happening was related in more than a small way to policies being
made by a government agency in Knoxville. At one point he sent
an aide from his office with an order to find 100 doctors before
winter to go to eastern Kentucky; the aide found none. As the
administration made other decisions related to the mountains, it
ignored the role that TVA had played in the havoc and could
play in the solution. In 1961, Kennedy named Aubrey Wagner
to the TVA board and appointed him chairman in 1962; in 1963,
he named Wagner to the President's Appalachian Regional Commission that was to study how to solve poverty in the mountains. There is no evidence that Wagner or anyone else was ever
questioned about, or did themselves question, TVA's role in
creating the coal market slump that had brought on the unemployment and the union busting in the mountain coalfields.
The UMW leadership, having failed even under Lewis's leadership
to get TVA to change its policies, had already turned to Cyrus
Eaton to get him to buy up TVA suppliers with union money.
By the early 1960's the union was as interested as the Chamber
of Commerce in trying to discredit media reports of poverty in
eastern Kentucky. TVA's bitter harvest would come home in
other ways.

By 1974 TVA was buying 37 million tons of coal a year to
fuel its 12 steam plants which were producing 80% of its power.
A full 72% of the coal was coming from Kentucky, one-half of
it strip mined. Disturbingly also, for an agency that once saw
itself as "democracy on the march," a full 83% of the coal was
now being supplied by a dozen firms, all of them owned by oil
or metal conglomerates. In that year, the giants turned on their
friendly benefactor. Prices more than doubled. Suddenly TVA's
cheap power was no longer so cheap. Giant TVA suppliers like
Island Creek, chaired by the once friendly Senator Albert Gore
and owned by Occidental Petroleum, demanded a $3 a ton profit
guarantee, with a 50-50 split of profit over $6 a ton. TVA signed.
Mapco (Mid-America Pipeline Co.), owner of Webster County
Coal Corp., raised its price from $8.50 per ton to over $30. TVA

signed.

Mr. Wagner condemned the price increases and damned publicly the increasing energy concentration. This was taken seriously in some quarters, but knowledgeable observers saw a clear connection between past agency policy and the prices. The *Mountain Eagle,* of Whitesburg, Kentucky, revealed that two coal companies owned in part by Ashland Oil had defaulted on a $25 million TVA loan guarantee made in secret by the TVA board in 1970. In rapid fire fashion, other puzzling coal deals by TVA came to light:

(1) it had selected Peabody Coal Co., the world's largest, to open a new deep mine on TVA property in western Kentucky and had agreed to equip the mine and pay Peabody a guaranteed fee per ton, despite the fact that in 1971 Peabody had the worst deep mine safety record in the industry;

(2) in 1974 it had signed contracts worth $58 million with a company it was alleging in federal court had defrauded it on past contracts;

(3) it was accepting truck loads of rock, mud, and slate disguised as coal at its Kingston Steam Plant, taking action to stop only after repeated exposures of the practice in the media;

(4) it had made a secret bid of $1 billion to purchase Peabody.

These actions were only a part of a disturbing pattern that began to emerge publicly in the early 1970s. In a June 17, 1974, speech, Wagner told the National Coal Association that portions of the Mine Health and Safety Act "should be eliminated" in the interest of production. But TVA's coal purchasing practices were bothering in other ways too.

Because of its policy of buying low heat (approximately 11,000 BTUs per pound as opposed to national utility average of over 12,000 BTUs.) and high sulfur coal, a combination TVA claimed was cheap, the agency was in trouble with the nation's air cleanup program. The Environmental Protection Agency told the agency either to find low sulfur supplies (at least lower than the 4.5% sulfur coal it buys from some suppliers) or install scrubbers. TVA refused to do either. Wagner called scrubbers "a billion dollar pig in a poke," and launched TVA on a program of building tall stacks at its steam plants to disperse, rather than clean up, its sulfur dioxide emissions. EPA officials, mindful that TVA emits 14% of all utility sulfur dioxide nationally and 52% of the poison in eight states of the South, refused in 1974 to compromise further its stand on constant controls. Aware that failure to clean up TVA would mean a license for private utilities also to defy the law, EPA took its stand in federal courts, where in 1976 it got final word from the Supreme Court that TVA's compliance program violated the clean air laws.

The end result of TVA's reliance on its traditional suppliers and low quality coal is that it now finds itself unable to buy enough low sulfur coal to comply with the law. In an October 1976 bid opening, the agency received no significant bid from old suppliers for low sulfur coal and got few worthy offers from other suppliers. Chairman Wagner now claims the reason is that suppliers are holding coal off the market for higher prices. State Representative Lewis McManus, the former speaker of the West Virginia House of Representatives, and a critic of TVA for failing to buy low sulfur coal in his state, says the reason is that the agency will not negotiate with that state's small producers. TVA general manager Lynn Seeber rejoins that the agency has to buy by competitive bidding. McManus points out that the TVA board declared an "emergency" in 1973-74 and re-negotiated most of its long term contracts at higher prices with the conglomerate suppliers. Alone of utilities, it is now negotiating on an "emergency basis" for low sulfur coal.

TVA's new trump is nuclear power. It has more nuclear capacity planned than any utility in the country. In March 1975 its Brown's Ferry plant was knocked out for over a year by a worker using a candle to check for air leaks in a cable room. In December 1976 a fire caused by an electric heater destroyed the building that would have been used for start-up operation in 1978 of the Sequoyah nuclear plant. Mr. Wagner says nuclear power is safer than highway driving, cheaper than coal, and that the agency has no intention of backing away from its present nuclear emphasis unless coal power becomes cheaper. And while it pursues the nuclear commitment, the agency is now testing low sulfur coal from Montana as a possible source of supply for its Shawnee steam plant; it is doing so despite the fact that the coal is non-union, low BTU, and higher priced than quality low sulfur deep mine coal being purchased by private utilities in Appalachia.

D. Economic Status in the TVA Region

The Tennessee Valley watershed covers 40,910 square miles of land in seven states and 125 counties. About half the counties overlap with ARC territory in Tennessee, Alabama, North Carolina, Virginia, Georgia, Kentucky, and Mississippi. The TVA power service territory covers the same states but includes 170 counties, making the total counties covered by TVA 201, with a population over 6.7 million. The combined TVA territory covers 80,000 square miles.

When TVA was founded in 1933, personal income in these 201 counties was 45% of the national average, or about $168 per capita. In 1974, the figure was $4,262, or 78% of the national level of $5,448. That compares with the southeastern U.S. level (excluding Florida) of 84% of the U.S. level, or $4,602.[1]

In 1933, 62% of the region's jobs were in agriculture; in 1973, 6%. Manufacturing jobs in 1933 accounted for 12% of the work force; in 1973, 33%. Total manufacturing jobs in the valley increased 73% from 1960 to 1973, or 18% faster than the national average. Much of the industrial growth occurred in resource development areas related to TVA's activities, but the direct correlation is not possible to measure.

While federal appropriations to TVA have averaged $65 million a year since TVA was founded, the Valley's receipt of federal expenditure ($10,822 per person) is still far below the national average ($16,759 per person) over the period of 1934-1970; and only one-tenth or less of the Valley's receipts of federal monies were for TVA. The TVA power program is financed from current revenues and from a bond ceiling set by Congress at $15 billion, approximately 3% of the national debt. Since the self-financing reforms of 1959, TVA has paid back to the Treasury all but about one-fourth of the total federal investment in the power system.

TVA's only demand on the U.S. Treasury is the approximately $135 million a year current budget which supports non-power projects like the National Fertilizer Development Center at Muscle Shoals, Alabama (the Center holds patents on three-fourths of the world's fertilizer formulas), a tributary area development program, flood control, and industrial development.

The TVA region lags far behind the nation in earnings per worker when compared with the national average on an industry-group basis. In the region 36% of the workers earn less than $8,000 per year; nationally 16% do. The number of TVA region workers earning between $10-$12,000 per year is 29%, compared with a national percentage of 44. Part of the explanation is that the region has a larger share than the nation of low-wage paying industries. For example, 27% of the valley workers are employed in apparel and textile industries compared with 3% nationally. A 1974 TVA economic outlook report concluded: "The new manufacturing job holders in the TVA region have not yet become the average consumers or owners of wealth of either the Southeast or the nation."

One area in which the TVA region clearly outstrips the nation is in the growth of energy-intensive industry. Industries in the first quartile of electric energy use per employee grew at a rate of 4% in the period 1959-64 in the region compared with a decline of 0.3% in the nation. From 1964-74, the same industries grew at a rate of 4% in the region compared with a 0.8% rise in the nation. The growth is unquestionably tied to the fact that TVA rates are at an average 40% below the national average.

In the growth of wood-using industries over the past decade the TVA region leads both the nation and the Southeast, the nation by nearly 3 to 1.

TVA estimates that 44,000 jobs have been created in manufacturing plants located at major terminal points on the Tennessee River. The agency itself currently employs over 25,000 people, most of them in construction trades.

E. Conclusion

TVA brought many benefits to its 201 counties. Its cheap power brought havoc to some of those counties and hell to other parts of Appalachia. While pursuing this policy the agency has raised the incomes in the TVA region to around 75% of the national average, *about the same figure as for all of Appalachia.* The agency now is its own chief argument against spreading TVAs across the land, and its reform is a necessary first step in making sense of national energy problems and economic problems of the Appalachian South.

NOTE

[1]All figures used in this section were supplied by the TVA Department of Information, Regional Research Department, and the Power Division.

HIDDEN TRAPS OF REGIONALISM

by
Phil Primack

Regionalism—that is, the designation of quite large geographical units for planning and administrative purposes—is very much a part of the American system now, its current surge the perhaps inevitable result of problems grown too large and complex for local units of government to handle alone. It could be a welcome development: Water and air pollution know no city bounds; isolated rural counties can provide more adequate medical services by pooling resources. But if one can point to notable examples of regionalism working for the common good, there also have been some outright failures as well as instances of expectations unfulfilled. Such is the case in the Appalachian region, where the progress of regionalism merits close review lest similar mistakes be unnecessarily repeated.

Successful attempts at regionalism have two common factors: They have had the tools and the mandate with which to proceed. Thus in the San Francisco Bay Area the population has long demonstrated a willingness for and understanding of the need and procedure for some regional cooperation. (See "Regional Transport: San Francisco Maps Our Future" by Mary Ellen Leary, *The Nation*, July 30.) The tools have been primarily fiscal or statutory, but the mandate has been the involvement and informed consent of the concerned population. Where that

SOURCE: The Nation, *(c) September 24, 1973, pp. 272-276.*

AUTHOR: Phil Primack, *an activist journalist, is a former reporter for* The Mountain Eagle. *He has monitored ARC activities in Washington and writes frequently for* The Nation.

ingredient has been missing, good intentions have often failed to produce effective regional action. In many places, certainly in Appalachia, regional mechanisms have tried to operate in a vacuum of citizen awareness and support.

The questions raised by the spread of regionalism are as important for the local populations involved as they are for the ultimate success of regionalism itself. Who determines where and how a regional body shall have authority? What is the role for citizens in such determinations? To whom are regional board members accountable, and how are they chosen? How are the agency's criteria and funding priorities set? To give such questions anything less than full attention is in itself poor planning.

Appalachia has long been a programmer's guinea pig, the testing ground for a wide array of federal and state efforts. It is significant, therefore, that alarms are ringing in Appalachia, where a small but apparently growing number of people perceive regionalism as a threat to their ability to control local affairs of daily importance. They say that power over such basics as schools and garbage disposal has passed from their own hands into the murky authority of something called a regional agency or district.

Appalachia became a testing ground for regionalism in the early 1960's when conditions there had become economically so critical that President Kennedy realized something had to be done about a situation which local and state governments appeared unwilling or unable to correct. The result was a commission charged with producing effective ideas and designing a mechanism by which to implement them. The Appalachian Regional Commission (ARC) was formally and fiscally delivered by President Johnson in 1965.

From the beginning ARC billed itself as a "unique federal-state partnership," relying upon gubernatorial support and strategy. Also from the beginning, residents of the area predicted long-range ineffectiveness for the new creature, because it chose to ignore what many felt to be the keys to any lasting economic and social independence for Appalachia: local control and use of the region's vast natural resources, the rape of which had been responsible for much of the area's plight in the first place. The governors and such key Congressional figures as Sen.

Jennings Randolph wanted no part of that kind of activity; accordingly, the ARC has specialized in the political safety of bricks and mortar.

At the same time, no broader example of regionalism has been operating in the country these past eight years. Appalachian regionalism has been on both the multi-state and substate level. As for the former, policy and spending decisions are supposed to be based on regional criteria. That is, the governors of the thirteen Appalachian states supposedly view needs on a multi-state, regional level first and consider their own immediate economic or political needs second. The theory is fine, but it hasn't worked out. "All you have is thirteen guys, some of whom see their governors maybe twice a year, sitting around the table trying to bring home their own slab of bacon," says one former high ARC official who feels the experiment is lost.

At the substate level, ARC has leaned heavily on its "co-ordinated investment strategy" of concentrating investments in those areas showing "the greatest potential for future growth," as opposed to the Economic Development Administration's criterion of greatest need. Programs are to be assessed on the prospect that expenditures of money and effort in a given area will spread the results beyond the immediate application. This has meant lumping towns and counties into "growth centers." And growth areas have been translated into political action by creation of the "local development district" (LDD).

These bodies are formed so that each will contain at least one "growth center." Often that is their only unifying factor, with some notable cases of bad grouping (foothills with mountain counties, coal with non-coal, high population with low). In any case, it is through the LDDs that ARC follows its coordinated investment strategy. Some planners see that strategy, and the LDDs which go with it, as a national model. But as a model it has received scant scrutiny.

For one thing, while some ARC officials sincerely believe that the investment strategy has worked to alleviate Appalachian poverty, statistics from that part of the region which prompted the Appalachian Act in the first place—the mountainous central area—belie any claims of marked improvement. And many observers of the eight-year operation say that investments have not been placed in areas of real potential growth but in those of real potential votes for the governor and Congressmen who announce each ARC grant. Recent moves by ARC's new executive director to reassert the role of the states in all ARC operations will, some disgruntled ARC staffers feel, further stifle whatever creativity and innovation there may have been by making the motive for funding political advantage rather than real need.

Critics make the same basic assessment of the LDD approach. It is through the LDDs that most nonhighway ARC dollars flow; it is from the LDDs that ARC professes to hear the voice of the local people. There's the rub. People in the mountains have become sharply attuned of late to possible threats to their way of life, and many see the LDDs as a major curb to their influence on governmental decisions at the local level. They object to the LDDs as an intermediate layer of government standing between them and the control levels for state and federal moneys. They know who sits on LDD boards—and who doesn't.

The contradiction is blatant: ARC views the LDD as the indicator of local will because it includes all the major elected officials in a development district; but some local citizens call the LDD an impediment to local will precisely because of that make-up. They contend that it's hard enough to deal with their own "courthouse gang"; merge six or eight or ten of them together in a single LDD and "you simply just don't have a chance," as one LDD observer put it recently.

If this, then, is to become a national model, some basic problems need to be solved. Who represents whom and how and according to what guidelines? No one has thought much about such questions, it having been assumed that, since the need for multi-jurisdictional cooperation was critical, getting something started came first. Therefore the tough questions have yet to be answered. How much constituted authority should the new regional mechanisms be given? And from what source should such power proceed? What matters will best be dealt with regionally, and what is more wisely left in local hands? In short, are these new bodies in any way more or less accountable to the wills of the resident population than the original governments whose function they are complementing or in some cases replacing outright?

In parts of Appalachia the matter has moved past theory. In western North Carolina, for example, a community observer sees the LDDs as little more than power-structure collectives, with vested interests parading as "elected officials" and "civic group representatives." They equate progress with profit, he says, and the effect of it well may be far afield from what well-intentioned backers of regionalization have in mind: "If the planners keep going, the effect will be to practically disinherit the small farmer who might have moved here generations ago to live out his time or escape service in the Civil War or whatever. And that citizen will be the last person to sit on the development district board."

The composition of board members tends to support the fear that LDDs in Appalachia are, at best, staffed from the top down. Even where representatives of the poor or of minority groups do sit on the board, they are generally so outnumbered that they fall silent. Besides, matters handled by LDD boards are often more within the scope of the banker than of the dirt farmer or auto worker. It is thus no surprise that the long-range planning or other actions of such boards often reflect a bias toward a corporate, "free enterprise" model of development— even where such a model is sadly inadequate or worse.

That's the most basic concern. Even though the majority on a board may be elected officials, they were not elected to serve on that board by that board's jurisdictional area as a whole. A new kind of political chemistry begins to operate when officials elected from different areas come together to make collective decisions for which they cannot be held individually accountable. People in Hill County did not elect their fiscal court judge to vote on matters involving eight other counties; and they surely did not authorize those nine other county officers to vote on affairs which affect Hill County.

Perhaps even worse, regional board decisions have often become legislation by the lowest common denominator of what everyone can agree upon. Because of the establishment-affiliated membership of most regional agencies, the criteria thus become what is politically and economically palatable to all vested interests involved. Proponents of regionalism argue that such has often been the case with local government, and they are right. A key difference remains: At the local level, aroused citizens had the ultimate level of the ballot box; on the regional level they don't.

Aside from basic questions of accountability, the lack of direct citizen involvement is not in the interests of regionalism itself. A regional board can make unnecessary mistakes simply because no one was there to spot an obvious blunder in the early stages. Citizens do show up at city council or fiscal court meetings when an important matter is at hand. But regional bodies are remote and little understood, so the interest isn't generated. Decisions of potentially major effect may thus be developed in a vacuum—a situation that is bad for the regional agency charged with problem solving, and far worse for the citizens living with the problem.

Once again, the premise that some regional cooperation can establish or improve needed facilities was and is sound. It is shortsighted to talk about a one-county garbage landfill when a larger and better one could be built to serve several counties at far less cost to the individual units. But it has proved to be equally shortsighted and wasteful to attempt any such regional effort without the real participation and consent of the several constituencies involved.

Indeed, results can be downright disastrous. In one eastern Kentucky LDD, the board unanimously and enthusiastically backed a plan for a regional sanitary landfill. The state had ordered the closing of all open burning dumps, so something had to be done. But bureaucratic bungling and shortsightedness in assessing local situations resulted in only one landfill being opened to serve all eight counties, and that one isolated, expensive to use, and known to turn into a quagmire entrapping even the most hardy of mountain pickups.

When the failure became obvious, local residents wanted to know whom to get mad at. And they heard their county judge—himself the chairman of the landfill board at the time—saying it wasn't his jurisdiction; it was the problem of the regional garbage authority. And who was that? That was established under the auspices of the development district. The what? The development district. Well, could the judge get something done? Folks are just dumping their garbage into the creeks because there's no other place to put it. Sure, the judge promised, I'll raise the problem at the next district meeting; we're all concerned about the problem, but we have to work it out together.

The garbage mess, as it became known, proved to be the tip of the iceberg of anger. The same development district had endorsed land-use studies for each of its counties. In one of them, residents rebelled at the suggestion in the plan that they move out of their precious hollows and off their hillsides to areas where such "blessings" as sewer and water could be provided. They made it clear that they liked their hollows, had no desire to move away from them unless it was their choice, and in short wanted no part of any regional land-use plan.

Mass-meeting pressure forced the county fiscal court not only to drop the land-use plan but to abolish the county planning commission for good measure. Nonetheless, the LDD itself soon came out with its own district wide land-use plan. People again expressed concern, but this time they really didn't know where to focus it.

Planners argue that no one unit of government is forced to accept a regionally drafted plan or program. That may be true in theory, but federal and state trends deny it in fact. There is, for example, something called the A-95 procedure of the federal Office of Management and Budget. The stated purpose of the A-95 Memorandum is to foster multi-jurisdictional cooperation in order to assure maximum benefits from an array of federal programs included under A-95's coverage. A-95, says OMB, simply seeks to encourage consistency based on solid planning.

Under A-95, each state which so chooses establishes "clearing houses" to review and comment upon all applications for assistance from federal agencies included under A-95. LDDs, for example, have become the A-95 bodies in most Appalachian states. The application goes to the clearing house, which then invites parties it feels appropriate to comment upon the application, and within thirty days the clearing house itself comments. Only then is the application, with comment, passed to the federal agency. Technically, that agency can ignore an unfavorable A-95 review, though under a new revision of A-95 it must now tell the clearing house why it chose to do so. Under the same revision, A-95 still remains noncompulsory; that is, states don't have to adopt the procedure. In fact, however, the increasing trend is to require the kind of regional review called for in A-95 whether or not it has been formally adopted.

A-95 decisions are supposed to be based on grounds of consistency and soundness of planning. But again, good intentions can be offset by realities. Many of the same questions heard in Appalachia about LDDs are being raised there and elsewhere about the A-95 bodies of review. Just who sits on the A-95 board, and who should? If the clearing house doesn't possess the overall plan upon which it is supposed to peg its decisions, on what is the review based? Vested interests of the board members? Personalities or politics of the applicants? If there is a plan, who developed it, and with whose active advice and concurrence? Were all segments of the population included in the planning effort? The questions comprise the list of what makes political units responsive to needs.

A-95 raises other basic questions of civil rights. For example, a city with 600,000 people has the same voting power on that A-95 board as a suburban member with 20,000. Aside from one-man, one-vote, the same problems of board composition that arise with LDDs apply here. They are perhaps even more critical with A-95 boards, since both civil rights review and environmental impact determination are left to the auspices of the A-95 body in key areas. Jim Draper, formerly of the Georgia Council on Human Relations, has argued with OMB that A-95 boards "have neither staff nor philosophic inclination" to give minority or low-income people a fair shake. "Moreover," he said, "in many cases there is no representation of these interests on A-95 bodies' boards of directors. Thus, inclusion of such considerations [as civil rights or environment] as criteria for review becomes utterly meaningless—the painting over of rotting wood."

Is this, then, a hopeless quagmire, with the potential value and real need for regionalism clouded by equally real inadequacies of accountability and responsiveness? ARC, for example, might well have become a viable and creative institution if it had followed the advice of many of its initial Appalachian backers and dealt with the real problems of basic economic inequity in Appalachia. Instead, it chose to go with the governors, with the entrenched political systems of thirteen states. Some good has resulted, such as ARC health programs, but had the key segments of the Appalachian population been sought out and included both at the federal-state and the substate levels, a more lasting and accountable mechanism might have made more than a dent in the problems. ARC's survival might then rest on real accomplishment rather than political muscle.

It is certainly not too late to learn lessons from the experience of ARC, its LDDs and such other manifestations of regionalism as A-95. And the need to learn is pressing, since regional plans are likely to spread in ways and to places which will directly affect many more people. Maybe it is necessary to separate regionalism at the urban level from efforts in rural areas where, particularly in the South, the word is that regional government is the government in a growing number of places. Maybe the geographical closeness and heavy populations of urban areas make regional efforts there more viable. Or maybe rural areas with their much more limited financing and resources are the places for real regional concentration. It's going on, in any case, in both parts of America.

Some obvious steps could be taken to insure at least the possibility of accountability. For a start, districts should be developed according to common realities, according to economic and social factors which might produce a certain jurisdictional cohesiveness. To combine units sheerly on the basis of geography (the north fork of the river) or politics (that's a Congressional district there) is shortsighted if the real goal is to use common facilities for the common solution of common problems.

Representatives to a development district should be elected on a one-man, one-vote basis specifically to that post by the people of each constituent unit. At present, elected officials are automatically placed on the boards on the assumption that they represent the will of the people. If special elections were held to fill slots in the regional creation, not only would the special abilities needed by said office be brought out but public attention to and interest in the process might be developed. Such concern does not now exist, except in the negative sense when a district has overstepped its bounds. If regional cooperation is to become a reality, it must begin with the most basic kind of involvement for the population—and that is the vote.

Other specific steps can be taken to assure that these new

bodies of government bear at least a resemblance to our traditional concept of democratic institutions. These include hearings
and public notification of review matters; A-95 does not require
such notice. Out-reach offices staffed by local residents to serve
as centers for complaints or suggestions is another obvious step.
Without such action, and others like it, any future efforts to
broaden the power and scope of multi-jurisdictional authorities
will obscure even further the role of the American citizen in the
affairs of his government.

Hearings may be held this year on a bill by Sen. Joseph
Montoya (D., N.M) "to establish a national development program
through public works in investment" (S.232). In introducing it
last year, Senator Montoya noted that "the inspiration for the
approach taken in this bill" is the ARC. He added that the bill
"builds on one of the most successful features of the Appalachian program, the strengthening of state and local governments
and making them an integral part of the decision-making process on public works investments." The bill would do that by
fostering the establishment of "area development districts"
nationwide. Public works investments would be made only in
those areas which have demonstrated a regional outlook based
on sound planning in seeking the money.

Significantly, a main witness at last year's Montoya bill
hearings (the bill died then for lack of action) was ARC States'
Regional Representative, John Whisman. Whisman's credentials
as an ardent backer of national regional development go back
well over a decade. Concepts developed by him to deal with
eastern Kentucky's late 1950s tragedies—multi-county efforts,
relying on local elected officials to reflect the people's will—
eventually translated into ARC and, Whisman has said "hope-
fully will go national as well." The Montoya bill may well be the
vehicle.

Testifying last year, Whisman acknowledged that ARC has
perhaps not accomplished what it was supposed to do—provide
economic opportunity for Appalachians. Indeed, he said, the
problems may well have gotten worse in the 1970's. So what
should we do? "To meet these new characteristics of our problems, we need to establish new institutional arrangements in
society." He added: "The purpose of the regional development
approach" is not primarily "to solve the problems of economic

lag or unemployment or poverty. Rather, the basic purpose is to solve problems of all kinds, mobilizing our know-how and our funds at all levels of government in a partnership that can forge new and effective solutions."

If that is the purpose, what Whisman is effectively talking about is a basic reconfiguration of government. In acknowledging that problems of poverty remain rampant in ARC's Appalachia, he contends that what we really need are new "institutional arrangements," which, of course, is what ARC was supposed to be in the first place. That reconfiguration is now coming upon us, and we simply have not thought through carefully enough its ramifications upon all strata of society, particularly upon the low-income groups and minorities who themselves are already saying they see it all as a new threat.

They may be right. The burden of proof is on the backers of regionalism to prove them wrong.

RETHINKING THE MODEL

Section V: Rethinking the Model

A somewhat facetious but thought-provoking essay by Dennis Lindberg, "Appalachia: A Colony Within a Colony," suggests that America itself may be a Japanese colony. He points to the model of an advanced technological society which results from efficient control and manipulation of labor and resources. Appalachia can be viewed in a broader sense as a colony of a technological society.

David Walls' article "Internal Colony or Internal Periphery?" compares three models: Culture of Poverty, Regional Development Model, and Internal Colony. He points to weaknesses in all three and suggests an alternative model which analyzes the area in terms of advanced capitalism. This broader perspective is a synthesis of the three models.

In the final article, "Extending the Internal Periphery Model," Thomas Plaut takes us further to consider the culture of the advanced capitalist or technological society and shows how the rationalist, achievement-oriented, "scientific" culture leads to the type of exploitation previously outlined and the degradation of life and culture. Plaut also points to the forms of resistance and opposition which are necessary if humanistic values can survive the processes of social change.

APPALACHIA: A COLONY WITHIN A COLONY?

by
Dennis N. Lindberg

Much has been written about Appalachia as a colony—a place where American magnates have come to draw upon the natural resources which make the gears of capital intensive industries outside the region turn.

But recent efforts to mine the high grade smokeless Sewell coal in Randolph County, West Virginia, suggest that history moves faster than theory. Appalachia may not be an American colony as much as America itself may be a Japanese colony.

The coal in question is found beneath the steep banks of the Shavers Fork of the Cheat River, which is reputed to be the finest trout stream in the Eastern United States. At the present time, and for rather complex political reasons that have little to do with ecology, the ecologists have won a battle over mining permits that have not been issued. But what is more interesting than the ecology battle is who has been after the coal.

It hasn't been Pittsburgh, where the mayor says no smokeless coal is available to bring the boilers in his city's police stations, fire stations, and schools up to his own air quality standards.

SOURCE: *This article first appeared in* The Village Voice, *September 24, 1970; additional material was written October 1973.*

AUTHOR: Dennis Lindberg *is an assistant professor of sociology at Davis and Elkins College, Elkins, West Virginia.*

The Japanese have been after the coal, some million and a half tons a year, enough to load 30,000 50-ton railroad cars, or 80 such cars per day.

In school we learned that long ago when there were colonies, they shipped raw materials to their mother country and in return provided a market for the mother country's manufactured goods, an arrangement that worked mostly to the advantage of the mother country. The mother country's superior technology and resultant lower costs soon destroyed the colony's traditional native industries.

So we ship coal to Japan and in return buy her finished products: steel, cameras, radios, tape recorders, machinery, ships, cars, and motorcycles—a classic colonial relationship. Of course, we can produce some of those finished products ourselves, but they are not competitive in quality or cost.

The developing relationship between the U.S. and Japan, I'm postulating (perhaps prematurely), is much like the old relationship between India and Britain, with the Japanese playing their role with far more subtlety than the British.

The British ran India with a system of indirect rule, whereby native political institutions were brought into the British structure and under its control. Natives were used to keep other natives in line, and the natives themselves paid for their own policing.

In Africa and Asia, the British were successful at this, and in a number of cases were able to keep control after the nominal independence of the countries involved. This is what is often called neo-colonialism. It should also be pointed out that generally in India, Britain did not loot the country directly, but let the wealthy natives keep their wealth and prestige, and did not directly interfere with the country's social structure.

Japan's dominance of the United States began at the end of World War II. She got the U.S. to finance the rebuilding of her industrial plant, and, perhaps more importantly, she got the U.S. to forbid her to rearm. This amounted to an agreement by the U.S. to assume the role of defending Japanese interests. Not only do the natives pay for and provide the manpower for their own policing, they also provide both the funds and the manpower to police the mother country's developing neo-empire. We have a mutual security treaty with Japan. We provide the security and they provide the mutual.

Jacques Ellul in *The Technological Society* is of great help in understanding why Japan has been able to neo-colonize the U.S. Technique is more than tools and machinery to Ellul. It encompasses everything which is done for the sake of greater efficiency. Since there is only one best or most efficient way of doing something, technique is totalitarian. Since maximum efficiency is the goal, an aristocracy of technicians arises to determine the one best way. "Planning in modern society," Ellul says, "is *the* technical method."[1]

The Japanese have developed an integration of government and the corporate economy, through joint planning and coordination, which most nearly approaches Ellul's model of an advanced technological society (either corporate or socialist):

> (a) take a firm hold on the economy, (b) manage it on the basis of exact mathematical methods, (c) integrate it into a Promethean society which excludes all chance, (d) centralize it in the frameworks of nation and state (the corporate economy today has no chance of success except as a state system), (e) cause it to assume an aspect of formal democracy to the total exclusion of real democracy, and (f) exploit all possible techniques for controlling men.[2]

Insofar as American leaders (corporate and government) realize the gap between Japanese technique and their own, they will move to centralize control and institute planning to a far greater degree than we have yet experienced. Again, all planning is totalitarian. To be carried out, a plan requires at least the threat of coercion. If a person or family is allowed freedom of decision, there is no plan.

There are still some significant obstacles in the U.S. to technical progress. The governmental system of checks and balances between Congress, the President, and the courts is inefficient. So is the partial freedom of state and local government from federal control. Corrupt politicians are inefficient, as are a free press, anti-trust laws, and the ability of citizens to sue government and corporations to block "progress."

Thus a small, efficient, tightly controlled, formally democratic island country can effectively exploit a larger, looser, less efficient, more really democratic, continental country. It's the British in India all over again, on a more sophisticated level.

Appalachia as a colony within a colony stands in relation to the "advanced," urban areas of the U.S. as the country as a whole stands to Japan. Government and business in the region are less efficient. Non-economic considerations like family and friendship often get in the way here. Short-term profit has yet to give way to efficiency as the basic goal of the economy (or even life), reflecting a rudimentary stage of technology. Some human activities remain valued which are not economic (reducible to a money value), and man, in this "backward" area, remains something more than producing, consuming, economic man.

Most strategies for change in Appalachia have been technological strategies, designed in one way or another to "develop" or "modernize" the region. All involve planning by experts. Opposition to these plans, be they for resort development, clear-cutting, dam or road building, for education, health, welfare, or economic development, is seen by the planners as irrational meddling. The plan is rational, be it the plan of the government agency or the plan of radical intellectuals.

> The complete identity, rather than the resemblance, between corporatism and planning ought to be noted. Corporatism is adapted to a traditional, cultivated, bourgeois mentality; planning to an innovating, proletarian, pseudo-scientific mentality. But the attitude of the two is fundamentally the same. And, speaking objectively, the result, insofar as the real structure of human society is concerned, will be identical.[3]

People are to be manipulated into supporting the plan. Councils, boards, legislatures and the Congress ideally should function as a democratic veneer, which is necessary to give people the illusion that they have some control.

True technique will know how to maintain the illusion of
liberty, choice, and individuality; but these will have been
carefully calculated so that they will be integrated into
the mathematical reality merely as appearances.[4]

"Development," however, may no longer be possible in
Appalachia. The standard of living of middle-class America is
now beginning to decline. This is due in part to the new colonial
relationship with Japan (i.e., inflation resulting from our having
to pay for having fought Japan's war in Vietnam, intense pressures on raw materials markets leading to higher prices, etc.).

More fundamental is the fact that the industrial nations of
the world are beginning to realize that the natural resources of
the world are limited. Donella and Dennis Meadows in *The
Limits to Growth* describe a dynamic model of the world, considering population, industrial output per capita, food per capita,
natural resources, and pollution as basic factors. The model is
programmed into a computer using historical data from 1900 to
1970 and then projected until the year 2100, assuming "no
major change in the physical, economic, or social relationships
that have historically governed the development of the world
system."[5] The result is what the Meadows call overshoot and
collapse: Resources are used up; food production rises until
all the land is worn out; industrial output rises rapidly and then
declines because of starvation. By 2050 industrial output per
capita and food per capita are both less than half of what they
were in 1900.

After numerous other model runs simulating all of the
popular remedies to the pollution-population-energy-etc. crisis,
the Meadows conclude that the only way to prevent the disaster
of overshoot and collapse is to immediately stabilize the world
by stabilizing population, setting capital investment equal to
capital depreciation, introducing extensive recycling of resources
and improved pollution control devices, and increasing the lifetime of all forms of capital. This equilibrium state is sustainable
far into the future with an average which is half the present
average U.S. income.[6]

It is thus impossible, considering population growth, arable
land, and the finite limits of the earth's resources, to extend the
levels of consumption of energy and material goods of the

American suburban middle class to the "poorer" sections of this country, let alone to the majority of the world's people who live in "under-developed" countries. The suburban middle classes are precisely those who have been most reduced to producing-consuming, economic men, valuing themselves through money and not likely to give it up.

The Meadows maintain that only through long-term planning can the equilibrium model be attained and disastrous collapse avoided. The sooner this planning begins (and the mandatory implementation of it), the less overtly authoritarian it can be. Since the model shows overshoot before the collapse, it is too late to do anything once the crisis is widely perceived. That is, you don't realize that the river is badly polluted until the fish are dead. Then it's too late to do much about those fish.

As long as major decisions in the world are made by those whose primary concern is that their industrial enterprises and national economies shall continue to grow, nothing will be done to move toward equilibrium. To return again to Ellul: "Anything and everything which technique is able to produce *is* produced and accepted by consumers"[7]; and "everything which is technique is necessarily used as soon as it is available, without distinction of good and evil."[8]

Most books about Appalachia tell us that the white settlers of the region were drawn largely from the prisons of England and Scotland and were rough bitter victims of the enclosure movement that was destroying medieval society in Britain. Some were debtors, some thieves, and some may have been Luddites. Trampled on at home and then again in the coastal plains of America, these outcasts went west to the mountains and stayed there to escape civilized society. They wanted no part of the civilized free market, wage labor, law, or class system. They valued most their freedom and independence. They were more than economic men and did not have to prove themselves through wealth. But they survived.

There are only two economic systems, according to Ellul. The first exploits technique (efficiency, the one best way, economic man, etc.), while the second "ascribes the chief place to nature."[9] This second orientation resembles what some middle-class writers about Appalachia (with technologized minds) have called fatalism. This understanding of the limits of man and the nature of the world, whether religious or not, is more in touch with the reality of the world as reflected in the Meadows' model than is "non-fatalistic" technological understanding which presumes that man can and should control nature.

Since the Industrial Revolution, westernized man has had to choose between freedom and wealth. Most have not understood the choice and have thought both were possible. Many have not perceived their loss of freedom. The first settlers knew from bitter experience and chose a real independence.

There are many families in the mountains today who remember the old ways of surviving and are relatively free of technological values. They are people for whom economic activity is still a means and *the* end of life. A strategy for survival in the Appalachia region in the face of the interrelated energy-food-population-pollution crisis would seek to support these families and help them protect themselves from "development."

The consequence of all "development" programs is to diminish the independence (hence the ability to survive) of the mountain family. All, no matter how well meaning and whether in health, education, economic development, or whatever, leave the family more dependent on outside institutions and more at the mercy of experts. Many of the social programs of the '60's (welfare rights, Head Start, medicare, etc.) had the unintended effect of luring people into an increasingly manipulative, totalitarian system and robbing them of their dignity and values. "No matter how liberal the state, it is obliged by the mere fact of technical advance to extend its powers in every way."[10]

Appalachia is a colony of technological society, first American and now also Japanese. Within the next 50-70 years, technological society will become increasingly totalitarian and manipulative. It quite possibly will collapse. Self-sufficient families and communities, knowing that nature (God) is greater than man, can survive and retain their independence. Suburbanites, thinking that man can conquer nature (God), being expert in one or two fields and unknowing and dependent in most areas of life, unable to buy gasoline, electricity or food with their money, may perish in great numbers.

Colonialism is an attack upon the land, the culture, and the soul of a people. The three are tightly bound. Losses in one affect the others. Families and communities can resist (passively or actively) or give in (gradually or quickly), disintegrating into a collection of individual consumers of mass-produced identities.

Seeing Appalachia as a colony is much more than seeing who controls the profits from the coal mined in the region. It is rather seeing a process of robbing people of their family, community, land, independence, and soul—robbery by people who mean well, and who know that they do it for your own good.

NOTES

[1]Jacques Ellul, *The Technological Society* (New York, 1964), p. 184.

[2]*Ibid.,* p. 186.

[3]*Ibid.*

[4]*Ibid.,* p. 139.

[5]*Ibid.,* p. 124.

[6]*Ibid.,* p. 165.

[7]*Ibid.,* p. 93.

[8]*Ibid.,* p. 99.

[9]*Ibid.,* p. 186.

[10]*Ibid.,* p. 235.

INTERNAL COLONY OR INTERNAL PERIPHERY?
A CRITIQUE OF CURRENT MODELS AND
AN ALTERNATIVE FORMULATION

by
David S. Walls

In the course of the 1960's, Appalachia was rediscovered as a social problem region. Efforts of mainstream social scientists to explain the stubborn persistence of poverty and underdevelopment in Appalachia can be categorized as two types: the subculture of poverty model, and the regional development model. In response to the inadequacy of these models, and the social policy that followed from them, radical intellectuals and activists developed an internal colonialism model for the Central Appalachian region. In recent years substantial gains have been made in the theoretical and empirical investigation of neocolonialism, dependency, internal colonialism, advanced capitalism, and the capitalist world system. The resulting clarification of these concepts suggests that the analysis of Central Appalachia as an internal colony needs to be reconsidered and a more adequate formulation developed. My conclusion is that Central Appalachia is best characterized as a peripheral region within an advanced capitalist society. Each of the three current models was first developed in the context of underdevelopment in the Third World and later applied by analogy to the Appalachian case. I will summarize and criticize these models, suggest pos-

SOURCE: *Dissertation Chaper (c) 1977.*

AUTHOR: David S. Walls, *former director of the Appalachian Volunteers, is on the faculty of the School of Social Professions, University of Kentucky, Lexington. He also works with the U.K. Appalachia Center.*

sible grounds for a synthesis, and argue for the alternative formulation suggested above.

The Subculture of Poverty Model

The subculture of poverty model identifies the internal deficiencies of the lower-class subculture as the cause of the problem. Oscar Lewis is the social scientist most closely identified with this model, and the most widely read exposition of the model applied to Appalachia is Jack Weller's *Yesterday's People,* which borrows an analytic framework from Herbert Gans.[1] The subculture of poverty model suggests remedial programs of education, social casework, and clinical psychology. Studies of Appalachian culture in these terms include works by psychiatrist David Looff, social worker Norman Polansky, and sociologist Richard Ball.[2]

The work on Appalachia in the subculture of poverty tradition has a very limited validity at best because of three problems that the authors fail to confront: deficient research methodology, a blurring of community and social class diversity in the region, and a lack of historical perspective and specification. The methodological approach in the works of Weller, Looff, and Polansky, for example, imports sociological or psychiatric categories and focuses on the pathological. They overgeneralize from problem families to the culture of one or more social classes. They fail to distinguish between the traditional Southern Appalachian subculture and a contemporary subculture of poverty. The limitations of these scientific, clinical classification systems are particularly evident in comparison to the work of such writers as Robert Coles, John Fetterman, Tony Dunbar, and Kathy Kahn, whose humanistic method uses their subjects' own words to characterize Appalachian life-worlds.[3] Their descriptions of individuals and families manage to capture the strengths as well as the shortcomings of mountaineers and the diversity of personality types within some common subcultural themes. These accounts of the contradictions in the lives and outlooks of mountain people bear out Helen Lewis' suggestion that many Appalachians are in fact bi-cultural; they take part in the traditional subculture in family and neighborhood life, and in the mainstream culture through employment, formal education, media entertainment, and contact with public agencies.

The subculture of poverty model in general has been subjected to devastating criticism.[4] In the Appalachian case, sociologist Dwight Billings has shown the model to be of little value
in explaining the lack of economic development in the mountain
section of North Carolina and the contrasting industrialization
of the piedmont, for example. Ironically, it was just when the
distinctiveness of the Southern Appalachian traditional subculture was fading that the subculture of poverty model was
popularized and applied to the region.[5] For all the controversy
generated in the debate over the subculture of poverty, this
model had less policy impact on Appalachia than one might
expect. The model did help to rationalize such national programs as Project Head Start, the Elementary and Secondary Education Act, and the great expansion of social services that took
place in the 1960's. But the subculture of poverty model was not
a major influence on the state and federal planners who devised
the Appalachian Regional Development Act of 1965.

The Regional Development Model

Although the literature on development includes disciplines
from social psychology to social ecology, the most influential
stream derives from neoclassical economics as amended by
central place theory.[6] The resulting regional development model
is concerned with providing economic and social overhead
capital, training people for skills for new industrial and service
jobs, facilitating migration, and promoting the establishment or
relocation of privately-owned industries through a growth center
strategy. A modernizing elite is seen as the agent of the developmental process. The major attempt to apply the model within
the United States is the work of the Appalachian Regional Commission (ARC) and its associated programs. Niles Hansen is
probably the best-known academic proponent of this approach.[7]

The Appalachian regional development advocates have an
academic base in the Departments of Sociology, Economics and
Agricultural Economics at West Virginia University, the University of Kentucky, and the University of Tennessee, and such related applied research institutes as the Appalachian Center at
WVU, the Center for Developmental Change at UK, and the
Appalachian Resources Project at UT. More significantly, this
model has a political base in the multi-county Local Develop-

ment Districts established under the ARC program. The LDDs serve primarily as a mechanism for arriving at consensus among regional elites. Through the dual federal-state structure of the ARC, the interests of regional and national elites are reconciled.

With its emphasis on mainstream economic theory and the technical aspects of development, the regional development model lays claim to being a scientific, value-free, and non-controversial approach. As such, it is an effective means of providing additional resources to the region without affecting the existing structure of resource control. Actions taken by regional and national planners are defended as technical decisions, rather than political choices among alternative courses of development. The most important decisions are the "non-decisions": the questions that are never raised and the subjects that never make the public agenda.[8] Examples include public ownership of the region's natural resources and worker or community-owned and controlled industry.[9]

The Internal Colonialism Model

The issues of power and privilege in Appalachia are never faced squarely by the subculture of poverty and regional development advocates. In reaction to this obvious shortcoming, radical academics and activists looked for a model that emphasized inequality and exploitation. They hit upon the internal colonialism model for reasons that had more to do with the focus of the New Left in the late 1960's—imperialism abroad and oppression of racial minorities at home—than the appropriateness of the model to the Appalachian situation. As the Appalachian radicals apply the internal colonialism model, it has been used to examine the process by which dominant outside industrial interests established control and continue to prevent autonomous development of the subordinate internal colony. The model suggests the need for an anti-colonial movement and a radical restructuring of society with a redistribution of resources to the poor and powerless.

Dependency and Neocolonialism

The internal colonialism model has emerged from a background of the history and theories of colonialism and imperialism and is most directly related to the theories of neocolonialism and dependency that have been developed in the post-World War II period. Dependency theory has been developed primarily by radical economists and sociologists concerned with Latin America, while the theories of neocolonialism and imperialism have been more concerned with Asia and Africa, or the Third World as a whole.[10]

A vital contribution of the dependency model is the notion of the "infrastructure of dependency," the structures internal to the dependent country including industrial organization, patterns of urbanization, and social classes. In the exposition by Suzanne Bodenheimer, two examples of the infrastructure of dependency are the patterns of dependent industrialization and the formation of clientele social classes. Characteristics of dependent industrialization include foreign domination of the most dynamic sectors of industry, increasing competitive advantage for foreign monopolistic enterprises over local firms, and the introduction of advanced, capital-intensive technology without regard to resulting unemployment. Clientele classes have a "dual position as partners of metropolitan interests, yet dominant elites within their own societies." They may include not only the industrial bourgeoisie but also the state bureaucracy and other sectors of the middle class when their positions are tied to foreign interests. The infrastructure of dependency is thus "the functional equivalent of a formal colonial apparatus," but insofar as it is internalized and institutionalized "much more difficult to overcome."[11]

Internal Colonialism

The success of the anticolonial movements in the Third World following World War II has undoubtedly contributed to the popularity of referring to a variety of exploitative situations within both developing and advanced industrial countries as internal or domestic colonialism. Through conceptual confusion or carelessness, internal colonialism has been used to designate situations of stratification by class, race, ethnicity, or geography, alone or in various combinations. It is also used to describe absentee industrial ownership, although this is a characteristic feature of uneven and polarized capitalist development.[12] Included among such internal colonies have been the U.S. South, northern New England, the northern Great Lakes region, the Southwest, the "Celtic periphery" of England, southern Italy, and so on.[13] One explanation may be that the vocabulary of colonization is more comfortable than that of class conflict, and regional or ethnic chauvinism is more acceptable than talk of socialism.

Internal colonialism is a useful concept if defined in a rigorous sense rather than used as an all-inclusive catchword. Two precise definitions with varying degrees of restrictiveness are advanced by Pablo González-Casanova and Pierre van den Berghe. González-Casanova seeks to distinguish internal colonialism from a class structure with a geographic or racial aspect:

> Internal colonialism corresponds to a structure of social relations based on domination and exploitation among culturally heterogeneous, distinct groups. . . .It is the result of an encounter between two races, cultures, or civilizations, whose genesis and evolution occurred without any mutual contact up to one specific moment. . . . The colonial structure and internal colonialism are distinguished from the class structure since colonialism is not only a relation of exploitation of the workers by the owners of raw materials or of production and their collaborators, but also a relation of domination and exploitation of a total population (with its distinct classes, proprietors, workers) by another population which also has distinct classes (proprietors and workers).[14]

In short, the González-Casanova definition requires a dual class structure: two class systems, one dominant and the other subordinate, each of which may be differentiated to a greater or lesser degree. This appears to be a useful minimal definition of internal colonialism, although it is broad enough to include a variety of dominant-subordinate group relationships.

The most restrictive definition of internal colonialism is developed by van den Berghe in a recent work. His view, in part a reaction to the overly broad use of the term, is worth quoting at length:

> In my opinion, the concept of internal colonialism, when

so diluted, loses all of its use for purposes of social science analysis. I shall therefore propose to treat internal colonialism as an ideal type with the following characteristics:

1)   Rule of one ethnic group (or coalition of such groups) over other such groups living within the continuous boundaries of a single state.

2)   Territorial separation of the subordinate ethnic groups into "homelands," "native reserves," and the like, with land tenure rights distinct from those applicable to members of the dominant group.

3)   Presence of an internal government within a government especially created to rule the subject peoples, with a special legal status ascribed to the subordinate groups. . .

4)   Relations of economic inequality in which subject peoples are relegated to positions of dependency and inferiority in the division of labor and the relations of production.

Such a definition of internal colonialism excludes mere regional differences in economic development, mere class differences in the system of production, and, *a fortiori*, differences based on age, sex, slave status, caste, sexual behavior (e.g., homosexuality), physical handicaps, and countless others. The usefulness of the concept to understand the situation of a group is a function of that group's approximation to the characteristics of the ideal type. For instance, in the United States, internal colonialism describes the position of Amerindians quite well, of Chicanos somewhat, of blacks poorly, of Appalachian whites hardly at all, and of women, old people, homosexuals and convicts only by the most fanciful stretch of the academic imagination. This is not to say that some of the groups excluded from my definition of internal colonialism may not be as badly or worse off than the denizens of the internal colonies. Their position is fundamentally *different*, however, and, hence, the internal colonial model is a poor one to understand their predicament. Internal colonialism is but one of many ways of getting the short end of the stick.[15]

González-Casanova's criterion of a dual class structure appears to include points one and four of van den Berghe's ideal type.

The latter would also require territorial separation and a special governing unit for full correspondence to the internal colonialism model. I find it most useful to adopt a definition between González-Casanova and van den Berghe, thus requiring economic exploitation, a dual class structure based on ethnic differences, within one or more distinct geographic regions. In other words, I would place internal colonialism as a special case within the theory of dependent capitalist development.

Internal Colonialism
Applied to Appalachia

I can find no use of the colonialism analogy to the Appalachians prior to the early 1960's. During the unionization battles of the 1930's, the Left press emphasized themes of exploitation and class conflict along classic Marxian lines in their articles about the Appalachian coalfields.[16]   Only after the internal colonial model had been applied to blacks did writers on Appalachia begin to speak in terms of colonialism. In his best selling 1962 study *Night Comes to the Cumberlands,* Harry Caudill makes only a passing reference to colonialism; by 1965 he begins to use the *internal* colonial designation.[17]   The theme was quickly picked up by activists and radical intellectuals in the Central Appalachian area, particularly the group associated with the Peoples' Appalachian Research Collective and its journal, *Peoples' Appalachia.*   Helen Lewis and her associates have attempted a detailed application to Appalachia of Blauner's model of the process of internal colonization of black Americans.

I find the application of Blauner's model of internal colonialism, broad as it is, to Appalachia to be strained at some key points.   The parallel to "forced, involuntary entry" by the colonizers is nowhere near as strong as the case of enslaved blacks from Africa or the conquered Native American tribes or the Mexican people of the Southwest. In the elaborated version of his argument, Blauner distinguishes between "colonized and immigrant minorities" and suggests that the circumstances of entry of white European ethnic immigrant groups is different in character from that of blacks and possibly other people of color in the United States. The situation of Appalachian people is clearly a third variant if they are to be treated as a minority at all; the mountaineers were an early settler group established for sixty to a hundred years before the expansion of industrial capitalism into the region. Blacks and immigrant ethnic groups have played an important role in the development of the Southern Appalachian coal industry, particularly in West Virginia, but the focus of the Appalachian internal colonialism theorists has not been on such groups.[18] The deception and fraud used in Appalachia by the vanguard of land, timber, and mineral agents do not appear to differ in kind from those techniques used generally by capitalists and their agents throughout the country in the period of industrial expansion.

On the question of "administration by representatives of the dominant power," the application of Blauner's internal colonialism model to Appalachia suffers from his emphasis on "police colonialism," the direct application of force by members of the dominant group. Blauner has not put enough emphasis on the neocolonial mechanism of an indigenous stratum of officials ruling in the interests of the dominant group. Helen Lewis suggests that the study of such local elite groups in the mountains is of great importance,[19] but this conclusion and suggestions of what mechanisms to look for flow more readily from the more general dependency model than from the narrower internal colonialism model.

The parallel to "racism as a principle of social domination" really breaks down in the Appalachian case. There may be prejudice against "hillbillies," but it is essentially based on bias against the lower classes, not all the people of the region.[20] There is no parallel to the dual class structures required by Gonzáles-Casanova's definition of internal colonialism. Mountaineers are able to "pass" into mainstream America both through migration and, for some, through integration into the business elite in the mountains.[21] White Appalachians generally have a potential for social mobility not matched by racial minorities. The traditional Appalachian subculture may be becoming a museum piece, but this is a situation far from white Appalachians as a group being accorded the near-caste position of some racial minorities in the United States.

Applying an additional characteristic of internal colonialism from van den Berghe's definition, I can find no evidence of "an internal government within a government especially created to rule the subject peoples." The Appalachian Regional Commission is not a functional counterpart of the Bureau of Indian Affairs. The people of Appalachia have no distinct legal status distinguishing them from other residents of the United States, as Native Americans do in some instances. Appalachia appears to provide a very poor fit to any strict definition of internal colonialism.

Cultural Hegemony and Capitalist Domination

Much of the attraction of the internal colonialism model, including its application to Appalachia, derives from its powerful analysis of the destruction of indigenous culture in the process of establishing and maintaining domination over the colonized group. Religion and education can play a major role in the destruction of traditional culture. The missionary movement in Appalachia can be seen as aiding, often inadvertently, the process of domination, as Lewis, Kobak and Johnson have described. James Branscome and Mike Clark have brought this analysis up to date by examining the effect of schooling on Appalachian culture in the current period.

These arguments hit the mark, but is cultural domination a distinctive feature of internal colonialism rather than class exploitation? A common and understandable misconception, derived in part from the stress on economic determinism in vulgar Marxist analysis, is that culture plays an insignificant part in the structure of class domination under capitalism. The colonial model is seen as distinctive by Blauner for its emphasis on this ignored area: ". . .the colonial attack on culture is more than a matter of economic factors such as labor recruitment and special exploitation. The colonial situation differs from the class situation of capitalism precisely in the importance of culture as an instrument of domination."[22] Orthodox Marxism has been particularly weak in its analysis of culture, and Blauner misses the importance of ideological hegemony in the establishment and maintenance of capitalist domination. For the beginnings of an adequate theory of the role of culture in capitalist societies we must turn to the Western Marxist tradition and such writers as Georg Lukacs, Antonio Gramsci, and the Frankfurt School theorists. The concept of cultural hegemony derives from Gramsci and emphasizes the obtaining of consent rather than the use of force in the perpetuation of class structures. Gwynn Williams provides a useful summary of Gramsci's notion of hegemony: "an order in which a certain way of life and thought is dominant, in which one concept of reality is diffused throughout society in all its institutional and private manifestations, informing with its spirit all taste, morality, customs, religious and political principles, and all social relations, particularly in their intellectual and moral connotation."[23]   The destruction of indigenous culture may be more conspicuous in the colonial situation, but a comparable process works to erode all ethnic and working-class cultures in advanced capitalist countries, a process which has perhaps advanced furthest in the United States.[24]

A few radical economists have attempted to avoid the problems of the colonialism analogy by returning to a traditional Marxian analysis of Appalachia in the context of capitalist exploitation and have suggested the fruitfulness of a longitudinal study of the removal of surplus value from the region over time. But this focus on economic relationships loses the valuable emphasis of the internal colonialism model on the role of cultural domination and the contribution of the dependency formulation on the "infrastructures of dependency." Perhaps the best formulation of a research project from the perspective of radical economics has been made by Richard Simon, who reviews the historical development of the West Virginia economy in the context of dependency theory, suggesting relationships with the social and political structures of that state and with the introduction of federal government programs in the 1960's.[25]   It is time to synthesize the best of the models so far put forward and develop a more accurate and comprehensive theory of poverty and underdevelopment in Central Appalachia.

Appalachia within an Advanced Capitalist Society

It is tempting to characterize the subculture of poverty, regional development, and internal colonialism models as, respectively, conservative, liberal, and radical models of barriers to social change. While this would contain a substantial amount of truth, the description would be misleading in one respect. From a perspective that I will develop briefly here, the three models are not, strictly speaking, mutually exclusive alternatives.

Interpreted in terms of a framework developed by Jürgen Habermas, they represent different dimensions of social existence.

A Framework for Synthesis

For Habermas, there are three fundamental conditions or media through which social systems are maintained: interaction, work, and power or domination. All human societies use these means to resolve the problems of preserving life and culture. Corresponding to each of these media are the human "interests" in mutual understanding, technical control, and "emancipation from seemingly 'natural' constraint."[26] A solution to the problems of Appalachian poverty and underdevelopment would have to be concerned with each of the three modes of culture, technique, and domination. Habermas' distinction provides a basis for viewing cultural adaptation, technical development, and redistribution of power as potentially complementary aspects of social development. Our models, therefore, are not merely three selected from a long list of possible models of poverty and underdevelopment. They represent fundamental dimensions of social life and may well be exhaustive of the possible alternatives if stated in a sufficiently general form (which none of the three current models are).

The subculture of poverty model can thus be seen as only one part of a broader framework of explanations rooted in the tradition of cultural idealism. Affirmative cultural approaches toward Southern Appalachia, exemplified by William G. Frost and John C. and Olive D. Campbell, are the obverse side of the coin from the pejorative tradition. Although they come to opposite conclusions about the virtue of the traditional mountain subculture, they are contending on the same turf. The regional development model, from this synthetic perspective, is seen as resting within the contemporary technocratic image and ideology of science. As John Friedmann points out, the regionalism movement of the 1930's, as personified by Howard Odum and others, was rooted in cultural idealism. The new regionalism of the 1960's, embodied in the ARC, discarded this grounding in favor of the technical reason of neoclassical economic theory.[27] The internal colonialism model is, similarly, one component of a broad range of theories that contribute to a critique of power and domination.

This synthetic view helps explain why writers widely considered to be champions of a certain model of Appalachian underdevelopment also draw on other models. Caudill, for example, is best known for his description of the Cumberland Plateau as an example of colonialism, but in *Night Comes to the Cumberlands* he also paints a pejorative picture of the subculture of the eastern Kentucky poor. In one essay Caudill appears to embrace many aspects of the developmental model, while in his most recent work he has re-emphasized a genetic explanation. From the other side, Weller is best known for his subculture of poverty characterization in *Yesterday's People,* yet he has recently described Appalachia as "America's mineral colony."[28] Such examples can be viewed as cases of inconsistency, confusion, or conversion. They can also be seen, at least in part, as attempts to grapple with the complexity of analyzing the problem of Appalachian development. To suggest that a dialectic of mutual interaction takes place among the modes of culture, technique, and power is, of course, not to argue that each of our three models of Appalachian underdevelopment is to be taken with equal seriousness.

I have suggested that the history of the Appalachian region is best understood in the context of industrial capitalist development. The internal colonialism model raises important questions about wealth, power, and domination without offering a satisfactory characterization of the situation of Central Appalachia. My synthesis of the three models leads to the conclusion that Appalachian poverty and underdevelopment need to be placed within a broader critique of domination. From this perspective, Central Appalachia must be analyzed in the context of advanced capitalism in the United States. In some instances (analyzing the role of the Japanese steel industry in providing capital for opening new coal mines in the region, for example), we may have to expand our horizon to the framework of the world capitalist system.

In a recent work Habermas formulates a model of advanced capitalism, which he characterizes by two features: the "process of economic concentration"—the growth of national and multinational corporations—and the "supplementation and partial replacement of the market mechanism by state intervention."[29] Habermas goes on to analyze advanced capitalist societies in terms of their economic, administrative (state), and legitimation

systems and the resulting class structures. Applying a similar
analysis will contribute to a deeper understanding of the position
of Central Appalachia.

The Economy

There is growing agreement among economists critical of
neoclassical theory that a three-sector model is necessary to
characterize the advanced capitalist economy in the United
States. John Kenneth Galbraith delineates the market system,
the planning system, and the state. As a rough demarcation,
Galbraith's planning system consists of the largest "one thousand
manufacturing, merchandising, transportation, power and financial corporations producing approximately half of all the goods
and services not provided by the state." Making up the market
system are the remaining twelve million firms which produce the
other half of the non-state output of goods and services.[30] The
market system includes farmers, small retail and service establishments, construction and small manufacturing firms, and the arts.
Whereas the workings of the market system bear some resemblance to the model of competition embodied in classical economics, the planning system is oligopolistic and its stability depends on the intervention of the state.

James O'Connor has developed a similar model with a much
deeper analysis of governmental activity. O'Connor also divides
private capital into two sectors: a competitive sector (roughly
parallel to Galbraith's market system) and a monopoly sector
(somewhat smaller than Galbraith's planning system). O'Connor's
state sector includes two categories: "production of goods and
services organized by the state itself and production organized
by industries under contract with the state."[31] Approximately
one-third of the labor force in the United States is employed
in each of these three sectors. The monopoly and state-contract
sectors tend to be capital-intensive industries, while the competitive and state service sectors tend to be labor intensive. As a
consequence, wages tend to be high in the monopoly and state
sectors and low in the competitive sector. Unions tend to be
strong in the monopoly and state sectors and weak in the competitive sector. Both product and labor markets tend to be un-
stable and irregular in the competitive sector, a circumstance
which has fostered the development of segmented labor mar-

kets.[32]

State sector expenditures, in O'Connor's model, are divided into two categories, social capital and social expenses, with social capital being of two kinds, social investment and social consumption. This distinction between social investment and social consumption roughly parallels Niles Hansen's distinction between economic and social overhead capital. *Social investment*, in O'Connor's terms, "consists of projects and services that increase the productivity of a given amount of labor-power and, other factors being equal, increase the rate of profit." Examples include government-subsidized roads, railroads, and industrial parks. *Social consumption* "consists of projects and services that lower the reproduction costs of labor and, other factors being equal, increase the rate of profit." Social consumption expenditures fall into two categories: goods and services consumed collectively and social insurance. Examples of the first include school, recreation and medical facilities, and the second, Social Security, workman's compensation, unemployment insurance, and health insurance. Most of the programs developed through the Appalachian Regional Commission are thus in the areas of social investment and the first, or collective, category of social consumption. Finally, *social expenditures* "consist of projects and services which are required to maintain social harmony—to fulfill the state's 'legitimization' function. They are not even indirectly productive." O'Connor includes welfare and military programs in this category.[33]

This model of the advanced capitalist economy in the United States has some obvious implications for an analysis of the Central Appalachian region, particularly in regard to the coal industry. The coal industry is unusual, though not unique, in having both substantial monopolistic and competitive sectors. Manufacturing and mining industries are generally concentrated in the monopolistic sector, while the competitive sector is primarily composed of small factories and services. The coal industry thus offers an opportunity for a comparative study of these two sectors within a single industry. Topics for investigation include relative rates between the two sectors of capital investment, wage levels, productivity, technological innovation, unionization, and influence on the legislative, administrative, and judicial institutions of the state that affect the coal industry. Contrasting business ideologies between the two sectors need to be explored. Since Central Appalachia contains the largest concentration of firms in the competitive sector of the coal industry, it is a particularly appropriate location for a study of the two sectors.

The Role of the State

The institutions that compose the state, to take Ralph Miliband's definition, are the executive, the legislative, the administrative (civil service bureaucracy), the military and police, the judiciary, and the subcentral governmental units. This system is part of a broader political system, which includes political parties, pressure groups, and a variety of other institutions not defined as political, such as corporations, churches, and mass media. A crucial question is the relationship between the state (and state elite) and the dominant economic class. Miliband recalls that "it is obviously true that the capitalist class, as a class, does not actually 'govern.' One must go back to isolated instances of the early history of capitalism, such as the commercial patriciates of cities like Venice and Lubeck, to discover direct and sovereign rule by businessmen."[34]

Contemporary analysts of the role of the state in advanced capitalism, including Miliband, O'Connor, and Nicos Poulantzas,[35] emphasize the relative autonomy of the state system. From their viewpoint, the familiar statement of Karl Marx and Frederick Engels that "the modern State is but a committee for managing the common affairs of the whole bourgeoisie" has been vulgarized. As Miliband comments, "The notion of common affairs assumes the existence of particular ones; and the notion of the whole bourgeoisie implies the existence of separate elements which make up that whole. This being the case, there is an obvious need for an institution of the kind they refer to, namely the state; and the state cannot meet this need without enjoying a certain degree of autonomy."[36] But the summary statement of Marx and Engels is still too abbreviated; the state reflects not simply the common interests of the whole bourgeoisie but a compromise between those interests and the interests of subordinate classes. The balance of the compromise depends in part on the level and extent of political struggle by the subordinate classes.

In a recent work that draws on Miliband, Poulantazas, and O'Connor, Ian Gough develops the role of state expenditures as concessions to working class struggles. The expansion of social services and social insurance since the Depression of the 1930's has meant that an increasing amount of the compensation of the labor force has come in the form of social wages. Indeed, "the strength of working-class pressure," he writes, "can roughly be gauged by the *comprehensiveness* and the *level* of the social benefits." Although such programs are tailored and modified to accommodate the interests of the dominant class, Gough notes:

> It is essential to distinguish their concrete historical *origins* from the ongoing *function* they play within that particular social formation. Social policies originally the product of class struggle will, in the absence of further struggle, he absorbed and adapted to benefit the interests of the dominant classes. On the other hand, whatever their particular function for capital at any time, the fact that social services are also an integral part of the real wage level of the working class means that they are fought for in much the same way as money wages, in economic and political class struggle.[37]

In a similar fashion, the class distribution of the burden of taxation also affects the real wages of the working class.

This recognition of the importance of social services, income transfer programs, and tax policy helps us understand and situate such social movements in the Central Appalachian region as the Black Lung Associations and their fights for workmen's compensation, clinical treatment programs, expanded benefits from the UMWA Health and Retirement Funds, and the severance tax on coal. It also illuminates the role of the federal bureaucracy and judicial system in the reform of the UMWA and its Health and Retirement Funds, the struggle for mine safety and health, and the expansion of a variety of benefits from social security to food stamps to community mental health services.

The Legitimation System

Habermas argues that formal democratic institutions which

allow universal adult voting in elections may obtain sufficient "diffuse mass loyalty" in the absence of substantive participation in public policy formulation if two conditions are present: "civic privatism" and an ideology that justifies elite rule. Civic privatism involves a withdrawal from the public realm into "career, leisure, and consumption." Both the "theory of democratic elitism" favored by mainstream American political science and the mystique of technical expertise promoted by theorists of public administration serve to legitimate the absence of public participation in political decision making.[38]

Among the working class in Central Appalachia, legitimation of the political system appears to be weak at the level of specific institutions yet remains strong at a diffuse level ("patriotism"). Cynicism about public officials abounds, with ample justification. The retreat to privatism is possibly facilitated by the extended family systems, which may provide sources for satisfaction even in the absence of substantial material comforts. Yet agencies of government frequently seek legitimation through a rhetoric of democratic participation. For example, TVA's claims of "grass roots democracy" disguised a policy of conceding the farm and related rural development programs to the local agricultural elites in exchange for a free hand for federal planners in public electrical power generation.[39] The ARC uses the Local Development Districts as the "local building blocks" of a program of federal-state cooperation. In Central Appalachia, such claims have seldom received an affirmative embrace from the working class, but they have met with acquiescence more often than active opposition.

The Class Structure

A common rhetorical excess is the description of the class structure of Central Appalachia as polarized into the wealthy and the poor. For Harry Caudill, there are "two Appalachias. . .side by side and yet strangers to each other. One, the Appalachia of Power and Wealth,. . .headquartered in New York and Philadelphia, is allied to mighty banks and insurance companies. . . .The second Appalachia is a land devastated. . . .Its people are the old, the young who are planning to leave and the legions of crippled and sick."[40] The reality, of course, is far more complicated. The question is not merely one of polemical license. Any strategy for social change must make a thorough assessment of the potential interest in change of the various class groupings in the region.

It is generally agreed that advanced capitalism has led to a proliferation of class and occupational groupings between the classic proletariat (the industrial working class) and the bourgeoisie of monopoly capital. The expansion of service industries with its accompanied increase in grey-collar and white-collar employment has been one aspect of this increase. The development of what Galbraith calls the "educational and scientific estate" is another. Despite the increased level of average per capita income, the distribution of shares of income and wealth has changed little in the past forty years. The "myth of the middle class" has been dispelled by careful analysis of confusing census occupational categories, and the continuing existence of a "working-class majority" has been established.[41]

In Central Appalachia, the expansion of state expenditures has helped create sizable intermediate class groupings of public workers (in education, local government, and public services) and workers in industries heavily subsidized by public funds (health services particularly). Unionization efforts have been made recently among municipal and hospital workers. These elements of the "new working-class" have taken their places alongside such long-established groups as coal miners, workers in small factories, small farmers, country merchants, county-seat retailers, bankers, professionals, independent coal operators, and managers for the nationally-based coal companies in the monopolistic sector, in addition to household workers, the welfare poor, and others outside the standard labor force. The class structure is obviously complex, and its changes need to be analyzed over time, particularly in relation to changes in the coal industry and the growth of state expenditures. Radicals must learn to paint portraits of the region in which a variety of working people can recognize themselves.

The Internal Periphery

In a market economy, certain regions within a country will experience economic rise or decline in response to such circumstances as demographic changes, technological advances, and the depletion of resources. On this the theorists of regional growth, urban hierarchies, and uneven capitalist development are agreed. As the core-periphery distinction is presently used by several schools of economic thought, it seems reasonable to me to apply the term peripheral to such regions within advanced capitalist countries as Appalachia which share many of the characteristics of underdevelopment, poverty, and dependency found in the peripheral countries of the Third World. Certainly the term is a more appropriate analogy than internal colony, which, as I have illustrated, should be restricted to a special case.

Immanuel Wallerstein has recently begun developing a more rigorous theory of the relationship of core and peripheral countries in the capitalist world economy and has elaborated an important intermediate case, that of the semi-peripheral countries (a distinction that corresponds in part to the levels of development within the Third World countries).[42]   In Wallerstein's view, the semi-peripheral countries perform two important functions for the capitalist world system, one political and one political and economic. The political function is to avoid a sharp polarization into rich and poor countries that would foster an alliance among the poor nations.   The intermedite sector develops a third set of interests based on its aim of making it into the core. The political-economic function of the semi-periphery is to provide an outlet for capital investment from core countries in low-wage industrial production.

The analogy between peripheral countries in the world system and peripheral regions within core countries obviously should not be pushed too far. As John Friedman points out, there are important differences between regions and countries, and between poor countries and poor regions in rich countries.[43] The most important difference is that countries have a relatively greater degree of closure in their boundaries. Through the use of tariff barriers, control over investments, and other means, countries can achieve a relative degree of insulation from the world economy. Constitutional and political limitations on the restraint of commerce prevent any state within the United States (much less multi-state regions without separate political authority) from following similar policies of restricting trade, investment, or population movements.

These qualifications noted, Wallerstein's three-tiered system may find an analogue within advanced capitalist countries. Regionalization and regionalism, the economic and ideological manifestations of peripheral status, may well join the racial, ethnic, and sexual aspects of the division of labor as functional barriers to class polarization of conflict over inequality.[44] The possibility of attaining semi-peripheral status may preclude a strong alliance of one region with another worse off. We see evidence of this in the successful move of the Northern and Southern Appalachian regions to standard semi-peripheral status within the United States while Central Appalachia remains behind. Given the general "fiscal crisis of the state," the federal government seems reluctant to commit resources to the elimination of regional inequality—the elevation to semi-peripheral status of all internal peripheral regions. The executive branch has resisted attempts of the Congress to expand the Title V regional commissions in the manner of the ARC. Peripheral regions remain functional for the system of advanced capitalism in the United States much in the way that poverty in general has positive functions.[45]

Conclusion

Analogies are valuable in social analysis insofar as they summarize and illuminate certain features of the subject under investigation. In this sense the analogy between the situation of Central Appalachia and that of colonized countries has been stimulating and fruitful. It has focused attention on the acquisition of the raw materials of the region by outside corporate interests and on the exploitation of the local work force and community at large resulting from the removal of the region's natural resources for the benefit of absentee owners. But analogies, while providing insights into some aspects of reality, can obscure or distort others. A loose analogy is no substitute, in the long run, for a precise theory that can lead to more detailed investigations. In this sense the internal colonialism model applied to Central Appalachia needs to be superceded by a model of peripheral regions within an advanced capitalist society.

The question is more than academic. At issue are the goals and strategy of a movement for social change. Writers using the internal colonialism model have been ambiguous about what solution is appropriate for Appalachian problems. Taking the term "colony" in its strongest sense, that of a suppressed nation, would prescribe an Appalachian nationalism aiming at secession and an independent nation-state. No one has proposed such a solution, although a weaker version—a state of Appalachia—has been mentioned.[46] Nor have many seriously suggested that the region would be better off if all the coal companies were owned by the local elite of "hillbilly millionaires"—a sort of bourgeois decolonization—instead of the national and international energy corporations, although an exclusive focus on absentee owner-ship might lead to that conclusion. If the heart of the problem is defined as private ownership of the coal industry, then the pos-sibility of public ownership, perhaps even limited to a regional basis, is suggested.[47] If the problem is defined as capitalist relations of production generally, then the alternative—some form of socialism—takes on a dimension that goes far beyond the nationalization or Appalachianization of the coal industry alone. It is this challenge of defining socialist goals and strategies that is presented by the model of peripheral regions within an advanced capitalist society.

NOTES

[1]Oscar Lewis, *The Children of Sanchez* (New York: Random House, 1961), pp. xxiv-xxvii; Jack E. Weller, *Yesterday's People: Life in Contemporary Appalachia* (Lexington: Univ. of Kentucky Press, 1965); and Herbert J. Gans, *The Urban Villagers: Group and Class in the Life of Italian-Americans* (New York: Free Press, 1962).

[2]David H. Looff, *Appalachia's Children: The Challenge of Mental Health* (Lexington: Univ. Press of Kentucky, 1971); Norman A. Polansky, Robert D. Borgman, and Christine DeSaix, *Roots of Futility* (San Francisco: Jossey-Bass, 1972); Richard A. Ball, "New Premises for Planning in Appalachia," *Journal of Sociology and Social Welfare*, 2 (Fall 1974), 92-101.

[3]See Robert Coles, *Migrants, Sharecroppers, Mountaineers*, especially Chs. 5, 6, 9 and 12, and *The South Goes North*, Ch. 6 (Boston: Little, Brown, 1972); John Fetterman, *Stinking Creek* (New York: Dutton, 1967); Tony Dunbar, *Our Land Too* (New York: Random House, 1969), Part II; Kathy Kahn, *Hillbilly Women* (Garden City, N.Y.: Doubleday, 1972). A good contrast of the two approaches is Mike Maloney and Ben Huelsman, "Humanism, Scientism, and Southern Mountaineers," *People's Appalachia*, 2 (July 1972), 24-27. The methodological basis of the humanistic approach is sketched in John R. Staude, "The Theoretical Foundations of Humanistic Sociology," in *Humanistic Society: Today's Challenge to Sociology*, ed. John F. Glass and John R. Staude (Pacific Palisades, CA: Goodyear, 1972), pp. 262-270.

[4]In addition to Charles Valentine's *Culture and Poverty*, see Jack L. Roach and Orville R. Gursslin, "An Evaluation of the Concept 'Culture of Poverty,' " *Social Forces*, 45 (March 1967), 383-392; the comments on Valentine in *Current Anthropology*, 10 (April-June 1969), 181-201; and the essays in *The Culture of Poverty: A Critique*, ed. Eleanor Burke Leacock (New York: Simon and Schuster, 1971).

[5]Dwight Billings, "Culture and Poverty in Appalachia: A Theoretical

Discussion and Empirical Analysis," *Social Forces,* 53 (December 1974), 315-323; and Thomas R. Ford, "The Passing of Provincialism," Ch. 2 in *The Southern Appalachian Region: A Survey,* ed. Ford (Lexington: Univ. of Kentucky Press, 1962), pp. 9-34.

[6]On regional development theory, see Harvey S. Perloff *et al., Regions, Resources, and Economic Growth* (Baltimore: Johns Hopkins Press, 1960); E. A. J. Johnson, *The Organization of Space in Developing Countries* (Cambridge: Harvard Univ. Press, 1970); and Harry W. Richardson, *Regional Growth Theory* (New York: Halstead, 1973). An Appalachian application is Mary Jean Bowman and W. Warren Haynes, *Resources and People in East Kentucky* (Baltimore: Johns Hopkins Press, 1963). See also H. Dudley Plunkett and Mary Jean Bowman, *Elites and Change in the Kentucky Mountains* (Lexington: Univ. Press of Kentucky, 1973).

[7]On the ARC, see Donald Rothblatt, *Regional Planning: The Appalachian Experience* (Lexington, MA: Heath, 1971); and Monroe Newman, *The Political Economy of Appalachia* (Lexington, MA: Heath, 1972). Niles M. Hansen's works include *Rural Poverty and the Urban Crisis* (Bloomington: Indiana Univ. Press, 1970); *Intermediate-Size Cities as Growth Centers* (New York: Praeger, 1971); an edited volume, *Growth Centers in Regional Economic Development* (New York: Free Press, 1972); and *Location Preferences, Migration and Regional Growth* (New York: Praeger, 1973).

[8]The idea of "nondecisions" is developed in Peter Bachrach and Morton S. Baratz, *Power and Poverty: Theory and Practice* (New York: Oxford Univ. Press, 1970), Ch. 3, pp. 39-51. See also Matthew Crenson, *The Politics of Air Pollution: A Study of Non-Decisionmaking in the Cities* (Baltimore: Johns Hopkins Press, 1971); and Roger W. Cobb and Charles D. Elder, *Participation in American Politics: The Dynamics of Agenda Building* (Boston: Allyn and Bacon, 1972).

[9]For an example of an alternative approach see John G. Gurley, Capitalist and Maoist Economic Development," in *America's Asia: Dissenting Essays on Asian-American Relations* (New York: Vintage, 1971), pp. 324-356. Some proposals for a socialist regional development strategy for Appalachia are outlined by Richard Simon and Roger Lesser, "A Working Community Commonwealth," *Peoples' Appalachia,* 3 (Spring 1973), 9-15. On the community development corporation and its potential for Appalachia, see Brady J. Deaton, "CDCs: A Development Alternative for Rural America," *Growth and Change,* 6 (January 1975), 31-37.

[10]See the articles in *Readings in U.S. Imperialism,* ed. K. T. Fann and Donald C. Hodges (Boston: Porter Sargent, 1971); in *Dependence and Underdevelopment,* ed. James D. Cockcroft, *et al.* (New York: Doubleday Anchor, 1972); in *Structures of Dependency,* ed. Frank Bonilla and Robert Girling (Palo Alto: Stanford Univ. Institute for Political Studies, 1973); and in the special issue on dependency theory of *Latin American Perspectives,* 1 (Spring 1974). A good review essay is the editors' introduction to *Latin America: The Struggle with Dependency and Beyond,* ed. Ronald H. Chilcote and Joel C. Edelstein (New York: Schenkman, 1974), pp. 1-87.

[11]Susanne Bodenheimer [Jonas], "Dependency and Imperialism: The Roots of Latin American Underdevelopment," in *Readings in U.S. Imperialism,* ed. Fann and Hodges, pp. 62-64.

[12]Thorstein Veblen, *Absentee Ownership and Business Enterprise in Recent Times* (1923; Boston: Beacon, 1967).

[13]See, for example, Joe Persky, "The South: A Colony at Home," *Southern Exposure,* 1 (Summer/Fall 1973), 14-22; Andre Gorz, "Colonialism at Home and Abroad," and Lee Webb, "Colonialism and Underdevelopment in Vermont," both in *Liberation,* 16 (November 1971), 22-29 and 29-33 respectively; Geoffrey Faux, "Colonial New England," *The New Republic* (28 November 1972), pp. 16-19; Dale L. Johnson, "On Oppressed Classes," in *Dependence and Underdevelopment,* ed. Cockcroft, *et al.,* p. 277; and Michael Hechter, *Internal Colonialism: The Celtic Fringe in British National Development, 1536-1966* (Berkeley: Univ. of California Press, 1975).

[14]Pablo González-Casanova, "Internal Colonialism and National Development," in *Studies in Comparative International Development,* 1 (1965), 27-37; rpt. in *Latin American Radicalism,* ed. Irving Louis Horowitz, *et al.* (New York: Random House, 1969), quote from pp. 130-132.

[15]Pierre van den Berghe, "Education, Class and Ethnicity in Southern Peru: Revolutionary Colonialism," in *Education and Colonialism: Comparative Perspectives,* ed. Philip G. Altbach and Gail P. Kelly (New York: McKay, forthcoming). Van den Berghe traces the origin of the term internal colonialism to a pamphlet by Leo Marquard, *South Africa's Colonial Policy* (Johannesburg: Institute of Race Relations, 1957).

[16]See, for example, three excellent collections of articles in pamphlet form: *The West Virginia Miners Union, 1931: As Reported at the Time in "Labor Age"; Harlan and Bell, Kentucky, 1931-2, The National Miners*

Union: As Reported at the Time in the "Labor Defender"; and *War in the Coal Fields, The Northern Fields, 1931: As Reported at the Time in the "Labor Defender" and "Labor Age"* (Huntington, WV: Appalachian Movement Press, 1972).

[17]Caudill, *Night Comes to the Cumberlands* (Boston: Little, Brown, 1963), p. 325; "Misdeal in Appalachia," *The Atlantic Monthly* (June 1965), p. 44; see also his "Appalachia: The Dismal Land," *Dissent*, 14 (November-December 1967), 718-719.

[18]See Kenneth R. Bailey, "A Judicious Mixture: Negroes and Immigrants in the West Virginia Mines, 1880-1917," *West Virginia History*, 34 (January 1973), 141-161; and Paul Nyden, *Black Coal Miners in the United States* (New York: American Institute for Marxist Studies, 1974).

[19]See her review of Plunkett and Bowman, *Elites and Change*, in *Social Forces*, 53 (September 1974), 139-140.

[20]A classic example of such bias is Albert N. Votaw, "The Hillbillies Invade Chicago," *Harper's Magazine* (February 1958), pp. 64-67. An excellent study of the hillbilly stereotype is Clyde B. McCoy, "Stereotypes of Appalachians in Urban Areas: Myths, Facts, and Questions," a paper presented at the Conference on Appalachians in Urban Areas," sponsored by the Academy for Contemporary Problems, Columbus, Ohio, 28 March 1974.

[21]Success through migration is class biased, however; see Harry K. Schwarzweller, *et al., Mountain Families in Transition* (Univ. Park: Pennsylvania Univ. Press, 1971), Chs. 6-9, pp. 121-205.

[22]Robert Blauner, *Racial Oppression in America* (New York: Harper & Row, 1972), p. 67; a revised version of his article "Internal Colonialism and Ghetto Revolt" appears as Ch. 2. For an application of the model to the Chicano population, see Joan Moore, "Colonialism: The Case of the Mexican-American," *Social Problems*, 17 (Spring 1970), 463-472. Another valuable discussion is Jeffrey Prager, "White Racial Privilege and Social Change: An Examination of Theories of Racism," *Berkeley Journal of Sociology*, 17 (1972-73), 117-150. For a critical view of the model, see Donald J. Harris, "The Black Ghetto as Colony: A Theoretical Critique and Alternative Formulation," *The Review of Black Political Economy*, 2 (1972), 3-33. An interesting change of viewpoint is evident in Robert Allen, who in *Black Awakening in Capitalist America* (New York: Doubleday, 1969) made extensive use of the internal colony model; see his review

"Racism and the Black Nation Thesis," *Socialist Revolution*, No. 27 (January-March 1976), pp. 145-150. Another view that emphasizes class over colony is Gilbert G. González, "A Critique of the Internal Colony Model," *Latin American Perspectives*, 1 (Spring 1974), 154-161.

[23]Gwynn Williams, "The Concept of 'Egemonia' in the Thought of Antonio Gramsci: Some Notes on Interpretation," *Journal of the History of Ideas*, 20 (October-December 1960), 587. For some of Gramsci's writings, see *The Modern Prince and Other Writings*, trans. and ed. Louis Marks (New York: International Publishers, 1957); or *Selections from the Prison Notebooks*, ed. and trans. Quinton Hoare and Geoffrey Nowell Smith (New York: International Publishers, 1971). Lukács' classic is *History and Class Consciousness*, trans. Rodney Livingstone (1921; Boston: MIT Press, 1972). On the Frankfurt School, see Martin Jay, *The Dialectical Imagination: A History of the Frankfurt School and the Institute of Social Research, 1923-1950* (Boston: Little, Brown, 1973); and his "Some Recent Developments in Critical Theory," *Berkeley Journal of Sociology*, 18 (1973-74), 27-44.

[24]On the role of the schools in maintaining capitalist hegemony, see Joel H. Spring, *Education and the Rise of the Corporate State* (Boston: Beacon, 1972); Martin Carnoy, *Education as Cultural Imperialism* (New York: McKay, 1974), especially Chs. 5-8, pp. 233-370 on the United States (although I would speak of education as cultural hegemony rather than internal colonialism, as Carnoy does); and Samuel Bowles and Herbert Gintis, *Schooling in Capitalist America: Educational Reform and the Contradictions of Economic Life* (New York: Basic Books, 1976). On the derogation of working-class culture, see Richard Sennett and Jonathan Cobb, *The Hidden Injuries of Class* (New York: Random House, 1972).

[25]See Keith Dix, "The West Virginia Economy: Notes for a Radical Base Study," *Peoples' Appalachia*, 1 (April-May 1970), 3-7; Emil Malizia, "Economic Imperialism: An Interpretation of Appalachian Underdevelopment," *Appalachian Journal*, 1 (Spring 1973), 130-137; Richard Simon, "The Development of Underdevelopment in West Virginia," an outline of a dissertation in progress dated 12 April 1973, also distributed as "Land History: Development of Underdevelopment in West Virginia," a Peoples Development Working Paper of the Regional Economic Development Commission of the Council of the Southern Mountains, Summer 1973.

[26]See particularly his Frankfurt inaugural address of June 1965, published as "Knowledge and Human Interests: A General Perspective," in the appendix to Jürgen Habermas, *Knowledge and Human Interests*, trans.

Jeremy J. Shapiro (Boston:　Beacon Press, 1971), pp. 301-317, quoted phrase from p. 311; and the brief explication of Habermas in the epilogue to Joachim Israel, *Alienation:　From Marx to Modern Sociology* (1968; Boston:　Allyn and Bacon, 1971), pp. 343-347.　See also his essay "Technology and Science as 'Ideology,' " in *Toward a Rational Society* (Boston: Beacon, 1970), pp. 81-122; and Trent Shroyer, "Toward a Critical Theory for Advanced Industrial Society," in *Recent Sociology No. 2:　Patterns of Communicative Behavior*, ed. Hans Peter Dreitzel (New York:　Macmillan, 1970), pp. 210-234.

[27]John Friedmann, "Poor Regions and Poor Nations:　Perspectives on the Problem of Appalachia," *Southern Economic Journal*, 32 (April 1966), 465-467.

[28]Caudill, "Jaded Old Land of Bright New Promise," in *Mountain Life & Work*, 46 (March 1970), 5-8, rpt. in *Appalachia in the Sixties*, ed. David S. Walls and John B. Stephenson (Lexington:　Univ. Press of Kentucky, 1972), pp. 240-246.　His genetic and subculture of poverty arguments are apparent in *Night Comes to the Cumberlands*, pp. 1-31 and 273-301, but are strongly emphasized in his latest work, *A Darkness at Dawn: Appalachian Kentucky and the Future* (Lexington:　Univ. Press of Kentucky, 1976).　Jack Weller, "Appalachia:　America's Mineral Colony," in *Vantage Point*, No. 2 (1973), a now discontinued tabloid issued by the Commission on Religion in Appalachia in Knoxville.

[29]Habermas, *Legitimation Crisis*, trans. Thomas McCarthy (1973; Boston:　Beacon, 1975), pp. 33-41; quote from p. 33.

[30]Galbraith, *Economics and the Public Purpose* (1973; New York: Signet, 1975), pp. 42-43; quote from p. 42.

[31]James O'Connor, *The Fiscal Crisis of the State* (New York:　St. Martin's, 1973), especially Ch. 1, "An Anatomy of American State Capitalism," pp. 13-39; quote from p. 17.

[32]See *Labor Market Segmentation*, ed. Richard C. Edwards, *et al.* (Lexington, MA:　Heath, 1975).

[33]O'Connor, *Fiscal Crisis of the State*, pp. 6-7, and Chs. 4-6, pp. 97-169.

[34]Ralph Miliband, *The State in Capitalist Society:　The Analysis of the Western System of Power* (London:　Quartet, 1973), Ch. 3, "The State

System and the State Elite," pp. 46-62; quote from p. 61.

[35]Nicos Poulantzas, *Political Power and Social Classes,* trans. Timothy O'Hagan (1968; London: New Left Books, 1973). Poulantzas draws heavily on the neo-orthodox structural Marxism of Louis Althusser. For the dispute between Poulantzas and Miliband, see Miliband, "Poulantzas and the Capitalist State," *New Left Review,* No. 82 (November-December 1973), pp. 83-92; and Poulantzas, "The Capitalist State: A Reply to Miliband and Laclau," *New Left Review,* No. 95 (January-February 1976), pp. 63-83. See also Poulantzas, *Classes in Contemporary Capitalism* (London: New Left Books, 1975).

[36]Miliband, "Poulantzas and the Capitalist State," p. 85n; the statement by Marx and Engels is from *The Manifesto of the Communist Party,* Part I.

[37]Ian Gough, "State Expenditure in Advanced Capitalism," *New Left Review,* No. 92 (July-August 1975), pp. 53-92, quotes from pp. 75, 76.

[38]Habermas, *Legitimation Crisis,* pp. 36-37; and his "The Scientization of Politics and Public Opinion," in *Toward a Rational Society,* pp. 62-80. See also Peter Bachrach, *The Theory of Democratic Elitism: A Critique* (Boston: Little, Brown, 1967).

[39]Philip Selznick, *TVA and the Grass Roots: A Study in the Sociology of Formal Organization* (1949; New York: Harper Torchbooks, 1966).

[40]Caudill, "O, Appalachia!" *Intellectual Digest* (April 1973); rpt. in *Voices from the Hills,* ed. Robert J. Higgs and Ambrose N. Manning (New York: Ungar, 1975), pp. 524-525. See a similar collapsing of a complex stratification system to a dichotomy in Roman B. Aquizap and Ernest A. Vargas, "Technology, Power, and Socialization in Appalachia," *Social Casework,* 51 (March 1970), 131-139.

[41]See Richard Parker, *The Myth of the Middle Class: Notes on Affluence and Equality* (1972; New York: Harper Colophon, 1974), for a division into poor, lower middle, upper middle and rich classes; Parker waffles and helps perpetuate the myth he attacks by not terming his "lower middle class" the working class. A more thorough analysis is done by Andrew Levison, *The Working Class Majority* (1974; New York: Penguin, 1975). A good collection of articles is *The Worker in "Post-Industrial" Capitalism: Liberal and Radical Responses,* ed. Bertram Silverman and

Murray Yanowitch (New York: Free Press, 1974). For a thoughtful exploration from an orthodox Marxist perspective, see Judah Hill, *Class Analysis: United States in the 1970s* (Emeryville, CA: privately printed, 1975). An excellent analysis is presented in Erik Olin Wright, "Class Boundaries in Advanced Capitalist Societies," *New Left Review,* No. 98 (July-August 1976), pp. 3-41; also available as reprint 219 from the Institute for Research on Poverty, University of Wisconsin at Madison.

[42]Immanuel Wallerstein, "Dependence in an Interdependent World: The Limited Possibilities of Transformation within the Capitalist World Economy," *African Studies Review,* 17 (April 1974), 1-26.

[43]Friedmann, "Poor Regions and Poor Nations," pp. 467-470.

[44]For a view of race, ethnicity and other such status-groups as "blurred collective representations of classes" in the world system, see Wallerstein, "Social Conflict in Post-Independence Black Africa: The Concepts of Race and Status-Group Reconsidered," in *Racial Tensions and National Identity,* ed. Ernest Q. Campbell (Nashville: Vanderbilt Univ. Press, 1972), pp. 207-226; see also his "Class-Formation in the Capitalist World-Economy," *Politics and Society,* 6 (1975), 367-375; and "The Rise and Future Demise of the World Capitalist System: Concepts for Comparative Analysis," *Comparative Studies in Society and History,* 16 (September 1974), 387-415.

[45]Herbert J. Gans, "The Positive Functions of Poverty," *The American Journal of Sociology,* 78 (September 1972), 275-289. On the Title V Commissions, see Ch. 5 in Martha Derthick, *Between State and Nation: Regional Organizations of the United States* (Washington, D.C.: Brookings Institution, 1974), pp. 108-133.

[46]The first proposal for something resembling a special legislature for the Southern Appalachians is made by George S. Mitchell, "Let's Unite the Pie!" *Mountain Life & Work,* 27 (Spring 1951), 19-20; he suggests an "annual representative meeting and a permanent staff. . . .Such a representative body ought to be. . .an annual assembly of all the mountain members of the state legislatures. Possibly the Members of Congress from the Mountains might be a sort of Upper House." Dwight Macdonald proposes a state of Appalachia in "The Constitution of the United States Needs to be Fixed," *Esquire,* 70 (October 1968), 246; but it would be formed by lumping together the present states of West Virginia, Kentucky and Tennessee as part of an overall consolidation of states for the purpose of obtaining larger administrative jurisdictions. The proposal has no relation to a policy

of overcoming the exploitation of the mountain region. Nor does the re-organization scheme of geographer G. Etzel Pearcy, which would form a state of Appalachia more appropriately from sections of southern West Virginia, southwestern Virginia, eastern Kentucky, and southeastern Ohio; see the article by Lee Harris from *The Los Angeles Times* rpt. as "A Plan to Reshape, Rename and Reduce U.S. States to 38," *The Courier-Journal & Times* (Louisville), 2 September 1973, p. E5.

[47]Gordon K. Ebersole brought the idea of the Public Utility Districts from the Northwest to the Appalachians; see his "Appalachia: Potential. . . With a View," *Mountain Life & Work*, 42 (Winter 1966), 10-12. Harry Caudill picked up the idea and gave it wide publicity; see his "A New Plan for a Southern Mountain Authority," *Appalachian Review*, 1 (Summer 1966), 6-11. Ebersole and Caudill were key leaders in the Congress for Appalachian Development. An issue of *The Appalachian South*, 2 (Spring and Summer 1967) is largely devoted to articles on CAD. On the history of CAD, see David Whisnant, "The Congress for Appalachian Development," *Peoples' Appalachia*, 3 (Spring 1973), 16-22.

EXTENDING THE INTERNAL PERIPHERY MODEL: THE IMPACT OF CULTURE AND CONSEQUENT STRATEGY

by

Thomas S. Plaut

A new bumper sticker has recently come into prominence in Yancey County, North Carolina: Black letters on a yellow field politely request, "NO PARK PLEASE." Such is the local response to an announced study by the National Park Service on the feasibility of turning the area around Mt. Mitchell, the highest mountain in the Eastern United States, into a sort of Yellowstone East.

A National Forest Service map of the Pisgah National Forest vividly demonstrates the "blocking in" process by which this agency purchases land for its Congress-ordained mission on a periphery of an authorized area and then moves inward, little green block by little green block, into the white open region of small farms.

In Randolph County, West Virginia, students plot the rapid land acquisition process by the AMAX coal company. When they ask company representatives to explain what they will do with this land, the official response is, "You tell us what you want to know, kid, and we'll tell you how to get along without it."

SOURCE: Paper written October, 1977, for this collection.

AUTHOR: Tom Plaut, associate professor and co-ordinator for sociology at Mars Hill College, is also on the staff of the Southern Appalachian Center.

These three examples, all current, can be matched by other vignettes from people all over Appalachia. They are representative of the process of social change that has been in evidence in the mountains since the mass cutting of timber began almost a century ago. They are part of a process which has cost much of the region its ability to provide a decent life for its people and which has been documented by previous selections in this volume.

The fact that by 1930 Appalachia had become an area where many people could not lead a life comparable in economic terms with the middle class American norm has resulted in social scientists and others seeking causes and models of causes for the "poverty" of the region. These models have been presented and criticized in the previous article by David Walls. In brief, a "deficiency model" blamed the mountaineers and their allegedly homespun "yesterday's people" culture for the announced "problems" of the region. Repeated incidents like the ones reported above and consequent outrage, together with a genuine love and respect for the people around us, led to the development of the colonial model as a dialectical response to the deficiency model. This model places the blame not on the people but on the external profit seekers who removed the region's vast wealth to Pittsburgh, New York, and Philadelphia, leaving an impoverished region behind them.

Walls also mentions the "development model," used especially by government agencies (and attendant state university research centers) who are in the development business and who find the region to be a good target for their efforts. I would extend this model beyond the government to include other groups and people who have an agenda to act out and find the mountains a good arena for the performance. William Goodell Frost, president of Berea College at the turn of the century, found the mountaineers to be underdeveloped in education and thus set out to develop them in this area. His example was followed by the establishment of scores of "settlement schools" throughout the region. Presbyterians, Methodists, and other denominations found the mountaineers suffering from an underdeveloped faith and thus labelled the region fertile ground for their missionary movement.[1]

Walls points out the strengths and limitations of each model and then combines them into his synthesis, which is a model of the region as an "internal periphery of an advanced capitalist system." The internal periphery model draws on the works of Galbraith, James O'Connor, and Jürgens Habermas to describe the region as essentially a resources preserve, complete with "native" leadership that serves the needs of the advanced industrial, resources, and recreation-hungry society that surrounds it. It is a helpful model in that it accounts for the external manipulations and the steady removal of wealth from the region as well as the internal quiescence and cooperation of a "dependency infrastructure" that facilitates the process. Thus it takes into account a wide range of cultural and socio-political phenomena.

Yet, the internal periphery model, as I now understand it, does not do what Walls would like it to do: help us arrive at "the goals and strategy of a movement for social change."

I would extend the internal periphery model by emphasizing that it posits, at least implicitly, the existence of two cultures: that of the "exploited" area and that of the "advanced capitalist" system that surrounds it. By culture I mean what Sir Edward Tylor defined as "that complex whole which includes knowledge, belief, art, morals, law, custom and other capabilities and habits acquired by man as a member of society," and their world view or *weltanschauung*.[2]

As Walls, Helen Lewis, Roger Lesser, Stephen Fisher, and others have pointed out, there is a great deal of literature on the culture of Appalachia, whether defined as a "culture of poverty" or as the "folk culture" of "Yesterday's People." But what about the culture of the other side: the "advanced capitalist region"? This has not been discussed, quite probably because it is part of what Alfred Schutz calls the "world-taken-for-granted" of the academics—even those outraged by the rape of the Appalachian region. We too have been socialized by the institutions of the advanced capitalist system. We accept the value system of a rationalist, achievement-oriented, "scientific" culture and are well conditioned members of the social system that inflicts so much pain and disorder in both internal and external peripheral regions. Culturally, we turn out to be the very people we've been warning each other about. We have been blind to our own folkways and thus have been unable to define them and assess their impact on social change.

Thus, we, and the rest of the world along with us, are inheritors of a change in cultural orientation so well described by Max Weber many years ago that it ought to be quoted at length here:

> Until about the middle of the past century the life of a putter-out was, at least in many of the branches of the Continental textile industry, what we should to-day consider very comfortable. We may imagine its routing somewhat as follows: The peasants came with their cloth, often (in the case of linen) principally or entirely made from raw material which the peasant himself had produced, to the town in which the putter-out lived, and after a careful, often official appraisal of the quality, received the customary price for it. The putter-out's customers, for markets any appreciable distance away, were middlemen, who also came to him, generally not yet following samples, but seeking traditional qualities, and bought from his warehouse, or, long before delivery, placed orders which were probably in turn passed on to the peasants. Personal canvassing of customers took place, if at all, only at long intervals. Otherwise correspondence sufficed, though the sending of samples slowly gained ground. The number of business hours was very moderate, perhaps five to six a day, sometimes considerably less; in the rush season, where there was one, more. Earnings were moderate; enough to lead a respectable life and in good times to put away a little. On the whole, relations among competitors were relatively good, with a large degree of agreement on the fundamentals of business. A long daily visit to the tavern, with often plenty to drink, and a congenial circle of friends, made life comfortable and leisurely.
>
> The form of organization was in every respect capitalistic; the entrepreneur's activity was of a purely business character; the use of capital, turned over in the business, was indispensable; and finally, the objective aspect of the economic process, the book-keeping, was rational. But it was traditionalistic business, if one considers the spirit

which animated the entrepreneur: the traditional manner of life, the traditional rate of profit, the traditional amount of work, the traditional manner of regulating the relationships with labour, and the essentially traditional circle of customers and the manner of attracting new ones. All these dominated the conduct of the business, were at the basis, one may say, of the *ethos* of this group of business men.

Now at some time this leisureliness was suddenly destroyed, and often entirely without any essential change in the form of organization, such as the transition to a unified factory, to mechanical weaving, etc. What happened was, on the contrary, often no more than this: some young man from one of the putting-out families went out into the country, carefully chose weavers for his employ, greatly increased the rigour of his supervision of their work, and thus turned them from peasants into labourers. On the other hand, he would begin to change his marketing methods by so far as possible going directly to the final consumer, would take the details into his own hands, would personally solicit customers, visiting them every year, and above all would adapt the quality of the product directly to their needs and wishes. At the same time he began to introduce the principle of low prices and large turnover. There was repeated what everywhere and always is the result of such a process of rationalization: those who would not follow suit had to go out of business. The idyllic state collapsed under the pressure of a bitter competitive struggle, respectable fortunes were made, and not lent out at interest, but always reinvested in the business. The old leisurely and comfortable attitude toward life gave way to a hard frugality in which some participated and came to the top, because they did not wish to consume but to earn, while others who wished to keep on with the old ways were forced to curtail their consumption.

And, what is most important in this connection, it was not generally in such cases a stream of new money invested in the industry which brought about this revolution—in several cases known to me the whole revolu-

tionary process was set in motion with a few thousands of
capital borrowed from relations—but the new spirit, the
spirit of modern capitalism, had set to work.[3]

Weber elsewhere documented the rise of the "spirit of
capitalism" in the rationally oriented bureaucracy in which the
human element was bent to the needs of the stated directions
and goals of the agency.[4]   Other social theorists have noted
other aspects of this process: Tonnies saw the move from
Gemeinschaft to *Gesellschaft* (from intimate, small community
to impersonal, complex society) accompanied by a shift in
the ways people viewed and treated each other.   The shift is
from *Wesenwille*, which can be described as a spontaneous,
emotional and committed base for interpersonal relations in
which a humanistic communal will encompasses rational
thought, to *Kurwille*, where rational thought and calculation
regulate social dialogue according to the use-value each party per-
ceives in the other.[5]   Durkheim noted the disintegration of
"moral" community and the consequent anomie, social disorder,
and increase in suicide rates.[6] Mid-century sociology had showed
the individual outcome of this trend in Mills' "Cheerful Robots,"
Reisman's "Other Directed Man" and Marcuse's *One Dimensional
Man*:

> With the technical progress as its instrument, unfreedom—
> in the sense of Man's subjection to his productive appa-
> ratus—is perpetuated and intensified in the form of many
> liberties and comforts.   The novel feature is the over-
> whelming rationality in this irrational enterprise, and the
> depth of the preconditions which shapes the instinctual
> drives and the aspirations of the individuals and obscures
> the difference between false and true consciousness.   For,
> in reality, neither the utilization of administrative rather
> than physical controls (hunger, personal dependence,
> force), nor the change in the character of heavy work
> . . .compensate for the fact that the decisions over life and
> death, over personal and national security at places over
> which individuals have no control.   The slaves of in-
> dustrial civilization are sublimated slaves, but they are
> slaves, for slavery is determined by. . .the pure form of
> servitude: to exist as an instrument, as a thing.[7]

The reality of the historical rationalist trend in what is now the culture of advanced capitalism is attested to by the rampant efforts to escape it or to discover human essence within it through movements such as youth culture, TM, EST, the Moonies, and Eslin.

Fritz Pappenheim and Philip Slater join Mills, Marcuse, Fromm, and Reisman in the assertion that in the advanced capitalist system, human beings are held captive as employees of large impersonal bureaucratic organizations that thunder about the countryside in pursuit of what Karl Mannheim has termed their own "functionally rational" goals:[8]

The U.S. Forest Service exists to enlarge and maintain a complex forest system.

The U.S. Park Service exists to create and maintain recreation facilities.

AMAX exists to extract coal in what its executives feel is the most efficient manner possible with existing technology.

What could be more "American" or more in line with a technology-intoxicated Protestant Ethic? What could be more devastating to the Appalachian Region? But it is also devastating the managerial technocrats in charge of the devastation, who define themselves in terms of their bureaucratic place and assigned position and mission within a bureaucratic hierarchy. Douglas Heath's longitudinal studies of "highly successful" American males indicate an inverse relationship between high intelligence scores (on the culture-bound tests of the rationalist, advanced capitalist culture), and the ability to be outgoing, supportive, and "mature" in personal interactions. Wives of some of these men called them "robots." One interviewee said "I've been married to him ten years now and still don't know what he really *feels*."[9]

One of the products of Western industrial culture has been the complex organization which in turn creates its own values, quasi-community, and its own kind of man. Recent essays by Richard Couto, John Gaventa, and Stephen Fisher, *et al.,*[10] draw upon the work of Peter Berger and Thomas Luckmann to suggest that the inability of Appalachians to make their interests and needs known in the larger policy arena is in some measure due to the fact that their social reality is determined by the defining institutions and mechanisms of the larger, dominating, advanced capitalist society.[11]   According to this argument, the media, educational systems, and government agencies define the Appalachians to themselves and to others as Lil' Abners and Snuffy Smiths—people incapable of responding to the complex issues of the "modern" world.   In being socialized to accept this definition of reality, Appalachians' ability to respond to issues and struggle for their interests is limited; they become quiescent even when they "seemingly have every reason to rebel."[12]

But Appalachian history is full of rebellions and rebels: of men and women who demand, in Camus' terms, that their existence be recognized.   From mine wars to roving pickets, Mother Jones to Widow Combs, Black Lung and Brown Lung movements, Appalachians have fought domination to a degree which has required the dominating culture to foster the sort of violent stereotype of the mountaineer depicted in the film *Deliverance.*

So the people whose reality is defined by the mechanisms of the dominant culture may well not be the residents of the "internal periphery" but of the dominant culture itself—people who, rather than defining and experiencing themselves as people, see and struggle to be "planners," "sound businessmen," "GS-13s" or other reifications of human endeavor which abnegate a sense of common humanity.   This is the process that creates monsters.   Adolph Eichmann was an expert only in rail transport and Robert McNamara was a systems specialist.   They were both organization men and good examples of Modern Man in the twentieth century: They killed people with tact, efficiency, and, most astoundingly, with some measure of well meaning.

Part of the problem Appalachia faces then lies not in its own culture but in the *weltanschauung* that accompanies the advanced industrial social system of large complex organizations in both the public and private spheres.

As perhaps is true of the everyday view of the world in most predominantly rural parts of the world, the way Appalachians construct and live in the world around them makes them vulnerable to the outside predator.   My own field observation in a coal fringe area in West Virginia and an agricultural area in Western North Carolina has found people busy and relatively content in lifestyles they find to be meaningful. The focus of their every-day life rests upon a network of people and problems physically and socially close to them. Lengthy daily discussions with one farmer in Madison County, North Carolina, over a period of five weeks revealed continual concern with family matters and his tobacco crop. He knew that a neighboring farm had been sold to Florida real estate speculators and subdivided and already sold to people mostly from New Jersey. He was not aware that in the past ten years 25 percent of the land in the county had been pur-chased by out-of-state people for second homes and that the Federal government held another 23 percent. He knew "land has gone high as a cat's back" but did not give any indication that he saw the implications of this increase on the future of farming or out-migration patterns in the area. This man's world view and orientation (whether it be a function of class or regional location or a combination of these variables) made him as insensi-tive to the implications of real estate speculation as VISTA volunteers were to the social structure and strengths of the com-munities they came to "help."

Supporters of the colonial model have tended to shy away from discussion of any possible limitations of mountain culture because advocates of the deficiency approach have made such devastating use of "culture of poverty" models in their efforts to "blame the victim."[13]   But it is fair to say, I think, that although the ways of life in rural Appalachia are rich and mean-ingful, they have been no match for the rationalist's, efficiency-oriented culture of advanced capitalism that has come into their territory. This sort of cross-cultural clash has not been limited to Appalachia; it has been a global phenomena recorded in the ruins of Mayan libraries and observatories, the beylik lands of Algeria, and the temples of Indo-China. Rationalism with its attendant social structure has levelled, bleached, and bled out a rich variety of human ways of being that have stood in its path.

Mike Clark, in trying to explain this phenomenon to stu-dents in Ohio last summer, turned to a speech by Chief Seattle, a leader of the Sequamish Indians, given in 1954 to mark the transfer of ancestral lands to the Federal government:

"How can you buy or sell the sky, the warmth of the land? The idea is strange to us. . .

We know that the white man does not understand our ways. One portion of the land is the same to him as the next, for he is a stranger who comes in the night and takes from the land whatever he needs. The earth is not his brother, but his enemy, and when he has conquered it he moves on. He leaves his father's graves behind; he does not care. He kidnaps the earth from his children. *He treats his mother, the earth, and his brother, the sky, as things to be bought, plundered, sold like sheep or bright beads.* [Emphasis mine.]   He will devour the earth and leave behind only a desert.

I do not know. Our ways are different from your ways. The sight of your cities pains the eyes of the red man. But perhaps it is because the red man is a savage and does not understand. . . ."[14]

"Some savage," commented Clark.   But if Chief Seattle could have compared notes with Marcuse, he might have better understood that when social institutions reduce men to commodities, men live only in the world of commodities—of things to be bought, sold, and used like sheep or beads or farmland. They have been deprived of the very qualities which would have enabled them to hear and understand the chief's concerns and world.

In summary, the internal periphery synthesis can be extended to incorporate the concept of two cultural traditions in conflict, with the historical record indicating that the social systems of complex organizations and attendant *weltanschauung* ultimately prevail.   It is our profound wish that it will not continue to do so, that some sense of humanistic balance and purpose can be introduced into the process of social change that inundates us.

Walls concludes his paper with the assertion that the internal periphery of advanced capitalism model leads us to "socialist goals and strategies" for a presumably humanistic "movement for social change."   But in adding the dimension of cultural orientation to his model, the posited struggle appears not to be between the "isms" as much as between community and increasingly centralizing, mass bureaucratic definitions of reality, control of life, and planning. The wide range of application of socialist concepts—from Sweden to Stalin, China, Cuba, Algeria, and Tanzania to Cambodia—indicate that socialism can come down on either side of this dichotomy. Of course with capitalism there is no question; centralization historically has proved to be one of its major dynamics. But the history of socialism requires us to be more specific; the diversity of its historical record indicates we cannot accept it on the basis of its stated humanist objectives alone.

The addition of the cultural orientation perspective to the internal periphery model requires us to begin to articulate some goals in terms of quality of life and the strategies for achieving those goals. At the same time, we can attempt to block or substantially modify proposals for the development authored by the impersonal bureaucratic structures of the advanced capitalist system that would continue the process of degradation and disintegration of Appalachian life and culture, the process that reifies human beings and human relations into things or commodities.

There is a growing history of successful opposition to development schemes of both public and private agencies. In the late sixties, for example, the Upper French Broad Defense Association rallied the citizens of Western North Carolina to block a TVA project which would have flooded 11,225 acres and dislocated 600 families. In another case, articulate opposition in public hearings in Tennessee resulted in the blockage of an AMAX Coal Company plan to strip mine 10,000 acres on the Cumberland Plateau.[15]

These victories were won by people who changed formerly legitimizing "public hearing" rituals into real forums where some collective evaluation of proposed projects and their social costs and benefits could take place. (There have also been defeats. I am reminded of a young surveyor who literally was run out of Randolph County, West Virginia, for speaking out in a public hearing in opposition to the construction of a coal washing facility on the Cheat River.) But the point is that we have the basis of a strategy here—to force participation in policy making into what previously have been legitimizing rituals or democratic pretense for private, elitist, and closed planning systems.

Secondly, we have to see "officialdom" as people who are judged and judge themselves in terms of the functional goals of the bureaucratic structures for which they work. Their sense of self worth, their income levels, status and life chances are in good measure tied to whether their agencies get that land, build that dam, or strip that coal. We thus cannot appeal to their "better natures," because to do so implies that they commit a sort of sociological suicide and resign from their perceived organizational communities. They are in good measure beyond reach; they are Heath's robots in action. At best we can try to redefine their interests for them; more likely we will have to oppose them.

Third, we should get on with the difficult process of defining the kind of life that is meaningful in the most profound sense of the term. (There is enough of the anthropologist in me to feel that we're dabbling here in a matter that extends well beyond our mental capabilities. Men like Levi-Strauss, Paul Radin and Stanley Diamond who delve into such things begin to sound like "primitive" shamans after a while—somewhat akin to Chief Seattle). But minimally and from a frankly humanistic and decentralist perspective, we can say that people should have a right to create and see the products of their creation, that they should not be separated from one another by overspecialization of task or great differentiation in wealth or status and that they should have community, a place of belonging and membership, where in collective association they can determine their future.

Elements for such a utopian vision can be found still in some "traditional" rural mountain communities, as George Hicks discovered in his study of Celo, N.C.[16] Celo stands almost at the foot of Mt. Mitchell where today one finds NO PARK PLEASE bumper stickers thick as galax.

NOTES

[1]David Walls, "On the Naming of Appalachia," a paper submitted to the Appalachian Symposium honoring Cratis D. Williams, April, 1976.

[2]Edward Tylor, *Primitive Culture* (New York: Harper and Row, 1958), I, 1.

[3]Max Weber, *The Protestant Ethic and the Spirit of Capitalism* (New York: Charles Scribner's Sons, 1958), pp. 66-68.

[4]H. H. Gerth and C. W. Mills, *From Max Weber: Essays in Sociology* (New York: Oxford University Press, 1946), pp. 196-240.

[5]Ferdinand Tonnies, *Fundamental Concepts of Sociology (Gemeinschaft und Gesellschaft)*, trans. Charles P. Loomis, American Sociology Series, Kimball Young, ed. (New York: American Book Company, 1940), pp. 194-195. An excellent discussion of these concepts can be found in Fritz Pappenheim, *The Alienation of Modern Man* (New York: Modern Reader Paperbacks, 1959), pp. 69-77.

[6]Emile Durkheim, *Suicide* (New York: The Free Press, 1951), note especially pp. 256-259.

[7]C. W. Mills, *The Sociological Imagination* (New York, Oxford University Press, 1959), p. 171. David Reisman, Nathan Glazer, and Reuel Denny, *The Lonely Crowd* (New Haven: Yale University Press, 1950). Herbert Marcuse, *One Dimensional Man* (Boston: Beacon Press, 1968), pp. 32-33.

[8]Karl Mannheim, *Man and Society in an Age of Reconstruction* (Cambridge: Harvard University Press, 1948).

[9]From correspondence and conversations with Douglas Heath. His findings have recently been published in D. H. Heath, *Maturity and Competence: A Transcultural View* (New York: Gardner Press, 1977), pp. 177-

178.

[10]John Gaventa and Richard Couto, "Appalachia and the Third Face of Power," a paper presented at the 1976 annual meeting of the American Political Science Association, Chicago, Illinois, September, 1976. Jim Foster and Steve Robinson and Steve Fisher, "Class Consciousness and Destructive Power: A Strategy for Change in Appalachia," a paper presented at the 1977 annual meeting of the APSA, Washington, D.C., September, 1977.

[11]Peter L. Berger and Luckmann, *The Social Construction of Reality* (New York: Anchor Books, 1967).

[12]Robinson, Foster and Fisher, p. 1.

[13]See William Ryan, *Blaming the Victim* (New York: Vintage Books, 1972).

[14]Mike Clark, "How Can You Buy or Sell The Sky," as reprinted in *The Mountain Eagle*, Whitesburg, Kentucky, June 23, 1977.

[15]Dave Whisnant, "The TVA Story: How Green is Your Valley." *Elements.* Also, see "Fact Sheet: AMAX in Tennessee, 1976," a mimeographed pamphlet jointly produced by Save Our Cumberland Mountains (SOCM) and Concerned Citizens of Piney, Spencer, Tennessee.

[16]George L. Hicks, *Appalachian Valley* (New York: Holt, Rinehart & Winston, 1976).

SUGGESTIONS FOR FURTHER
READING AND RESEARCH

The articles in this last section by Lindberg, Walls and Plaut represent some of the efforts to study and revise the Colonialism model and to search for new ways of understanding problems of development, exploitation and dependency. There is a need for further exploration and research into the social, political and economic implications of industrial, technological development throughout the world. Those interested in further reading and research are directed to the following readers and general introductions to economic imperialism, and problems of capitalist development theory.

Robert I. Rhodes, ed., *Imperialism and Underdevelopment*, New York, Monthly Review Press, 1970. This book contains a good bibliography for studying imperialism with special sections on Africa, Asia, and Latin America as well as a general section on capitalist development and underdevelopment.

James D. Crockcraft, et al., eds., *Dependence and Underdevelopment*, New York, Doubleday Anchor, 1972.

K. T. Fann and Donald C. Hodges, eds., *Readings in U. S. Imperialism*, Boston, Porter Sargent, 1971.

Frank Bonilla and Robert Girling, eds., *Structures of Dependency*, Palo Alto: Stanford University Institute for Political Studies, 1973.

Latin American Perspectives, I, Spring, 1974, A special issue on dependency theory and internal colonialism.

Richard C. Edwards, *The Capitalist System*, New York, Prentice-Hall, 1972.

Some of the classic works on neo-colonialism which remain important statements on the nature of colonialism and its effects on those who are colonized are suggested below. These have been very influential in the development of the research included in this reader.

Frantz Fanon, *Dying Colonialism*, New York, Grove Press, 1967.

Frantz Fanon, *The Wretched of the Earth*, New York, Monthly Review Press, 1967.

Harry Magdoff, *The Age of Imperialism*, New York, Monthly Review Press, 1969.

Dominique O. Mannoni, *Prospero and Calabani, The Psychology of Colonization*, New York, Praeger, 1956.

Albert Memmi , *Colonizer and the Colonized*, Grossman, 1965.

Kwame Nkrumah, *Neo-Colonialism: The Last Stages of Imperialism*, London: Nelson, 1965.

Pierre Jalee, *The Pillage of the Third World*, New York, Monthly Review Press, 1968.

Vladimir Lenin I., *Imperialism: The Highest Stage of Capitalism*, International Publishing Company, 1965.

Those interested in more reading on the Appalachian case are referred to the notes and bibliographies included with each of the articles in the reader.

In addition to the application to Appalachia, the colonialism model has been applied to other regions on sub-groups in the United States. Some of these are:

Joe Persky, "The South: A Colony at Home," *Southern Exposure*, I, Summer/Fall, 1973, 14-22.

Andre Gorz, "Colonialism at Home and Abroad," and Lee Webb, "Colonialism and Underdevelopment in Vermont," both in *Liberation,* 16, November, 1971, 22-29 and 29-33 respectively.

Geoffrey Faux, "Colonial New England," *The New Republic,* 28, November, 1972, 16-19.

Robert Blauner, "Internal Colonialism and Ghetto Revolt," *Social Problems,* 16, Spring, 1969.

A similar application to a sub-region of Great Britain is Michael Hechter, *Internal Colonialism: The Celtic Fringe in British National Development,* 1936-1966, Berkeley, University of California Press, 1975.

More recent analyses and reinterpretations of historical materials have relied heavily on the neo-colonial perspective. Important examples of these are:

Eugene D. Genovese, *Roll Jordan Roll: The World the Slaves Made,* New York, Pantheon, 1974.

Edwards Galeano, *Open Veins of Latin America, Five Centuries of the Pillage of a Continent,* Monthly Review Press, 1973.

Basil Davidson, *Africa in History,* Macmillan, 1974.

William Appleman Williams, *The Roots of the Modern American Empire,* Random House, 1969.

Further research and continued rethinking of the model are important to provide tools for analysis of the process which affects and changes our lives. Without a clear analysis of the dynamics of the social changes which are reshaping and, in many cases, destroying peoples and cultures throughout the world, we are helpless to direct or actually participate in these changes.

Other Books Published and/or Distributed by

APPALACHIAN CONSORTIUM PRESS

Boone, North Carolina 28607

"*. . .a right good people,*" by Harold Warren

Artisans/Appalachia/USA, text and photographs by David Gaynes

Arts and Crafts of the Cherokee, by Rodney L. Leftwich

Bibliography of Southern Appalachia, edited by Charlotte T. Ross

Bits of Mountain Speech, by Paul M. Fink

Blanford Barnard Dougherty, Mountain Educator, by Ruby J. Lanier

Down to Earth—People of Appalachia, text and photographs by Kenneth Murray

Hiking Virginia's National Forests, by Karin Wuertz-Schaefer

King's Mountain, by Hank Messick

Laurel Leaves, an occasional journal of the Appalachian Consortium

Mountain Measure, by Francis Pledger Hulme with photographs by Robert Amberg

Music of the Blue Ridge (LP Recording), by Bob Harman and the Blue Ridge Descendants

New Ground, co-edited by Donald Askins and David Morris

100 Favorite Trails of the Great Smokies and Carolina Blue Ridge (large scale map), compiled by Carolina Mountain Club and Smoky Mountains Hiking Club

'Round the Mountains, by Ruth Camblos and Virginia Winger

Symposium on Trout Habitat Research and Management Proceedings

Tall Tales from Old Smoky, by C. Hodge Mathes

Teaching Mountain Children: Towards a Foundation of Understanding, by David N. Mielke

"That D----d Brownlow," Being a Saucy and Malicious Description of William Gannaway Brownlow, Knoxville Editor and Stalwart Unionist, Who Rose from a Confederate Jail to Become One of the Most Famous Personages in the Nation, Denounced by his Enemies as Vicious and Harsh, Praised by his Friends as Compassionate and Gentle, Herewith Revived by Steve Humphrey, a 20th Century Newspaperman and Former Associate Editor of the Knoxville Journal, Desendant of the Whig.

The Birth of Forestry in America, by Carl Alwin Schenck

The Good Life Almanac, edited by Ruth Smalley

The Smokies Guide, by George Myers Stephens

The Southern Appalachian Heritage

The Southern Mountaineer in Fact and Fiction, by Cratis D. Williams

The Wataugans, by Dr. J. Max Dixon

Toward 1984: The Future of Appalachia, Southern Appalachian Regional Conference Proceedings

Trains, Trestles & Tunnels: Railroads of the Southern Appalachians, by Lou Harshaw

Unto the Hills, by Margaret Walker Freel

Voices from the Hills, edited by Robert J. Higgs and Ambrose N. Manning

Western North Carolina: Its Mountains and Its People to 1880, by Ora Blackmun

Western North Carolina Since the Civil War, by Drs. Ina W. and John J. Van Noppen

DESCRIPTIVE CATALOG AVAILABLE

Often referred to as the leader of inspiration in Appalachian studies, HELEN MATTHEWS LEWIS linked scholarship with activism and encouraged deeper analysis of the region. Lewis shaped the field of Appalachian studies by emphasizing community participation and challenging traditional perceptions of the region and its people. She has served as the director of the Berea College Appalachian Center, Appalshop's Appalachian History Film Project, and the Highlander Research and Education Center. She is co-author of *Mountain Sisters: From Convent to Community in Appalachia*. She has retired to Abingdon, Virginia.

DONALD ASKINS, an Alabama native, taught at Clinch Valley College in Wise, Virginia, before becoming the first Executive Director for the Appalachian Coalition, whose main focus was the elimination of strip mining. He is responsible for taking the aerial photographs of the mining operations in this collection in 1977 through 1979 as documentation of the effects of strip mining. Later, he pursued a criminal law degree and was elected Commonwealth attorney in 1991 until 2000. He retired to Clintwood, Virginia in 2000. He passed away at his home in Clintwood on March 30, 2015.

LINDA JOHNSON was the co-coordinator of the Grace House Learning/ Training Center in St. Paul, Virginia. She passed away in 2002.

CPSIA information can be obtained
at www.ICGtesting.com
Printed in the USA
LVHW041820280119
605527LV00002B/222/P

9 781469 642048